COUNTRY
PROJECTS *for*
WOODWORKERS

COUNTRY
PROJECTS *for*
WOODWORKERS

The Editors of *The Woodworker's Journal*

PJS Publications, Inc.

Printed in the United States of America.

Fifth Printing: January 1995

PJS Publications, Inc.
News Plaza
P.O. Box 1790
Peoria, IL 61656

Contents

Acknowledgment

The editors wish to thank the following individuals who contributed projects to this book:

Sam Allen, Rough-Sawn Cedar Clock; *Jon W. Arno,* Candle Box; *Warren W. Bender, Jr.,* Canning Jar Shelves; *Steve Benjamin,* Early American Wall Cupboard; *C.W. Comfort,* Key Holder; *Donald E. Cornue,* Country Kitchen Cabinet; *Thomas A. Gardner,* 19th Century Cherry Table; *Paul Levine,* 18th Century Trestle Table, Pine Spoon Rack, Cider Press Lamp, and Woodpile Trivet; *Robert C. Lewis,* 18th Century Lawyer's Case; *Robert A. McCoy,* Candle Holder; *Larry Miller,* Quilt Rack; *R.B. Rennaker,* Writing Desk; *Roger E. Schroeder,* Stepped-Back Hutch, Buckboard Seat, and Hutch Clock; *Raymond Schuessler,* Fireplace Bellows; *James R. Spence, Jr.,* Dovetailed Footstool; *John M. Wilson,* Blanket Chest; *Richard Wonderlich,* 19th Century Kitchen Clock.

Also, our thanks to *Joe Gluse* who did the technical art for the Half-Round Table, 18th Century Sleigh Seat, and Shaker Sewing Stand; *Gene Marino III* who did the technical art for the 19th Century Step-Chair, 19th Century Washstand, Early American Wall Cupboard, Early American Wall Secretary, and Shaker Woodbox; and *John Kane* of Silver Sun Studios for the cover photo, back cover photo, and many of the project photos.

Introduction

It is with some apprehension that many of us view the approach of a new century. The rapid technological, social and environmental changes of the past several decades have been perhaps a bit overwhelming. As time and design propel us into the future, we find ourselves delving more into the past, dreaming of an age when warmth, simplicity, hard work and honest value prevailed.

The resurgence of interest in the country way of life is a reaction to the frenetic time we live in now, and whether or not this reactionary thinking (we can simply call it nostalgia) has any impact on our future, the fact remains that decorating in the Country style provides an atmosphere that is comforting to those who need it.

In the 18th and early 19th centuries there were no suburbs. Professional cabinetmakers worked in the large cities and built their highboys, sideboards and other impressive pieces for wealthy clients. Out in the country, farmers and other rural folk either built what furnishings they needed themselves or bartered with local craftsmen who were skilled in woodworking. Necessity was the mother of invention in those days and there wasn't a lot of money or time to be spent on frivolities and decorative details. The furnishings were for the most part simple, functional and sturdily built of native woods. Those are the characteristics of country furniture and if time is the test of any style, it's safe to say that country furniture is here to stay.

The designs in this book cover a broad range of projects, all of which can be built by anyone with a modest degree of woodworking skill. Some pieces are authentic copies of actual antiques while others are simply in the Country style with no real counterpart from earlier times.

It is hoped that this book will encourage more people to try their hand at woodworking, to offset the cost of realizing their dream and to find the same satisfaction and sense of pride as their ancestors in knowing that they've built the furniture themselves. The 85 plans collected here provide more than enough projects and ideas to make any home the showcase of a country dream.

The Editors

Doughbox End Table

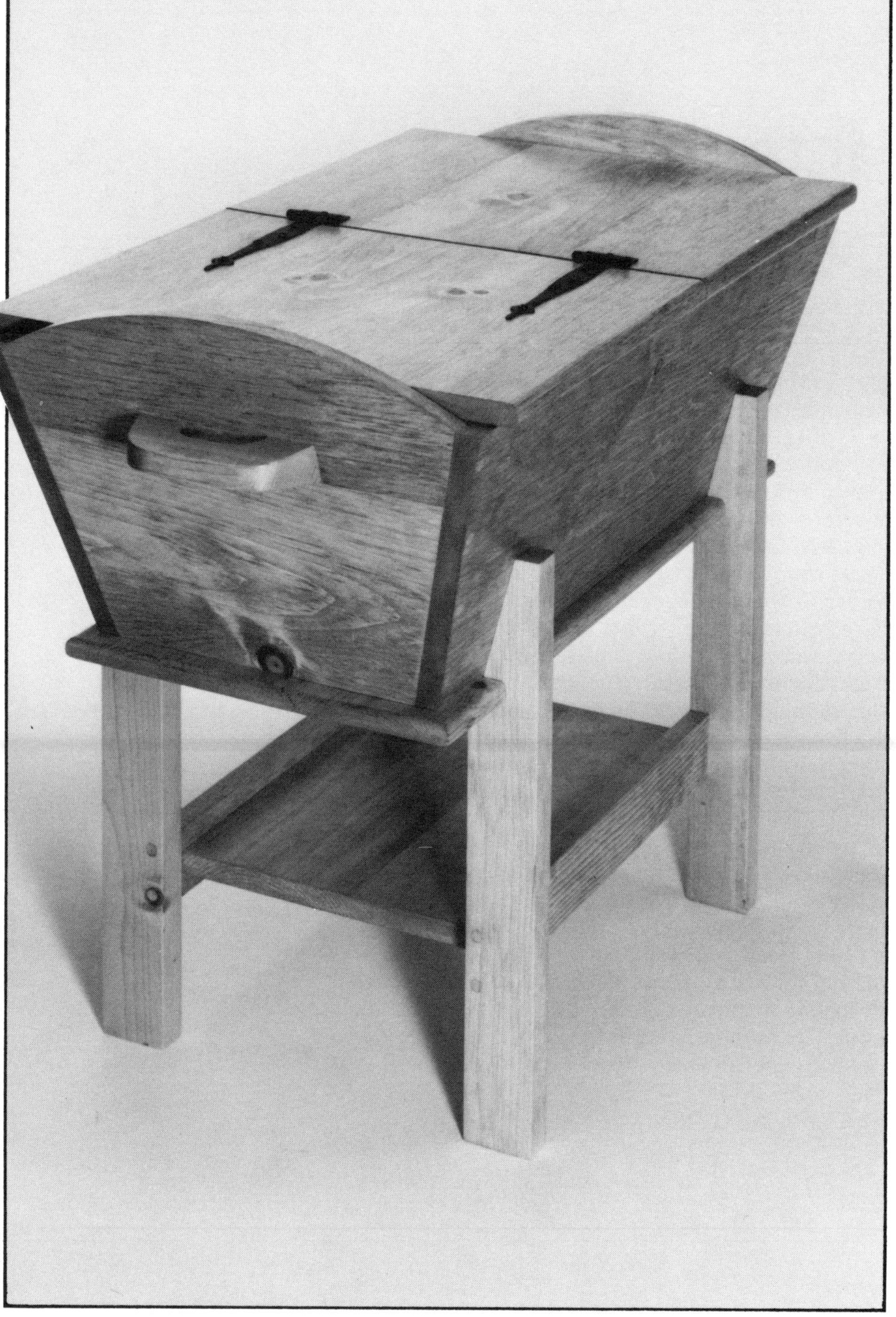

Doughboxes have always had considerable nostalgic appeal. Although they are no longer needed for their original purpose, many fine antiques and reproductions are in use as chairside tables. Their large storage compartments are ideal for magazines or knitting.

Our adaptation, crafted in pine, is a very pretty piece and its construction is just challenging enough to be interesting.

Begin by gluing up stock for the sides (A), ends (B), tops (C), bottom (E), and shelf (I). After flattening all edge-joined stock, tilt the table saw blade 15 degrees, and establish the 15-degree bevel on the top and bottom edges of the sides, and on the bottom edges of the ends. When a butt-joined piece, such as the doughbox, has sides and ends that are both tilted out, then these parts must have compound angles cut on their ends. Compound angles are made by both tilting the table saw blade and angling the miter gauge. Although the compound angle tables tell us that the precise setting for a butt-joined piece with sides tilted at 15 degrees would be 3¾ degrees for the blade and 14½ degrees for the miter gauge, we found that if you can't be that accurate on your table saw a setting of 4 degrees for the saw blade and 15 degrees for the miter gauge should result in a good, tight joint.

Next, lay out the 15 in. radius on the top edge of the ends, rough cut with the band saw, and then clean up the cut and bevel the edge with the disc sander. After finish sanding the various edges and inside surfaces, assemble parts A and B with screws and plugs.

Now cut the bottom and shelf to size, and machine the legs (G), and stretchers (H). Note that the 1 in. deep notches in the bottom will allow the bottom to expand and contract in relation to the legs and doughbox. The ½ in. deep grooves in the stretchers serve the same purpose for the bottom shelf, which is glued into one stretcher, but floats in the opposite stretcher groove. Slotted holes in the bottom allow it to be mounted to the doughbox. Both the bottom and shelf should be stained and finished before they are assembled to their respective assemblies.

After cutting, shaping and fitting the cleats (D) and handles (F) to the doughbox, screw the bottom in place, complete the leg/stretcher/shelf assembly, stain and finish the remaining components, and screw the upper subassembly to the lower subassembly. Eight screws, driven into the legs from the inside of the doughbox, join the upper and lower subassemblies.

Lastly, attach the top with screws through the slotted holes in the cleats, and mount the 7 in. long decorative wrought iron strap hinges (J). We purchased the hinges from Paxton Hardware, Ltd., 7818 Bradshaw Rd., Upper Falls, MD 21156. Order their part no. 5934.

Bill of Materials

Part	Description	Size	No. Req'd.
A	Side	¾ x 9½ x 28⅝	2
B	End	¾ x 11¾ x 15	2
C	Top	¾ x 17¾ x 13¾	2
D	Cleat	¾ x 2 x 15	2
E	Bottom	¾ x 13 x 25½	1
F	Handle	see detail	2
G	Leg	1⅛ x 2¼ x 17¾	4
H	Stretcher	¾ x 2¼ x 16	2
I	Shelf	¾ x 11⅜ x 16	1
J	Strap Hinge	7 in.	2

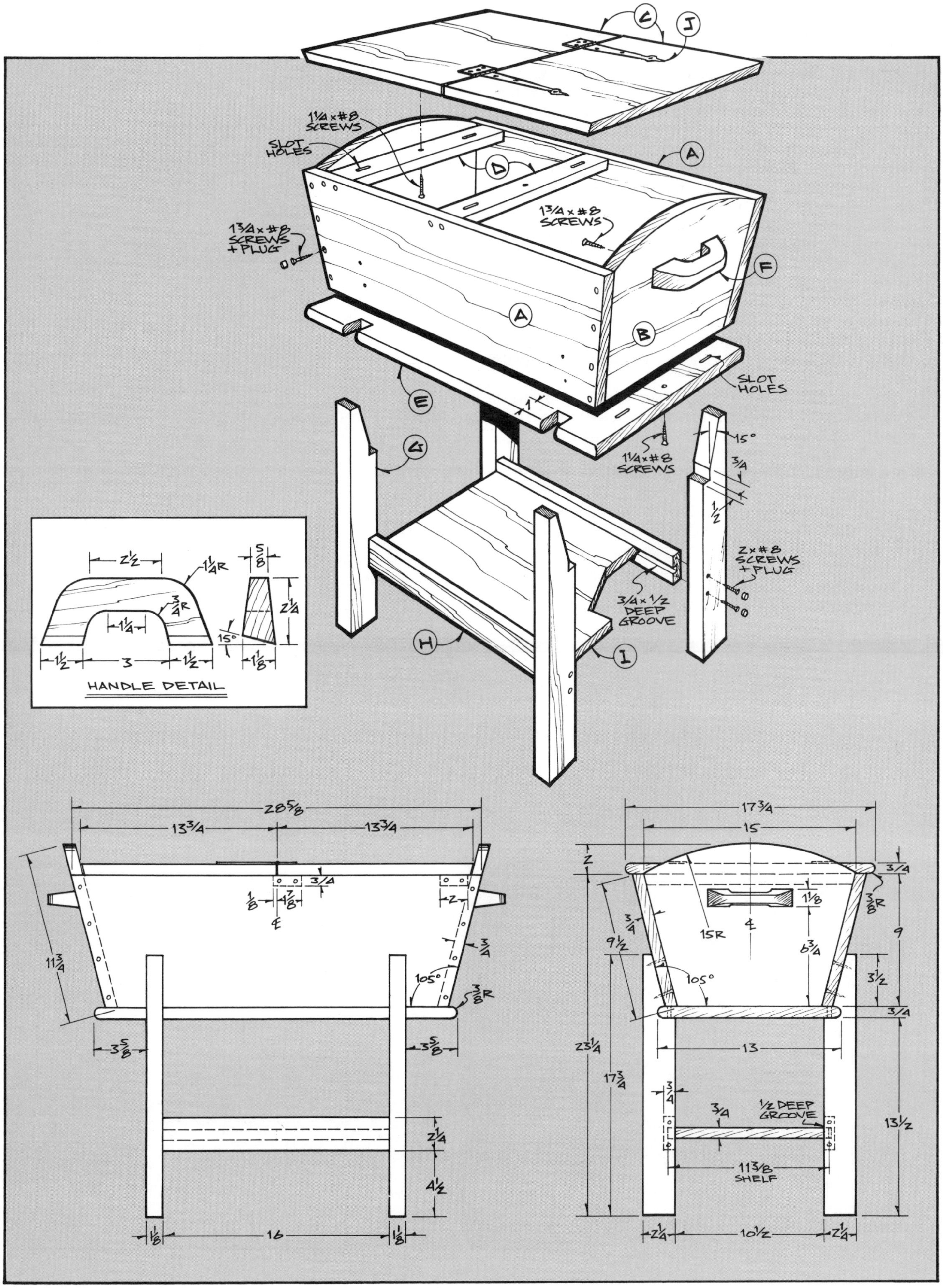
C
J
1¼ x #8 SCREWS
SLOT HOLES
A
D
1¾ x #8 SCREWS
1¾ x #8 SCREWS + PLUG
F
A
B
SLOT HOLES
E
1
G
15°
¾
1¼ x #8 SCREWS
½
2 x #8 SCREWS + PLUG
¾ x ½ DEEP GROOVE
H
I
2½
1¼R
⅝
¾R
2¼
1¼
15°
1½
3
1½
1⅛
HANDLE DETAIL
28⅝
13¾
13¾
¾
⅛
⅞
℄
2
11¾
¾
105°
⅜R
3⅝
3⅝
2¼
4½
1⅛
16
1⅛
17¾
15
2
¾
1⅛
⅜R
¾
9½
15R
℄
6¾
9
105°
3½
¾
23¼
13
17¾
¾
¾
½ DEEP GROOVE
13½
11⅜ SHELF
2¼
10½
2¼

Pine Wall Box

Small pine boxes were found in many Early American homes. They probably enjoyed this popularity because they not only provided a convenient place to store small items, but they also served as very lovely wall decorations. Our wall box, made almost entirely from ½ in. pine, is a fine example of those charming designs.

Begin by cutting the top (A) and bottom (B) to size, then use a router with a ¼ in. beading bit to cut the decorative molding on the front and side edges. Adjust the cut so that the lip is slightly heavier on the outside edge (see detail). Since ½ in. stock does not provide enough bearing surface for the router pilot, the pilot will burn into the stock. To prevent this, clamp scrap stock underneath and flush with the edge to be routed. This provides the additional bearing surface needed to get a good clean cut. After completing the moldings, the ½ in. by 11 in. notch can be cut out from the top.

Next, cut the divider (D) and two sides (C) to proper length and width. The back (E) is made up of two pieces of edge-glued stock.

Cut all drawer components to size, noting that ¾ in. stock is used for the front (F), ½ in. for the back and sides (G, H), and ⅛ in. plywood for the bottom (I). A ⅛ in. wide by ¼ in. deep groove is routed for the bottom in the front and two sides. The groove is located ¼ in. from the bottom. Also a ½ in. wide by ¼ in. deep dado is cut in the sides for the back. The dado is located ¼ in. from the very back.

Sand all parts completely before assembling with glue and finishing nails. Set nails, fill nail holes, then final sand and stain to suit. Two coats of polyurethane provide the final finish.

Part	Description	Size	No. Req'd.
A	Top	½ x 5½ x 13	1
B	Bottom	½ x 5½ x 13	1
C	Side	½ x 5 x 6½	2
D	Divider	½ x 4½ x 11	1
E	Back	½ x 11 x 13⅜	1
F	Drawer Front	¾ x 3 x 11	2
G	Drawer Side	½ x 3 x 4⅛	4
H	Drawer Back	½ x 2⅝ x 10½	2
I	Drawer Bottom	⅛ x 3¾ x 10½	2

Bill of Materials

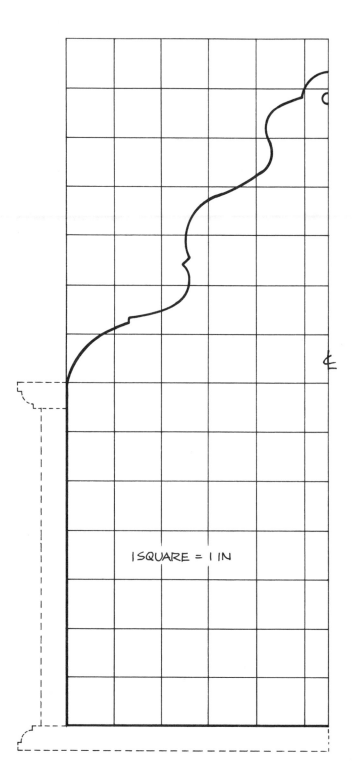

1 SQUARE = 1 IN

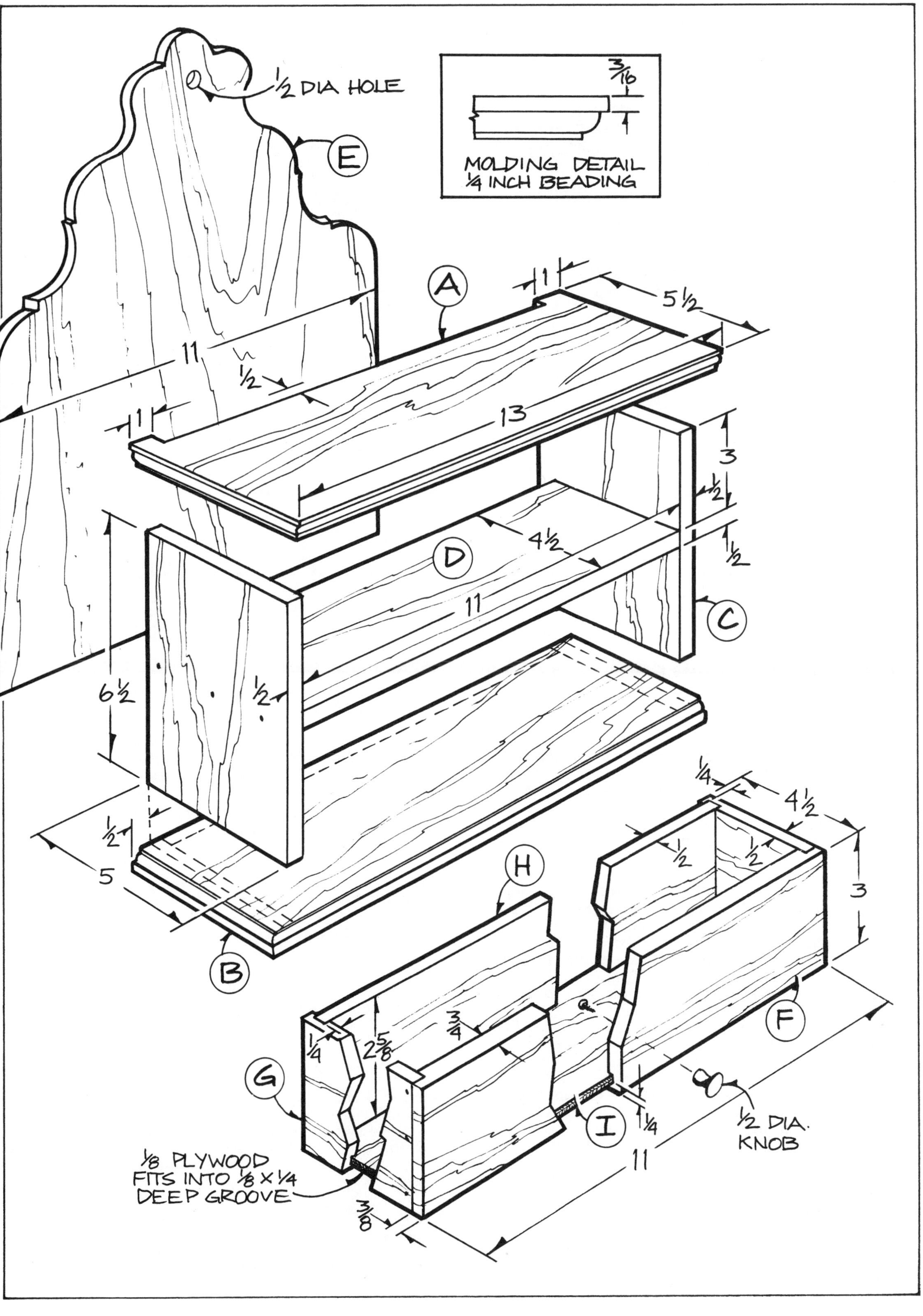

1/2 DIA HOLE
E
3/16
MOLDING DETAIL
1/4 INCH BEADING
A
1
5 1/2
11
1/2
13
1
3
1/2
4 1/2
D
1/2
11
C
6 1/2
1/2
1/2
5
B
1/4
4 1/2
H
1/2
1/2
3
F
3/4
1/4
2 5/8
G
I
1/4
1/2 DIA. KNOB
1/8 PLYWOOD FITS INTO 1/8 X 1/4 DEEP GROOVE
11
3/8

Cobbler's Bench Coffee Table

If Early American is your favorite furniture style, you may want to consider this for your next project. It's a fine example of an old time cobbler's bench, with overall dimensions that make it ideal for use as a modern day coffee table.

Start construction with the bottom piece. You probably won't find a board that's 18" wide, therefore it will be necessary to edge-glue two or more narrow boards to get the needed width. Glue and clamp firmly, allowing to dry overnight, then trim to finish size of 5/4 (1⅛" actual) x 18 x 42. Lay out the curve as shown on the grid pattern, then cut out with a jig saw.

The four legs are 15⅛" long and square tapered. They measure 2" at the base, narrowing down to 1¼" at the top. The tenon is about 1 3/16" long. To make the leg, cut a piece of 2" square stock a bit longer than necessary. Use a lathe to turn the ¾" dia. tenon. Allow extra length on the tenon for later trimming. If you don't have a lathe, the tenon can also be hand made with rasp. Trim to final length and bevel the leg bottom so it sits flat on the floor, then use a sharp plane to cut the tapers.

After cutting the two cleats to size (5/4 x 3 x 16) make the splayed leg drilling jig, following the three-step direction. A ¾" bit is used to bore the vertical hole through the squared block. Align the jig so that the center of the drill bit will start 1½" in from the edge of the cleat (see drawing). Also align the jig so that it's centerline is at 45 degrees to the cleat edges. When properly aligned, clamp in place and drill tenon holes with ¾" bit. Repeat procedure for other three holes.

The two sides are made from ¾" x 5" x 16" stock. Refer to the grid pattern to cut the curve. Also a ½" x 3½" slot is cut in one of the sides. The slot starts ½" from the edge and ¼" from the top.

The back and main divider can be made next. The back measures ¾ x 5 x 18, while the main divider measures ¾ x 3⅛ x 18. Note that each has a ¼" x ½" x 11¼" long stopped dado located ¼" down from the top edge. The slide itself is cut ½ x 3½ x 13½. Next, make the ½ x 3⅛ x 3 slide box divider and the 2" high small dividers.

Before assembly, give all parts a thorough sanding, making sure to remove all planer marks. Clean up any saw marks on the curved cuts. Use a spokeshave or drawknife to give an "antiqued" edge to the four legs.

Begin assembly by joining the four legs to cleats. Apply glue to both leg tenons and cleat holes, then mate together. Rotate leg so that bottom bevel will sit flat on floor. Allow to dry overnight, then trim any excess tenon that protrudes through cleat top. Now the cleat and leg assembly can be joined to the bottom with 1¾" x #10 wood screws. Note that the cleat is located 1" from the back, front and side edge of the bottom piece.

Attach the two sides and the back to the bottom with glue and 2" finishing nails set below the surface. Be sure the slotted side is in front. Next, add the main divider and slide box divider, again using glue and finishing nails. Check the sliding top for a good fit, and make adjustments as necessary. The small dividers can now be glued in place as shown in the drawing.

Make two drawer slides (see detail) and attach to the underside of the bottom with 1½" x #8 wood screws. The drawer itself has a ¾" x 4 x 8 front, with ½" thick sides and back. The bottom is ¼" plywood. The leather drawer pull is a nice detail, quite appropriate for the bench of a cobbler. Simply cut a narrow slot in the drawer front, then loop a 1" strip of leather and insert through the opening. Use a couple of small tacks to secure it in place.

Final sand all surfaces, giving corners and edges a good rounding to simulate years of wear. Be sure to remove glue smudges. Apply a stain that reproduces the look of old pine (Minwax Early American is one). Allow to dry, then complete the project with two coats of polyurethane varnish.

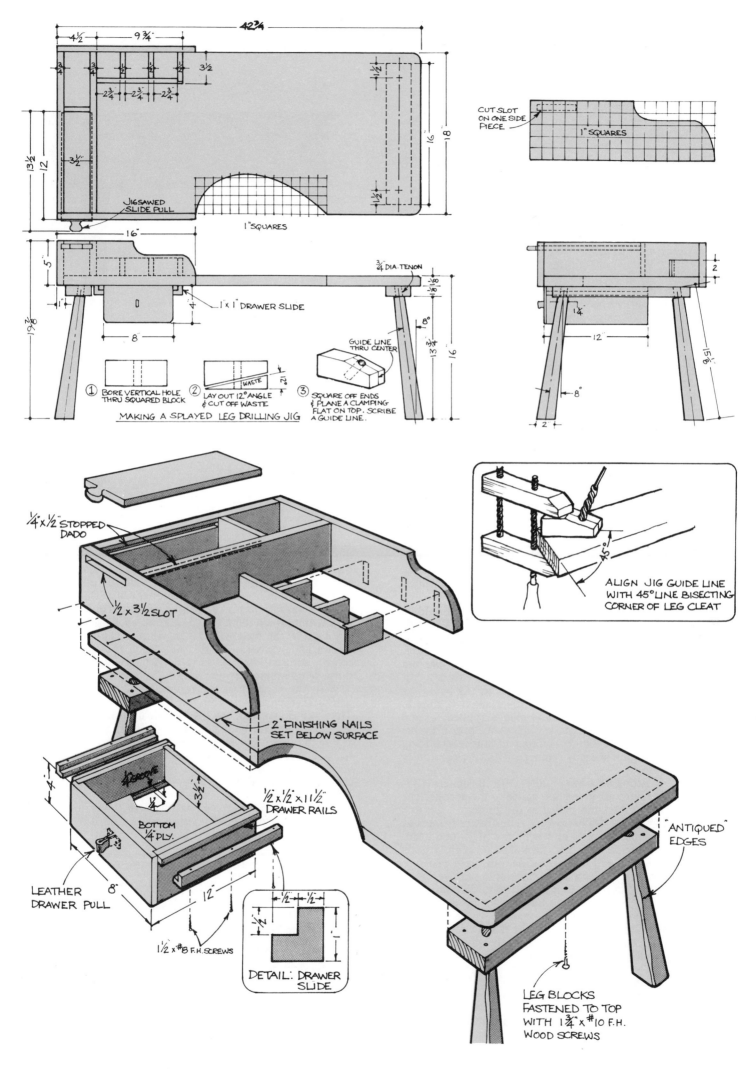

42¾

4½

9¾

3½

3½

2¾ 2¾ 2¾

13½

12

3½

JIGSAWED
SLIDE PULL

1" SQUARES

18

16

½

½

CUT SLOT
ON ONE SIDE
PIECE

1" SQUARES

16"

5"

19⅝

1"

¾ DIA. TENON

1"x 1" DRAWER SLIDE

8"

4

GUIDE LINE
THRU CENTER

8°

13¾

16

2

1¼

12"

15⅝

8°

2"

① BORE VERTICAL HOLE
THRU SQUARED BLOCK

② LAY OUT 12° ANGLE
& CUT OFF WASTE

12°

WASTE

③ SQUARE OFF ENDS
& PLANE A CLAMPING
FLAT ON TOP. SCRIBE
A GUIDE LINE.

MAKING A SPLAYED LEG DRILLING JIG

¼"x ½" STOPPED
DADO

½ x 3½ SLOT

45°

ALIGN JIG GUIDE LINE
WITH 45° LINE BISECTING
CORNER OF LEG CLEAT

2" FINISHING NAILS
SET BELOW SURFACE

4"

¼ GROOVE

3½

BOTTOM
¼ PLY.

½ x ½ x 11½"
DRAWER RAILS

"ANTIQUED"
EDGES

LEATHER
DRAWER PULL

8"

12"

½ x #8 F.H. SCREWS

½

½ ½

DETAIL: DRAWER
SLIDE

LEG BLOCKS
FASTENED TO TOP
WITH 1¾" x #10 F.H.
WOOD SCREWS

7

19th Century Cherry Table

The photo shows a cherry table of about 1850 vintage. Nicely proportioned, with its elegant turned legs, this piece is of a style sometimes referred to as "Country" furniture.

While the table is entirely of cherry wood, other hardwoods may be substituted for reproduction. The second choice would be mahogany. As for structural details, dowel joints can be substituted for the apron and rail tenons and lap joints used instead of drawer dovetails.

The legs are turned from 2 inch stock to finish at 1⅞ inches square at the tops. Most turning dimensions are shown in the leg detail. When turning is completed, this writer prefers to apply a sealer before removing the turning from the lathe. This protects the surface from damage and prevents glue marks that are hard to remove.

Next, cut side and back aprons A and E to rough length, including tenons at each end. While ⅞ inch stock is called for, ¾ inch material may be substituted but other adjustments will have to be made.

All six double apron tenons can be cut with the same saw settings. Use a piece of scrap to check blade height for the ¼ inch depth of the shoulders. Make two long shoulder cuts on each apron. The tenon length is completed by drawing the apron away from the fence and making repeated passes over the blade, first on one side and then on the other until a full length tenon has been made. The upper shoulder is made using the same procedure. Waste between tenons is removed with backsaw and chisel. When completed, sand the aprons and apply a sealer.

Parts D1 and D2 are next cut and tenoned as shown. The two parts are alike and joined to front legs with shoulders facing down.

The next step is the fitting of the aprons and drawer rails to the legs. To prevent errors, mark each surface of the legs with corresponding marks on the aprons and rails. Use a mortise gauge to lay out mortises; remember that the aprons should be flush with the outside surface of the legs. This departs from the usual practice of having the aprons inset slightly. Mortises can be cut with a router, or by drilling holes the entire length of the mortise and finishing with a chisel.

Before making the top and drawer, the carcase should be completely finished and assembled. First, fit all parts together temporarily to check joints for fit and squareness. As a safety factor when gluing, use the following method. Glue back legs to their apron and front legs to the upper and lower rails, without clamping. Do not set aside to dry, but immediately fit the front legs and aprons to the back legs *without glue.* Clamp and check for squareness. If square, the unglued parts are separated and glue is applied. Clamp and again check for squareness. This procedure prevents any leg from twisting out of alignment under clamping pressure. Excess glue is easily removed from the previously sealed surfaces.

Cutting and fitting of drawer guides (B) and runners (C) is a simple job. Guides are glued and nailed to the aprons. The runners are then glued and nailed to the guides.

Construction of the drawer is next. The drawer front is of ⅞ inch stock while the sides and back are of ⅜ inch hardwood. One suggestion in fitting dovetails . . . slightly bevel the sides of the pins and they will slide into place easier.

Cut grooves on the sides and the back of the drawer front to hold the drawer bottom. This groove should be started ¼ inch up from the bottom edges and sizes for an easy fit of the ¼ inch plywood bottom.

Before assembling the drawer, cut the false beading on the front. This can be done with a mortising gauge or inlay router. Glue and assemble all parts, checking for squareness and flatness. The drawer bottom should slide easily into place. Secure it with a few nails up into the drawer back. The original drawer pull is of brass but a 1 inch dia. turned cherry pull would be fine.

Several pieces are jointed and edge glued to make up the

top. After drying, cut to finish size and round the front and side edges. To allow the top to expand and contract with seasonal changes in humidity you'll need to cut a pair of ¼ in. wide by ½ in. long slots in the upper rail as shown. Also it will be necessary to make two pair of slotted glue blocks (see detail) and attach them to the side and back aprons. The top is joined to the base with 1½ in. x no. 8 round head wood screws and washers. There's not much room to drive the screws, so it will be helpful to use a box wrench and one of those removable screwdriver tips.

With the construction completed, thoroughly sand first with 100, then 180 or 150 and finally with 220 grit paper. Then rub down with steel wool. Most antiques were either shellaced or varnished. This piece calls for a varnish finish.

For many woodworkers, there is no better varnish than the polyurethanes. They are water and alcohol resistant and very durable. The first coat acts as a sealer and should be thoroughly sanded with 220 or 340 grit, then steel wooled. Follow with one or two coats of satin varnish (two for the top). Lightly sand between coats with #600 wet or dry paper and 4/0 steel wool. Finish with a coat of hard wax.

Bill of Materials (All Dimensions Actual)

Part	Description	Size	No.
A	Side Apron	⅞ x 5¼ x 15 (Incl. 1" long tenons)	2
B	Drawer Guide	1 x 2 x 13	2
C	Runner	⅞ x 1 x 13⅞	2
D1,D2	Upper & Lower Rails	⅞ x 2 x 18¾ (Incl. 1" long tenons)	2
E	Back Apron	⅞ x 5¼ x 18¾ (Incl. 1" long tenons)	1
F	Leg	See Detail	4
G	Top	¾ x 17⅜ x 21¾	1
H	Drawer	See Detail	1

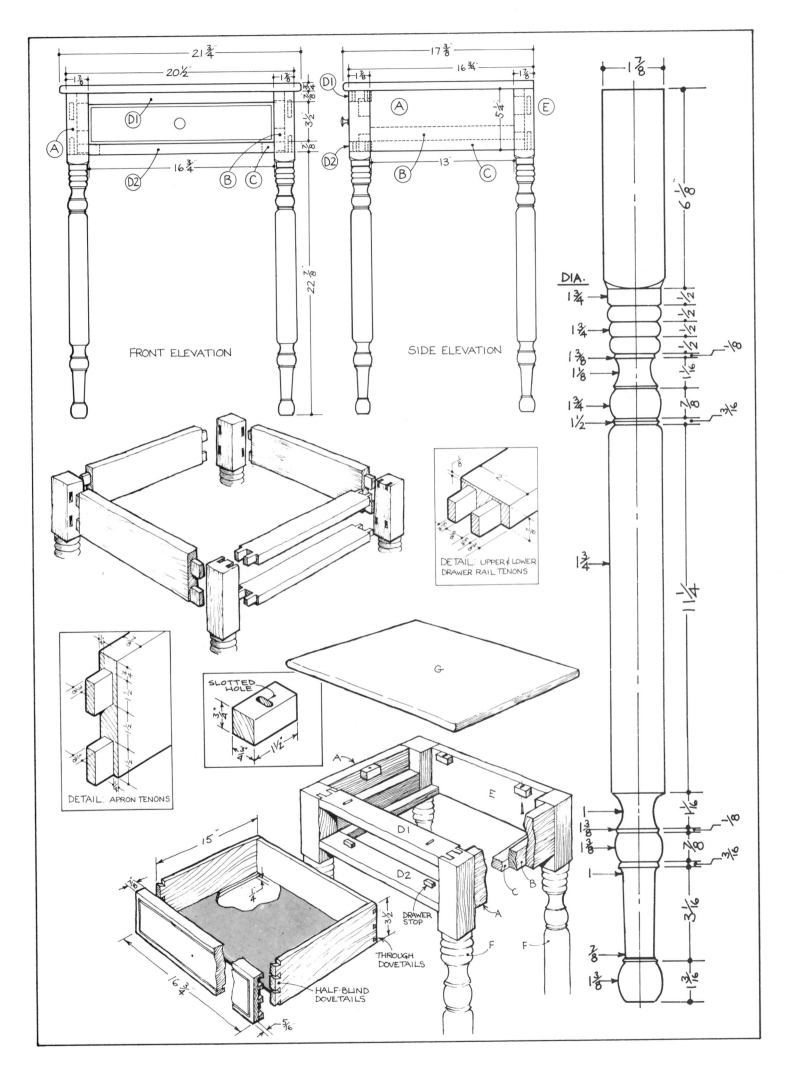

FRONT ELEVATION

SIDE ELEVATION

DETAIL: UPPER & LOWER
DRAWER RAIL TENONS

DETAIL: APRON TENONS

SLOTTED
HOLE

DIA.

DRAWER
STOP

THROUGH
DOVETAILS

HALF-BLIND
DOVETAILS

9

Pine Schoolhouse Desk

This small desk-bench unit was inspired by the old-fashioned schoolhouse desks now commanding high prices at antique shops. Built of easily obtained 5/4 inch pine (1⅛″ actual thickness) along with a few pieces of ¾ inch stock, it's proportioned for children of about 8-11 years and provides a convenient surface for both schoolwork and play. It's also an attractive piece of furniture for a child's room.

Start by jointing and edge-gluing three lengths of 5/4 x 8 inch stock for the desk top. Clamp until dry and then trim to finish dimensions of 20 x 26¾ inches. Plane and sand the slab flat, and round off the front and end top edges.

The shaped uprights supporting the desk and seat are cut from 5/4 x 10 inch and 5/4 x 8 inch stock respectively. Lay out a 1 inch grid pattern on cardboard of approximate size and enlarge one half of the profiles. Cut along your penciled profile and use this half-template to trace the shape on the workpieces.

Before cutting the curves, lay out and cut the rabbet at the top ends of the large upright. Also lay out and cut the dadoes to hold the bookshelf and footrest. These cuts can be easily done with a table saw and dado head or by making repeated passes over an ordinary blade.

The feet, which are also of 5/4 inch stock are next shaped as shown in Fig. 1, and dadoed to receive the seat and desk uprights. The bookshelf and footrest are next cut from ¾ inch stock. These are both cut to 9¼ x 22½ inches; however, the footrest is partially cut away along the front edge for a more decorative appearance.

Sand all parts well and glue and clamp feet, shelves and uprights together, maintaining squareness while counter-boring for ½ inch dia. plugs and drilling pilot holes for the screws fastening feet to uprights as shown in Fig. 3.

Cut the top brackets from ¾ inch thick pine and trim the ends to 36 degrees (see Fig. 4). Referring to the same detail, lay out, mark and drill the ½ inch dia. by 1¼ inch deep counterbored screw hole on each end, then bore the ³⁄₁₆ inch shank dia. as shown. Also, locate and drill a ⅜ inch dia. by ⅝ inch deep dowel pin hole at the center of the bracket (7 inch from each end). The brackets can now be glued and screwed to the upright rabbets. Note that the screws are counterbored and covered with ½ inch dia. plugs.

Cut a backboard slightly long from ¾ inch stock for the rear of the bookshelf. Trim so it fits snugly between the uprights, flush with back and top edge of uprights. Secure with glue and finishing nails driven up through the book shelf.

Turn the assembly upside down and center it on the underside of the top, then locate the centerpoints of the two ⅜ inch diameter bracket dowel holes. Bore these holes ⅝ inch deep in the underside of the top to accept ⅜ inch dia. by 1¼ inch long dowel pins. Apply glue to the dowel pins and clamp the top to the brackets (don't glue any other area as the top must be free to expand and contract with seasonal changes in humidity. Next, drive the 1½ inch x no. 10 round-head wood screws and washers (Fig. 4). The shank hole is bored oversized (³⁄₁₆ inch) to allow some room for the top to move with those inevitable seasonal changes in width.

The top backboard is shaped from ¾ inch stock and fastened as shown in Fig. 3. The bench top is then cut to finish size, sanded and screwed to uprights. Finally, rout or gouge a 12 inch long by ¼ inch deep pencil groove near the back edge of top.

Use a plug cutter to cut ⅜″ long plugs from the face grain of pine scraps or use birch dowel stock cut to length. The plugs may be trimmed and sanded flush or left protruding slightly and rounded off.

Go over the piece carefully, rounding off all corners to give it an antique appearance and to discourage splintering. After finish sanding, apply the stain and sealer of your choice.

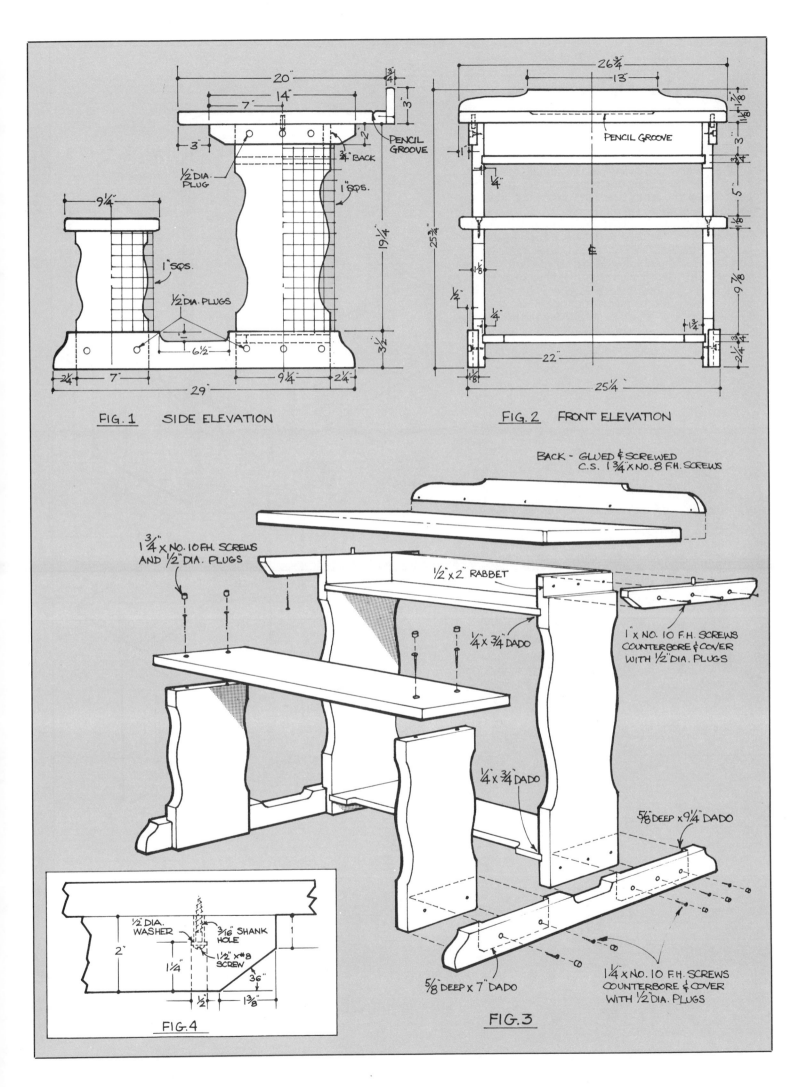

FIG. 1   SIDE ELEVATION

FIG. 2   FRONT ELEVATION

PENCIL GROOVE

½ DIA. PLUG

¾" BACK

1" SQS.

½ DIA. PLUGS

1" SQS.

PENCIL GROOVE

BACK – GLUED & SCREWED
C.S. 1¾" x NO. 8 F.H. SCREWS

1¾" x NO. 10 F.H. SCREWS
AND ½" DIA. PLUGS

½" x 2" RABBET

¼" x ¾" DADO

1" x NO. 10 F.H. SCREWS
COUNTERBORE & COVER
WITH ½" DIA. PLUGS

¼" x ¾" DADO

5/8" DEEP x 9¼" DADO

½" DIA. WASHER

3/16" SHANK HOLE

½" x #8 SCREW

FIG. 4

5/8" DEEP x 7" DADO

FIG. 3

¼" x NO. 10 F.H. SCREWS
COUNTERBORE & COVER
WITH ½" DIA. PLUGS

11

Grain Scoop

Wall decorations always make popular gift items. Using pine stock, this one is made in the form of a grain scoop and looks especially nice with a small arrangement of dried flowers.

A small piece like this often looks best with a light appearance, so we used 5/16″ stock for all parts except the handles, but ¼″ or ⅜″ stock can also be substituted without any problem. If you don't have a power planer, sharpen up your hand planes and go to work on a piece of ¾″ stock. A board about 8″ wide and 7″ long will take care of the side stock, and one 5¾″ wide x 11½″ long will suffice for the back, bot-

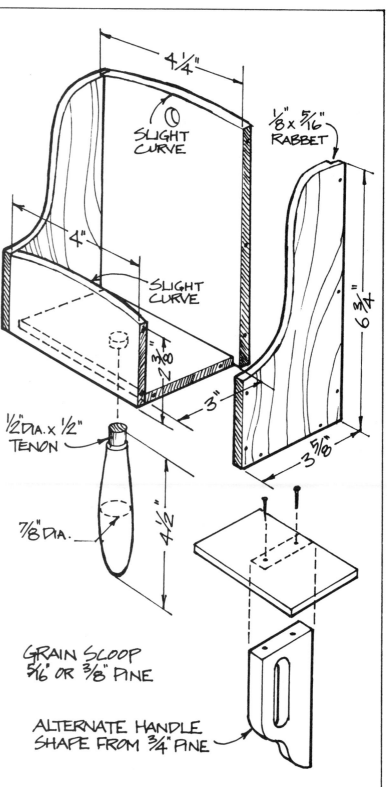

4¼″

SLIGHT CURVE

4″

SLIGHT CURVE

1/8″ x 5/16″ RABBET

6¾″

3 ⁵⁄₈

3″

3/16″

1″

½″DIA. x ½″ TENON

7/8″ DIA.

4½″

GRAIN SCOOP 5/16″ OR ⅜″ PINE

ALTERNATE HANDLE SHAPE FROM ¾″ PINE

tom, and front.

Cut all parts to dimensions shown, noting that each side leg has a ⅛″ x 5/16″ rabbet. If you use ¼″ or ⅜″ stock, adjust the rabbet to fit.

The handle is either lathe turned or handcarved to the dimensions shown. If you don't have a lathe, or prefer another style handle, we've included an alternate shape.

Sand all parts, then assemble with glue and countersunk finishing nails. After filling the nail holes, resand all surfaces before staining and finishing to suit.

Quilt Rack

With today's interest in quilting, there are many households that have several beautiful quilts sitting in storage closets and chests where no one is able to see or appreciate the time and handiwork they represent. The maple quilt rack shown here was developed after my grandmother expressed an interest in having a place to display her beautiful quilts.

From 2″ square stock, turn two spindles to dimensions shown. The two lower rungs (A) are made next, each turned to 1″ dia. from 1⅛″ square stock. Use the parting tool to establish the 24⅛″ length between shoulders, then finish by turning ⅜″ dia. x ¾″ long tenons each end. Using a diamond point chisel, four light cuts will form the decorative bead at the center. Repeat the same techniques to make the upper rung (F), except note that shoulder to shoulder length is 24″, and tenon should be made ½″ dia. x 1″ long. The stretcher (B) can now be made from 1″ (¾″ actual) x 3½″ x 24″ stock.

Next cut the arms (C) and legs (E) from 5/4 x 4″ x 12″ stock. For maximum strength, the grain direction should be the same as the arrows on the drawing. Before assembly apply a ¼″ radius to the exposed edges of arms, legs, and stretcher - then give all parts a thorough sanding. Drill ⅜″ dia. holes in part (C) as shown.

The stretcher (B) is attached to (D) with ⅜″ dowels. Be sure that these dowels do not interfere with dowels that join legs (E). Also, a ½″ dia. hole is drilled in the spindle for (F).

Now attach legs (E) to part (D) with ½″ dowels. To insure that all four legs will sit flat on the floor, take extra care and use a doweling jig when drilling holes. Clamping is difficult because of the lack of parallel flat surfaces, so a clamping jig cut to the shape of the leg should be used. If care is exercised when originally cutting out the arms and legs, the scrap can be used as the clamping jig.

Assemble part (A) to arms (C), then join this sub-assembly to the spindle (D). A clamping jig will also help here.

Final sand the entire project. The finish is your choice, but maple looks beautiful when given at least two coats of Watco Danish Oil finish, then waxed.

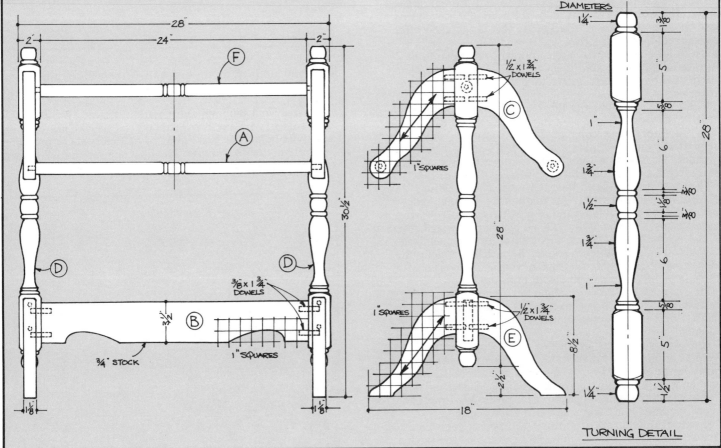

TURNING DETAIL

Ratchet Table Lamp

An 18th century ratchet candlestand provided the inspiration for this attractive combination end table and reading lamp. The ratchet device permits the lamp height to be varied from 38 to 50 inches from the floor, thus converting the piece to a floor lamp. And it's as interesting to build as it is to look at.

Oak was used for our model but maple, birch or cherry can be substituted. Although the posts and ratchet bar are of 1⅛ inch stock, thinner one inch (13/16″ actually) can be used. For stability, the feet should be about 2 inches thick and can be laminated from 1 inch stock.

Start by cutting feet to length, then lay out and cut the half-lap notches centered on each piece. Cut these for a snug fit. Lay out and cut two mortises to take the post tenons. Sand feet and join with glue.

The two posts are next cut slightly long and tenons formed on each end. Leave upper tenons a bit long so they can be trimmed flush later. Chamfer the posts as shown.

The ratchet bar is cut to length and width and a ⅜″ x ¾″ deep groove is cut, centered along its length. Drill a ⅜″ dia. x 2″ deep hole in the top in line with the groove. Connect groove and hole by drilling another ⅜″ hole into the back of the groove and angled up to intersect the nipple hole near its bottom.

Lay out and cut the ratchet teeth. Before starting each angled cut, chisel a small notch to help start the blade.

A ⅜″ x ⅜″ filler strip is cut to fit snugly in the long groove flush with the outer surface. Tap the strip in place temporarily and cut the tenon at the end of the bar. Remove the strip and feed lamp cord into the angled hole and out the top of the bar. Tie a loose knot in the cord so it won't slip back down while you glue the filler strip in place.

The notched spreader which is mortised to the end of the ratchet bar and keeps it centered between the posts is cut next. Notch it to fit around posts and mortise it to receive the tenon. Also cut and bevel the upper plate which is mortised to fit the post tenons and the ratchet bar. The mortise for the ratchet bar should be cut so that the bar slides easily. The cam assembly is made from ⅜″ dia. dowel and hardwood resawed to ⅜″ thickness. This is installed after assembly of the stand.

Carefully sand all parts and temporarily join posts to base with the spreader between them. Add the beveled top plate and ratchet bar to ascertain that all parts fit well and the bar moves easily.

If all looks well, cut the table support cleats and screw them to the posts. Make sure they are level and 22 inches from the floor. Glue lower post tenons into base and peg them as shown. Also glue and peg the ratchet bar to its spreader. Do not glue the upper tenons into the top plate until after the table top has been fitted.

The top consists of two boards which, after jointing, are 8¹⁄₁₆ and 6¹⁵⁄₁₆ inches wide. Cut the boards to rough length and, using the assembled stand as a guide, carefully lay out the locations of the posts and ratchet bar on the jointed edge of the wider board. Notch this board to fit around the uprights. The post notches should be a tight fit while the ratchet bar notch is a bit oversize. Edge-join the boards with glue and ⅜″ dowel pins and clamp until dry.

Trim top to finished size and after removing the upper plate, drive the top down over posts and fasten it to the cleats. The beveled upper plate can now be glued to post tenons.

The cam is attached by drilling a ⁷⁄₁₆″ hole, centered on one post and 6 in. above the table top. Assemble the cam as shown in the exploded view. Note that one dowel is 3 inches long and protrudes to serve as a handle. The cam sides should be parallel and snug against the posts. All dowel ends except the handle are trimmed flush after gluing.

A pair of nuts on the 1½″ nipple will permit you to use a wrench to screw it about ½ inch into the top of the ratchet

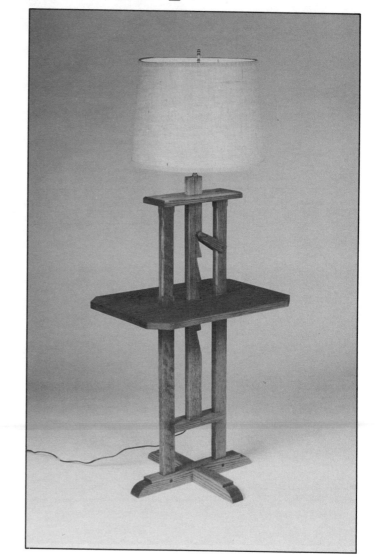

bar. Add lamp hardware as shown. The small opening at the top of the groove can be filled with a wood plug glued in place.

After a final sanding, apply stain if desired. We used one light coat of Minwax Provincial oil stain as the natural oak was quite light. This was followed by two coats of urethane varnish applied to all parts. The final coat was rubbed down with 4/0 steel wool.

Bill of Materials		
(All Dims. Actual)		
Description	**Size in Inches**	**No. Req'd**
Foot	2 x 2 x 21	2
Post	1⅛ x 1¾ x 34½ (includes tenons)	2
Ratchet Bar	See Detail	1
Spreader	¾ x 3 x 8	1
Upper Plate	¾ x 4½ x 12	1
Cam	See Detail	2
Support Cleat	¾ x 1½ x 14	2
Top	¾ x 15 x 20	1

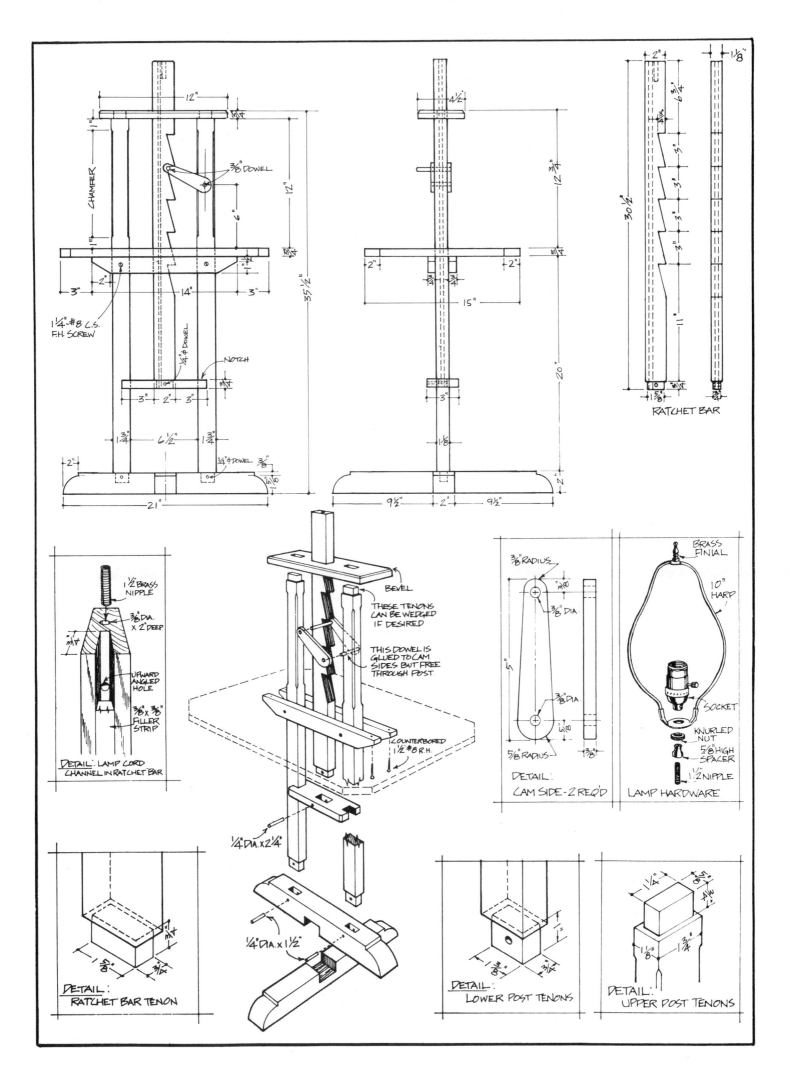

CHAMFER

12"

3/8" DOWEL

12"

6"

1 1/4"-#8 C.S.
F.H. SCREW

1/4" ∅ DOWEL

NOTCH

3" 2" 3"

3/4"

6 1/2"

1 3/4"

2"

1/4" ∅ DOWEL 3/8"

21"

35 1/2"

14"

4 1/2"

12 3/4"

2" 3/8" 3/8" 2"

15"

3"

20"

9 1/2" 2" 9 1/2"

1 1/8"

2"

2" 1 1/8"

30 1/2"

3/8" 3" 3" 3" 3" 3" 3"

6 1/4"

3 3/4"

RATCHET BAR

5/8"

1 1/2" BRASS
NIPPLE

3/8" DIA.
X 2" DEEP

UPWARD
ANGLED
HOLE

3/8" X 3/8"
FILLER
STRIP

DETAIL: LAMP CORD
CHANNEL IN RATCHET BAR

BEVEL

THESE TENONS
CAN BE WEDGED
IF DESIRED

THIS DOWEL IS
GLUED TO CAM
SIDES BUT FREE
THROUGH POST.

COUNTERBORED
1 1/2" #8 R.H.

1/4" DIA. X 2 1/4"

1/4" DIA. X 1 1/2"

3/8" RADIUS

3/8" DIA.

3/8" DIA.

5"

5/8" RADIUS

3/8"

DETAIL:
CAM SIDE - 2 REQ'D

BRASS
FINIAL

10"
HARP

SOCKET

KNURLED
NUT

5/8" HIGH
SPACER

1/2" NIPPLE

DETAIL:
LAMP HARDWARE

5/8" 3/4"

DETAIL:
RATCHET BAR TENON

3/4" 3/4"

DETAIL:
LOWER POST TENONS

1/4" 3/4"

1 1/8" 3/4"

DETAIL:
UPPER POST TENONS

15

18th Century Trestle Table

The 17th century was a time of deep unrest and turmoil in Europe. Religious persecution in Swiss Alsatia and Palatinate Germany forced the emigration of Amish and Mennonite peoples to Pennsylvania where they had been invited by William Penn in 1682.

Living in secluded areas, guarding their fragile cultural heritage, these industrious Germanic people soon learned to adapt to their new country.

They lived, as many early settlers did, in small cabins with one large room. This room served as a place to cook, eat, sleep and pass the time with friends. In this cramped lifestyle, pieces of furniture had to serve multiple purposes. Settles became beds, chair backs would fold down to become tables, and tables would drop leaves to become smaller and get tucked away.

The table shown in the photo can be disassembled and stored away. Made of American black walnut sometime before 1750, its medieval character served the gentle and simple ways of the country people generally referred to as Pennsylvania Dutch.

Although the table looks massive in the photo, and indeed has a certain rugged beauty, an examination of the dimensional drawings will show that it is in fact a small table. The original was made entirely of American black walnut, but the use of oak, maple or even pine will be authentic and considerably less expensive.

Begin with the legs (B). Make a full size pattern and transfer this onto the stock which should be at least 1⅛ inches thick. A bow saw with a fine blade is ideal for cutting the curves as their large size and detailed curvature may be a problem for some bandsaws. Don't forget to leave enough material at the end for the tenons.

The outside rail D and feet A come next. Note that although the curves are identical, part D is shorter. Also note that the rails consist of two pieces D and E, glued together. On the end elevation view (left side), the dotted lines showing parts D & E have been made solid, making it easier to lay out their profiles. Mortises for the leg tenons are then laid out and cut into the feet and top rail assemblies.

The top (H) comes next. These tables usually had tops made of one wide board but you will probably have to edge-joint and glue up two or more boards to achieve the width. The decorative edge on the top can be added with a molding plane or a router with rounding over bit.

Set the top on the leg assemblies so that part D is an equal distance from the ends of the top and measure for the stretcher (G) length. Allowing for the two long tenons, cut the stretcher and

Photograph courtesy
The Metropolitan Museum of Art,
gift of Mrs. Robert W. deForrest, 1933

again detail the corners with a plane or router.

After making the tenons and wedges (F), temporarily assemble the table and locate the dovetail troughs at each end of the top just outboard of the D rails. These can be easily cut with a router and dovetail bit. Cleat C is cut to fit these troughs across the full width of the top. If the dovetail routine seems too difficult, cut part C flat on top, counterbore them and screw them to the top. Use three screws per rail, one in the center and one near each end. The end screw holes should be elongated to allow for seasonal movement of the top.

The top can now be set on the leg assembly and holes drilled through parts C and D for the four ¾ inch diameter pegs (I) which secure the top to the leg assembly. These pegs can be

lathe turned as were the originals, or whittled.

The finishing touch is the drawer. Early drawers had large dovetails and bottoms of ¾ or ⅞ inch stock set into rabbets in front and sides. Not authentic, but far more practical is the use of ¼ inch plywood for the bottom panel as shown. The drawer runners M are glued and screwed to the sides to fit in the grooved rail assemblies.

Finishing of the table will depend upon the type of wood used but in general, the finish should be of a low luster type; either well rubbed varnish or perhaps one of the penetrating oils such as Watco Danish Oil. Be sure to give the underside of the top the same treatment as the topside. A brass pull similar to the style shown completes the project.

Bill of Materials (All Dims. Actual)			
Part	Description	Size	No. Req'd
A	Foot	2 x 2¾ x 25¼	2
B	Leg	1⅛ x 15½ x 24⅝ (includes tenons)	2
C	Cleat	1⅛ x 2⅜ x 26½	2
D	Outside Rail	1⅛ x 2¾ x 24	2
E	Inside Rail	1⅛ x 2¾ x 21	2
F	Wedges	½ x 2 x 5	2
G	Stretcher	2 x 2½ x 33½ (includes tenons)	1
H	Top	1⅛ x 26½ x 41¼	1
I	Pegs	¾ dia. x 6″ long	4
J	Drawer Front	⅞ x 5½ x 23	1
K	Drawer Back	¾ x 4¾ x 23	1
L	Drawer Side	¾ x 5½ x 18⅛	2
M	Drawer Runner	⅞ x ⅞ x 17	2

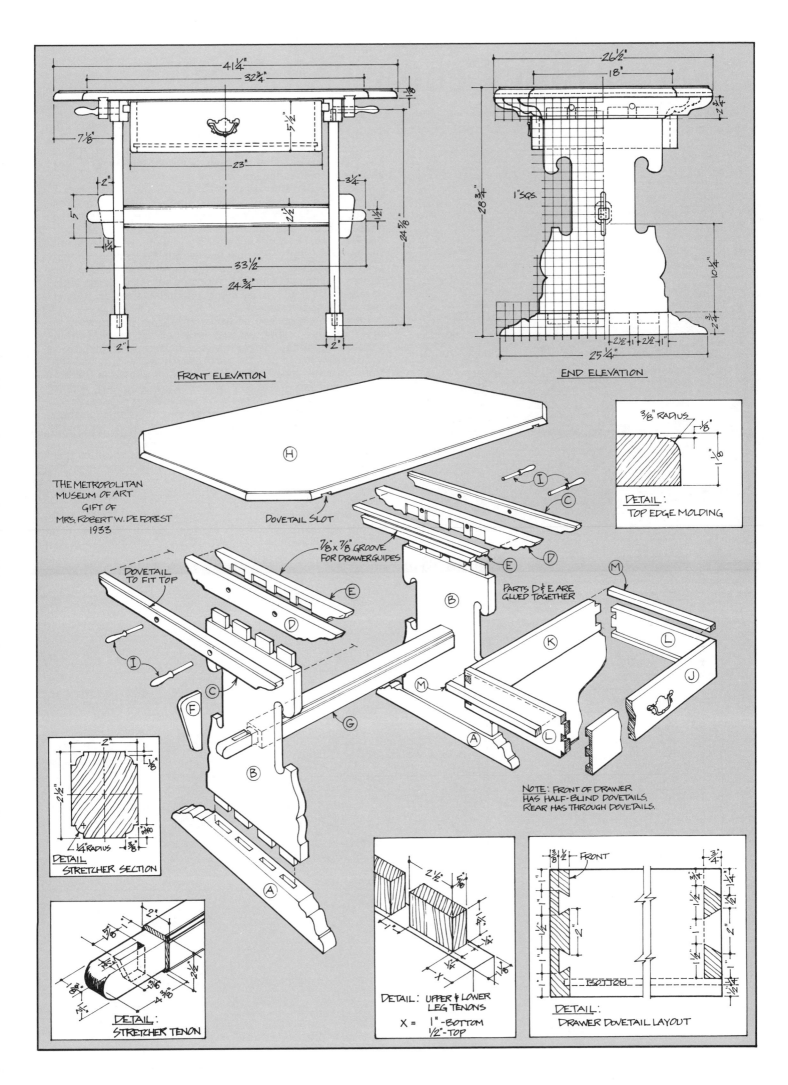

FRONT ELEVATION

41¼"
32¾"
7⅛"
2"
5"
1¼"
23"
5½"
2½"
33½"
24¾"
3¼"
½"
24⅞"
2"
2"

END ELEVATION

26½"
18"
2¾"
1" SQS.
28¾"
10¼"
3¾"
2¾"
25¼"
2½" 1" 2½" 1"

THE METROPOLITAN
MUSEUM OF ART
GIFT OF
MRS. ROBERT W. DE FOREST
1933

H

DOVETAIL SLOT

DETAIL:
TOP EDGE MOLDING

3/8" RADIUS
1/8"
1/8"

⅞" x ⅞" GROOVE
FOR DRAWER GUIDES

I
C
E
D

DOVETAIL
TO FIT TOP

PARTS D & E ARE
GLUED TOGETHER

M

E
D
B
I
C
F
M
A
G
B
K
L
J

NOTE: FRONT OF DRAWER
HAS HALF-BLIND DOVETAILS.
REAR HAS THROUGH DOVETAILS.

DETAIL
STRETCHER SECTION

2"
2½"
¼" RADIUS
3/8"

A

DETAIL:
STRETCHER TENON

2"
2½"
4⅜"

DETAIL: UPPER & LOWER
LEG TENONS
X = 1"-BOTTOM
½"-TOP

2½"

DETAIL:
DRAWER DOVETAIL LAYOUT

FRONT
3½"
¾"
BOTTOM

17

18th Century Shelves

The design of this classic piece is based on a colonial original. Solidly constructed from ¾″ pine, there are three good size shelves that provide plenty of display area. It's an enjoyable project that will add a handsome look to just about any room in the house.

Make the two sides first, cutting each one to ¾″ thick x 5½″ wide x 34″ long. Standard lumberyard 1 x 6 stock (which actually measures ¾″ thick x 5½″ wide) can be used here. Lay out and mark the location of the three shelf dadoes, then cut them ¾″ wide x ¼″ deep. It's best to cut the dadoes slightly less than the ¾″ shelf thickness, so that after the shelves are sanded, the fit will be perfect. The dadoes can be cut by making repeated passes with the table or radial saw blade, or by using a dado head cutter. Also, a router will do the job well.

Now, the curves can be transferred from the drawing to the stock. Use a saber saw, bandsaw or coping saw to cut to shape, keeping the sawblade on the waste side of the line.

The shelves can now be cut to length and width, and the front corners nipped off at 45 degrees as shown in the detail. If you wish to use 5½″ wide stock throughout, simply make the front edge of the shelf flush with the side curve.

Now sides and shelves can be given a thorough sanding. Make sure any planer marks are removed. Also, especially concentrate on the curved front edges of the sides.

Minwax Early American is a good choice of stain for this project. Apply two coats, let dry, then finish with two coats of satin polyurethane varnish.

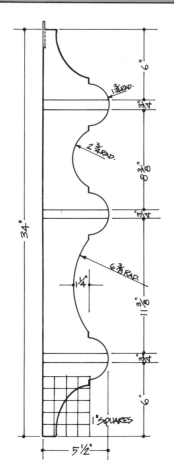

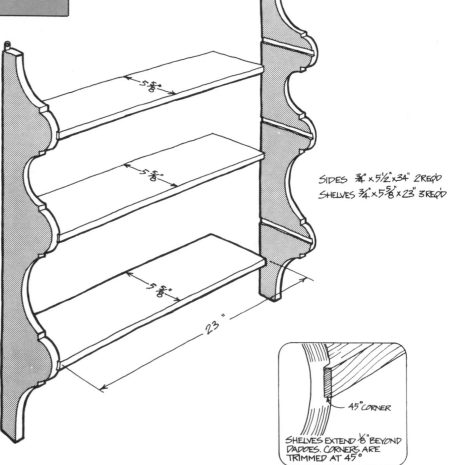

SIDES ¾″ x 5½″ x 34″ 2 REQ'D
SHELVES ¾″ x 5⅝″ x 23″ 3 REQ'D

SHELVES EXTEND ⅛″ BEYOND DADOES. CORNERS ARE TRIMMED AT 45°

Matchbox

Hang this small box by the fireplace or woodstove and you won't have to go searching for a match when it's time to start the fire. It provides lots of space to store a generous supply of wooden matches.

Cut the back, sides, and front to size from ⅜″ thick pine. A small triangular block is also cut to serve as a bottom. Sand all parts thoroughly.

Assemble sides to front and back with glue and small finishing nails. Apply a thin coat of glue to the triangular bottom and assemble to the bottom as shown.

Final sand all surfaces and edges, then apply a stain of your choice. Final finish with two coats of polyurethane varnish, followed by a rub down with 4/0 steel wool.

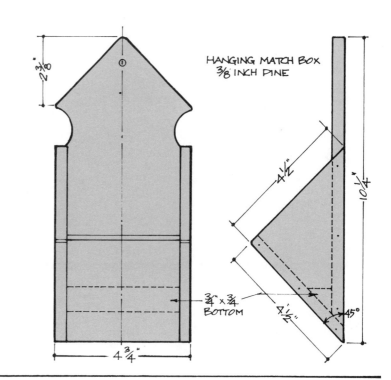

HANGING MATCH BOX
⅜ INCH PINE

This charming wall shelf is a scaled down version of a lovely antique piece. Made from ½″ pine, it can be completed in just one or two evenings in the workshop.

Parts A and B are cut from ½″ thick by 12″ long stock. Note that side A has a ¼″ deep by ½″ wide rabbet on one end, which means that side A must be cut ¼″ wider than side B. Also note that sides A and B also have a ½″ wide dado and rabbet cut for the shelves. A jig or saber saw will cut the curved scrollwork.

Now, using the grid pattern provided, cut out the top and bottom shelves as shown. Be sure to give the sides and shelves a thorough sanding, taking special care to smooth the curved surfaces.

Assemble all parts, final sand, then stain to suit. Two coats of polyurethane will complete the project.

Corner Shelves

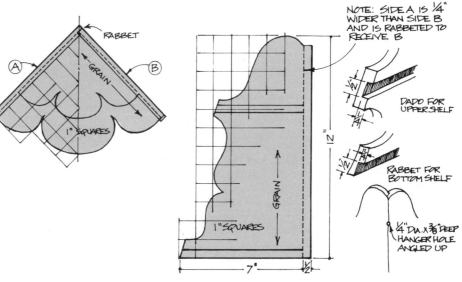

Pine Shaker Cupboard

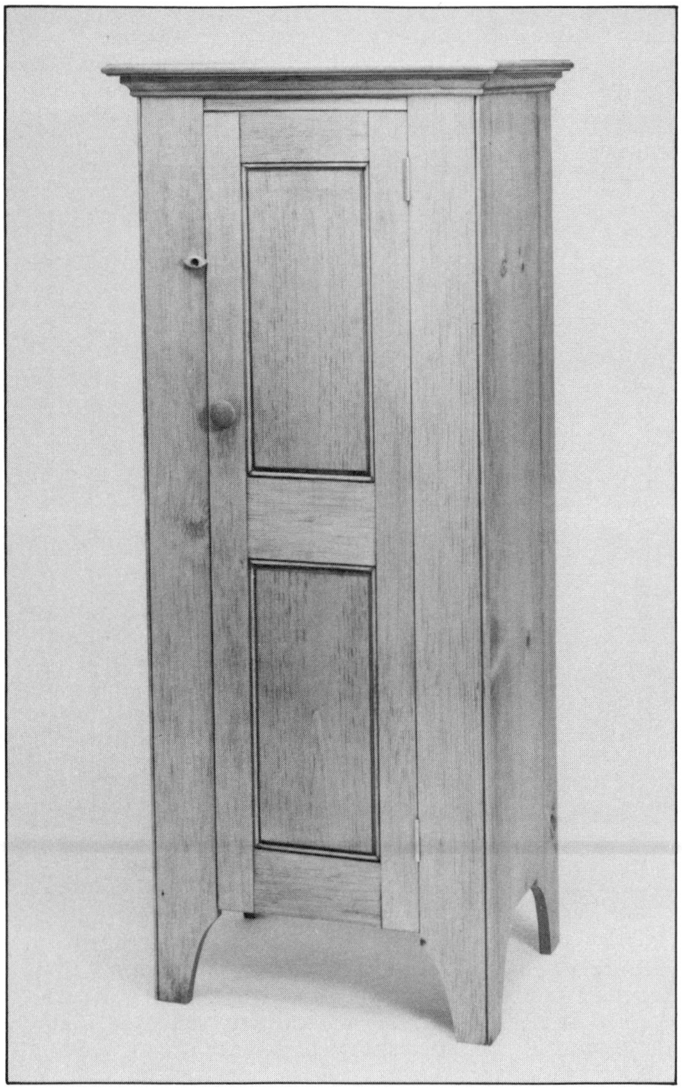

Many elements of fine Shaker design can be found in this charming pine cupboard. Although not an exact reproduction, our plans are based on an authentic Shaker piece — and we have made only minor dimensional and construction changes. For example, the top molding on the original was probably cut using several special molding planes. To reproduce it, we revised the design slightly to permit the use of standard moldings. The result is an unusual and attractive detail that is reasonably easy to make.

Our method of applying beading to the door rails and stiles is also a bit unusual in that it results in a mitered bead. Normally this is not easy to do, at least not with a molding head cutter, but we managed to work out a technique that makes the operation fairly simple.

A project like this looks best if knots are kept to a minimum, especially in front, so choose your pine carefully. If possible, select door panel stock that has pleasing wood figure. Notice ours is cut so that the figure is centered on the panel, and that the lower panel is a continuation of the upper one. Of course, there's no hard and fast rule that says you must do it this way, but we do feel it can add a great deal of interest to a piece.

Start construction by edge-joining enough stock to take care of two sides (B), four shelves (C), and the top (E). Two or three boards will have to be joined to get the needed width.

The front pieces (A) are cut to length and width, then mortised for a ⅜″ thick x 1½″ wide x 1¼″ long tenon. Cut the leg curve, then use a Sears Craftsman, ¼″ 3-bead molding head cutter (No. 9-2352) to apply a bead along the outside edge. Part D is now cut 2½″ wide x 14½″ long, including the ⅜″ thick x 1½″ wide x 1¼″ long tenons on each end.

Make the frame-and-panel door next. Note that steps 1 - 4 summarize the method used to cut the mitered rails. If you don't have a molding head cutter, you can still produce the effect of a panel beading. Simply cut the panel (part K) rabbet about ⅞″ wide. This extra room provides a place to glue a ¼″ half-round molding around the panel. For a clean look, be sure to miter the corners of the molding.

To bead the panels as we did, refer to the bill of materials and cut door stiles (G) and rails (H, I, and J) to overall length and width (rail length includes tenons). Now, noting the door rail tenon details, cut tenons as shown, then use the molding head cutter to apply a ¼″ bead (step 1) on parts G, H, I, and J as shown. Next, a ¼″ wide x ⅜″ deep groove (step 2) is routed along the same parts. Notice that the groove does not extend along the entire length of part G, but rather is stopped short to keep the groove from running out the ends.

Use a miter square with a 45-degree angle (step 3) to lay out the 5/16″ miter cuts on the rails, then cut out on the waste side of the line with a backsaw. To insure a perfect 45-degree angle, construct the jig as shown (step 4). Locate the jig exactly on the miter line and use a sharp chisel to pare excess stock.

Lay rails (H, I, and J) in position on parts G. Using the rails as templates, mark the exact location of the mortise and miter cuts on parts G. Cut the mortises first, then use the backsaw and chisel to remove most of the miter cutout. Now, again use the special jig to pare the miter.

Select panel stock (K) and cut to size, then form a ¼″ x ½″ rabbet around the edge. After giving all parts a complete sanding, the door can be assembled with glue and clamps. It's most important that the door be both square and flat, so pre-assemble the parts and check it over. After gluing and clamping, check it once again, and make adjustments as necessary.

After a thorough sanding, the rest of the cabinet can be assembled. The shelves are glued in dadoes and further secured with two countersunk wood screws. Use plugs to cover holes. Attach the back with screws driven into the shelves. Glue and finishing nails, countersunk and filled, hold the top and the top molding to the carcase.

Final sand all parts, then stain to suit. We used two coats of Minwax Provincial wood stain, followed by two coats of Minwax Antique Oil finish.

Bill of Materials (All Dimensions Actual)

Part	Description	Size	No. Req'd
A	Front	¾ x 4 x 51	2
B	Side	¾ x 14¼ x 51	2
C	Shelf	¾ x 13½ x 19	4
D	Case Rail	¾ x 2½ x 14½ (inc. 1¼″ long tenons)	1
E	Top	¾ x 14¼ x 19¼	1
F	Back	¾ x 9⅝ x 45⅛	2
G	Stile	¾ x 2½ x 43	2
H	Top Rail	¾ x 3 x 10⅛ (includes tenons)	1
I	Center Rail	¾ x 5 x 10⅛ (includes tenons)	1
J	Lower Rail	¾ x 4 x 10⅛ (includes tenons)	1
K	Panel	½ x 7⅝ x 16⅛	2

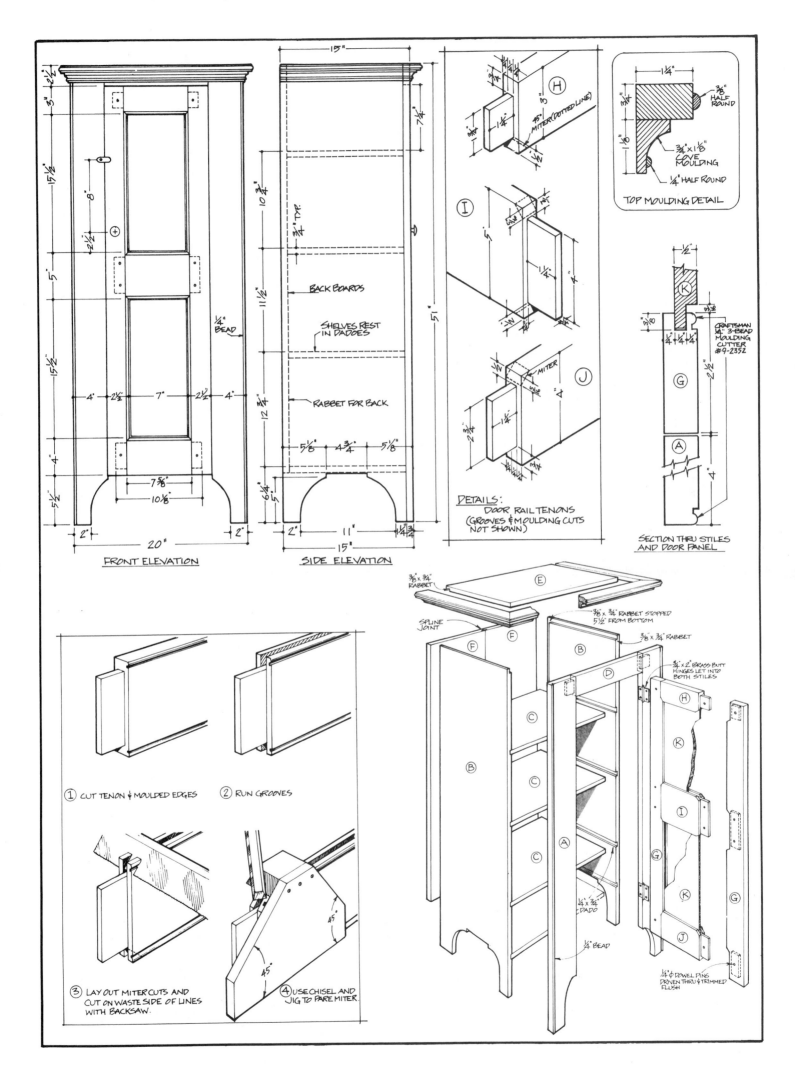

FRONT ELEVATION

2½"
3"
15½"
8"
2½"
5"
15½"
4"   2½"   7"   2½"   4"
¼" BEAD
7⅝"
10⅛"
4"
5½"
2"   20"   2"

SIDE ELEVATION

15"
7¼"
10¾"
¾" TOP
11½"
BACK BOARDS
SHELVES REST IN DADOES
9¾"
RABBET FOR BACK
12¼"
51"
5⅛"   4¾"   5⅛"
6¼"
5"
2"   11"   1¾"
15"

H
¾"   ¼"
¾"
3"
¼"
45°
MITER (DOTTED LINE)
½"

I
5"
1¼"
¼"
4"
¼"

J
MITER
¼"
2¼"
1¼"
4"
¾"

DETAILS:
DOOR RAIL TENONS
(GROOVES & MOULDING CUTS NOT SHOWN)

1¼"
⅜" HALF ROUND
¾"
¼"
¾" x 1⅛" COVE MOULDING
¼" HALF ROUND

TOP MOULDING DETAIL

½"
K
⅜"
¼" ¼" ¼"
CRAFTSMAN ¼" 3-BEAD MOULDING CUTTER #9-2352
G
2½"
A
4"

SECTION THRU STILES AND DOOR PANEL

① CUT TENON & MOULDED EDGES
② RUN GROOVES
③ LAY OUT MITER CUTS AND CUT ON WASTE SIDE OF LINES WITH BACKSAW.
④ USE CHISEL AND JIG TO PARE MITER.
45°
45°

⅜" x ¾" RABBET
E
SPLINE JOINT
F
F
⅜" x ¾" RABBET STOPPED 5½" FROM BOTTOM
B
⅜" x ¾" RABBET
D
¾" x 2" BRASS BUTT HINGES LET INTO BOTH STILES
B
C
H
C
K
A
I
C
G
¼" x ¾" DADO
K
¼" BEAD
J
G
¼" ⌀ DOWEL PINS DRIVEN THRU & TRIMMED FLUSH

21

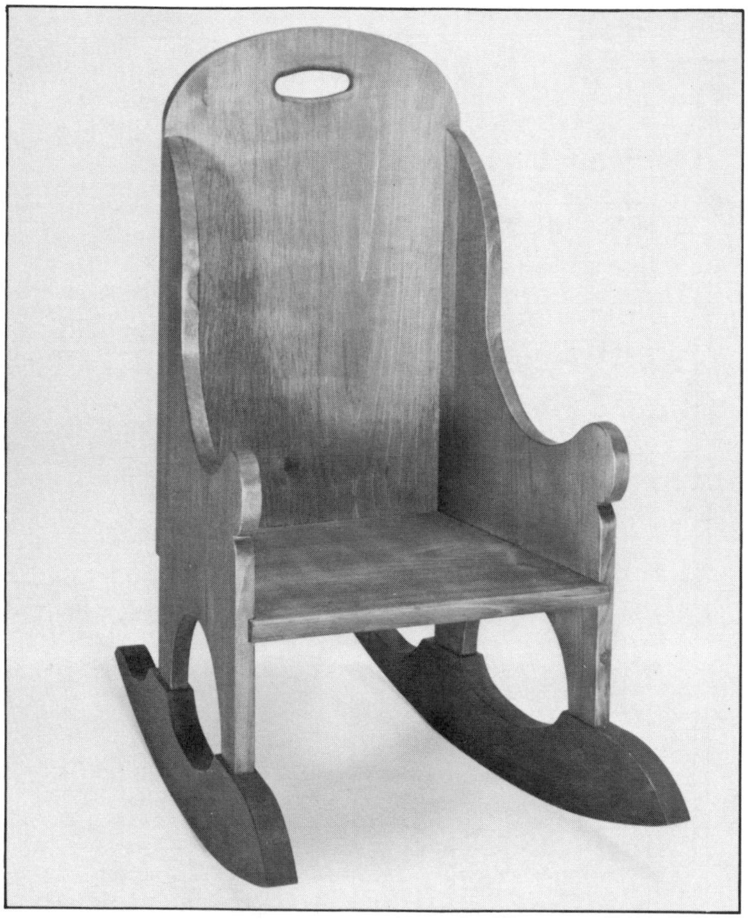

Child's Rocker

Worn out small fry will find this rocker a cozy place to rest tired legs...at least for a few minutes. The design is based on a composite of several early 18th century rockers, and the result is a piece that's solidly constructed yet reasonably easy to build. It's dimensioned to fit a child of about kindergarten age, so if you have a younger or older child, you may want to revise the dimensions a bit. Pine is used for all parts.

Start by cutting the sides to size (4/4 x 12⅜ x 22¼). It will probably be necessary to edge join 2 or more boards to get the 12⅜″ width. Using the detail as a guide, lay out and cut the tenons as shown, then lay out and cut the ¼″ deep x ¾″ wide seat dado. Bevel the back edge to the angle shown, then lay out and cut all remaining curves.

The back is cut to 4/4 x 13 x 20 and again edge gluing will probably be needed. Cut hand hole and top curve as shown. The rocker is cut from 5/4 x 4 x 23 stock. Lay out and cut mortises, then cut curved shapes as shown. Next the seat is made from 4/4 x 12¼ x 14½ stock. Cut to the angle shown to fit against side dadoes.

Before assembly give all parts a complete sanding. Use special care on the curved edges, making sure to remove all rough spots.

Assemble the side tenons to rocker mortises. Secure in place with ¼″ dia. dowel pins. The seat is secured to the sides with glue and wood screws, countersunk and covered with wood plugs. Attach back with glue and countersunk finishing nails.

Give all surfaces a final sanding, making sure to remove any glue squeeze-out. Stain to suit, then apply two coats of polyurethane varnish. Allow to dry, then rub down with 0000 steel wool.

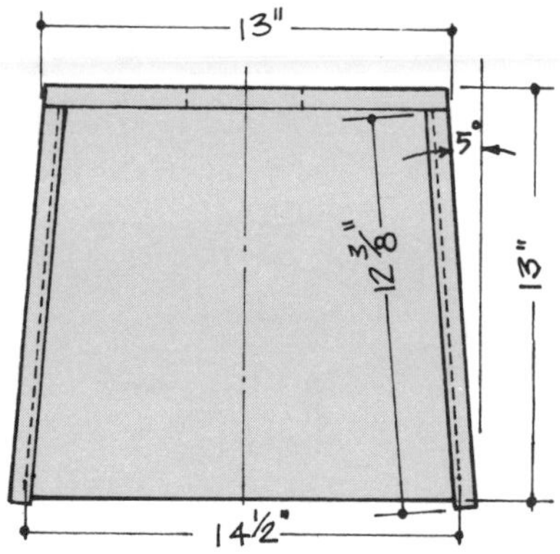
13"
5°
12 3/8"
13"
14½"

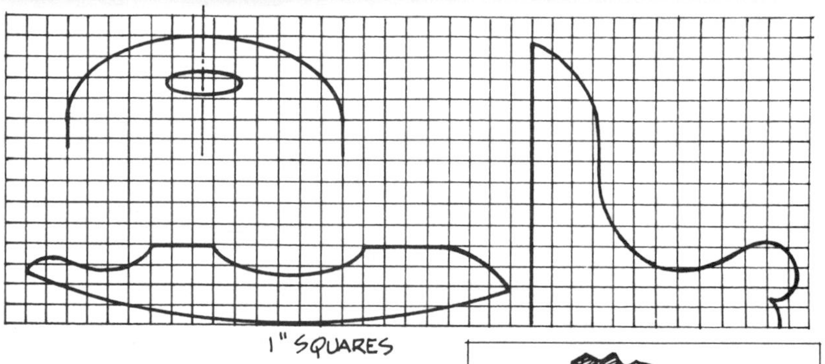
1" SQUARES

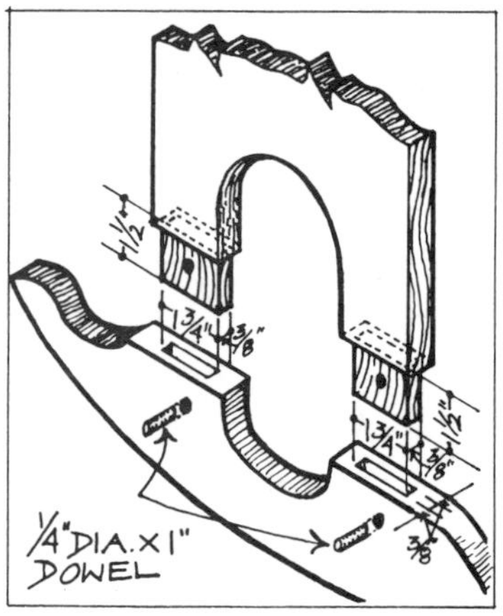
1½"
1¾"
3/8"
1¾"
1½"
3/8"
¼"DIA.X1"
DOWEL

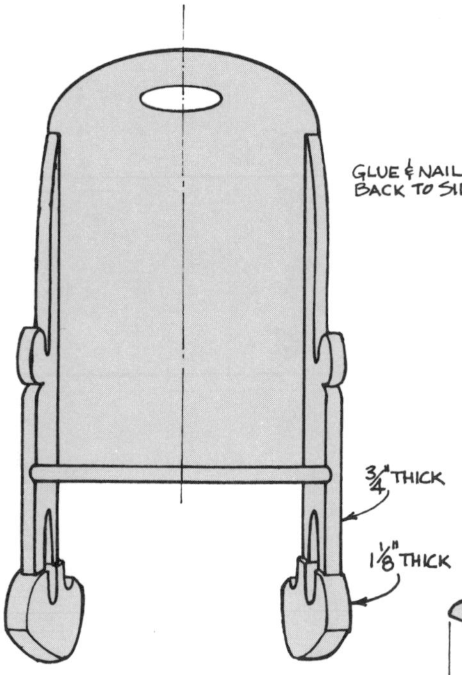
GLUE & NAIL
BACK TO SIDES
¾" THICK
1⅛" THICK

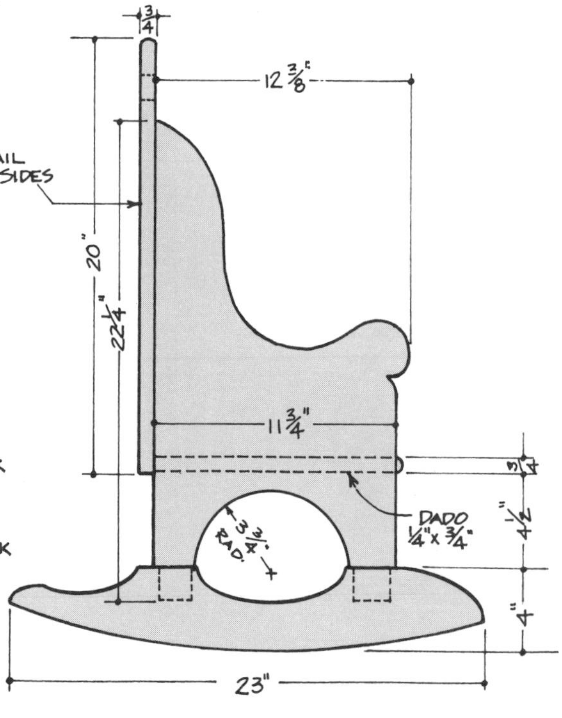
¾
12 3/8"
20"
22¼"
11¾"
¾
DADO
¼"x¾"
4½"
3¾" RAD.
4"
23"

Child's Rocker
Bill of Materials
(All Dimensions Actual)

Description	Size	No. Req'd
Side	¾ x 12⅜ x 22¼	2
Back	¾ x 13 x 20	1
Rocker	1⅛ x 4 x 23	2
Seat	¾ x 12¼ x 14½	1

Half-Round Table

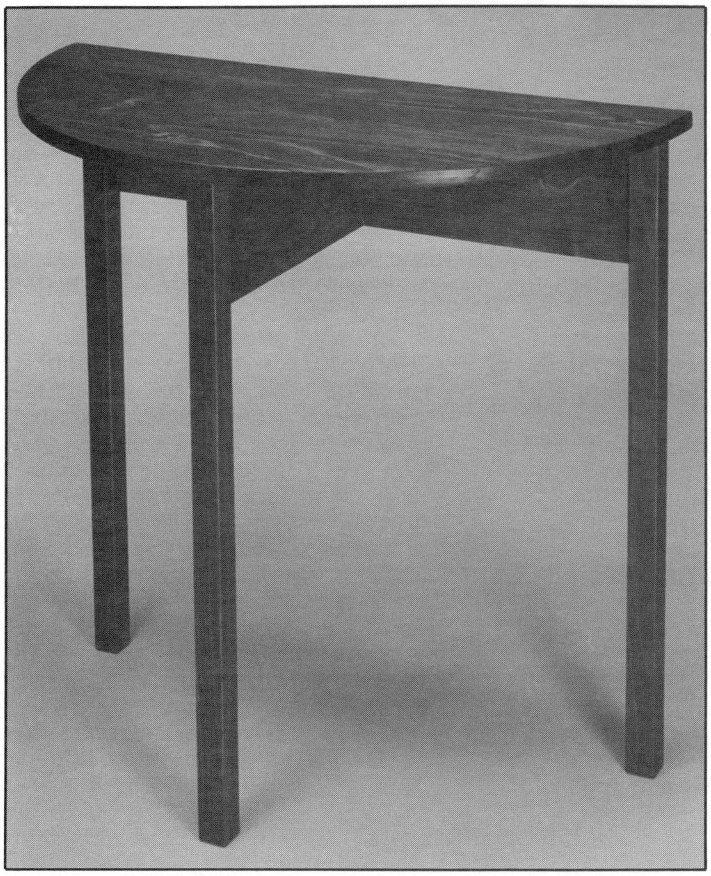

We based the design of this lovely pine table on an authentic colonial piece. It's been simplified somewhat by substituting dowel joints in place of mortises and tenons; however, more advanced woodworkers will probably choose to use the latter technique. No matter what way it's built though, the resulting table will be a very charming example of colonial style furniture.

Begin with the legs. If you can't get 1¼" stock, they can be made by face gluing two pieces of 1" (¾" actual) x 5 x 27½ stock. Use enough clamps to insure good surface contact. After drying, rip the piece to 1¼" widths. This results in a leg measuring 1¼" x 1½". To get a 1¼" square leg, rip ⅛" from each side of the 1½" wide surface. Now, trim each leg to a finish length of 27¼".

Cut the center apron (¾ x 5½ x 11¾) and rear apron (¾ x 5½ x 25½) to size, then add the rear apron dado as shown. Now the legs and aprons can be drilled for ⅜" x 1½" long dowel pins.

The top is made by edge joining enough stock to get the needed width. Lay out the 15" radius, then cut to shape. A quick compass can be built using a thin strip of wood. On one end a brad serves as a pivot point. Measure 15" from the brad and drill a small hole for a pencil point.

Before assembly, give all parts a complete sanding. At this point, we added a coat of Minwax Special Walnut wood finish. When dry, glue and clamp all dowel joints, then check to be sure all parts are square.

The top is joined using glue blocks as shown. To be sure that the top fits firmly to the aprons & legs, we actually located the blocks about 1/16" below the top edge of the aprons.

Finish with 2 coats of Minwax Antique Oil Finish, then final rub with 0000 steel wool.

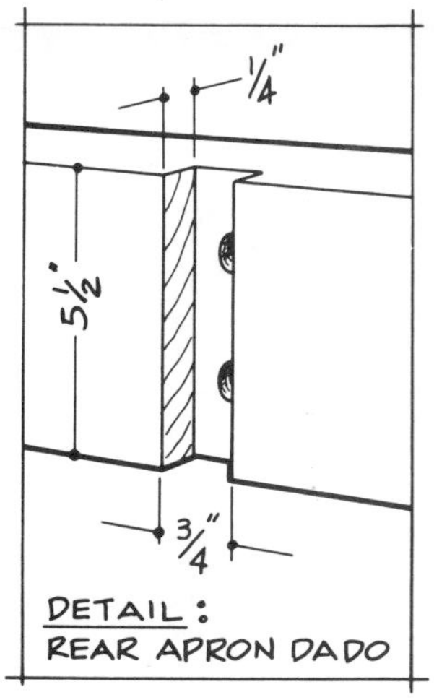

1/4"
5 1/2
3/4"
DETAIL: REAR APRON DADO

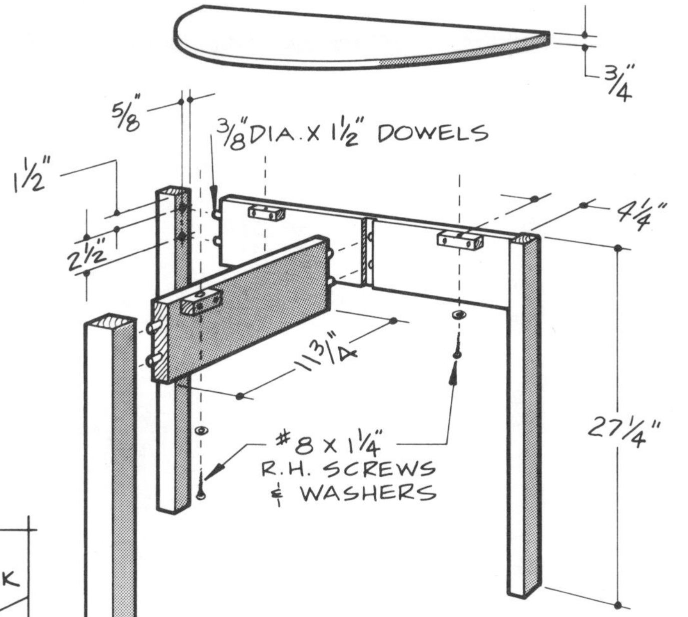

3/4"
5/8"
3/8" DIA. X 1 1/2" DOWELS
1 1/2"
2 1/2"
4 1/4"
11 3/4"
27 1/4"
#8 X 1 1/4" R.H. SCREWS & WASHERS

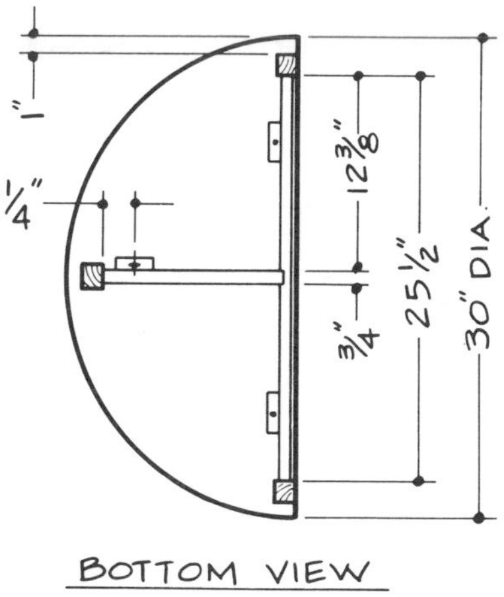

1"
2 1/4"
12 3/8"
25 1/2"
30" DIA
3/4"
BOTTOM VIEW

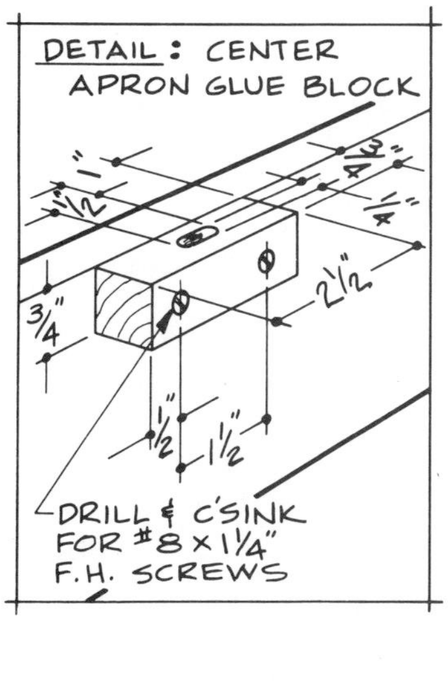

DETAIL: CENTER APRON GLUE BLOCK
1"
1/2"
4 1/4"
1/4"
3/4"
2 1/2"
1/2"
1 1/2"
DRILL & C'SINK FOR #8 X 1 1/4" F.H. SCREWS

Half-Round Table Bill of Materials (All Dimensions Actual)		
Description	Size	No. Req'd
Leg	1¼ x 1¼ x 27¼	3
Center Apron	¾ x 5½ x 11¾	1
Rear Apron	¾ x 5½ x 25½	1
Top	¾ x 15 x 30	1
Glue Block	See Detail	3

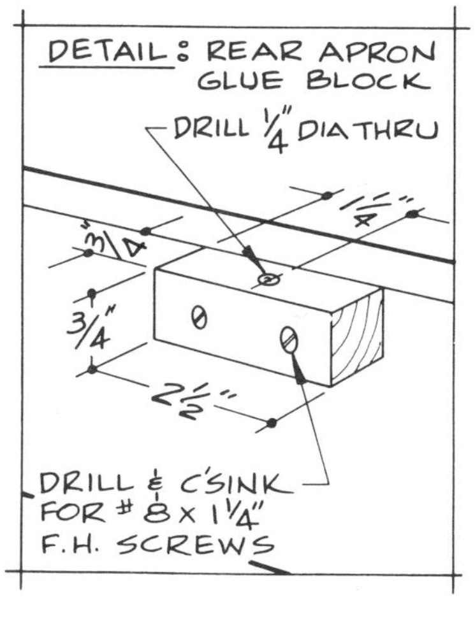

DETAIL: REAR APRON GLUE BLOCK
DRILL 1/4" DIA THRU
3/4"
1/4"
3/4"
2 1/2"
DRILL & C'SINK FOR #8 X 1 1/4" F.H. SCREWS

Pine Spoon Rack

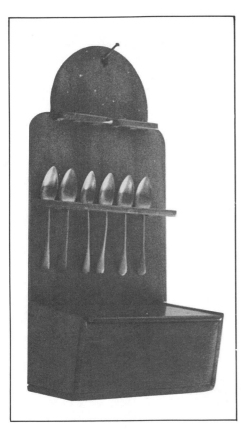

This beautiful, clean statement in wood hangs in a small warm kitchen. The room is well lit, with two large windows overlooking a garden. To add to the cozy feeling, a large fireplace dominates the adjacent wall.

From this description it is hard to imagine that upon walking out into the garden one discovers that this house is sandwiched between two skyscrapers. This is the Abigail Adams Smith Museum, located at 421 East 61st Street in New York City. Now restored to a tranquil home setting and filled with American furniture, this warm house and the warm people who care for it invite you into another time.

With its simple elegant lines, the spoon rack graces this setting as it did when first made in the early 1800's. To make a replica of this antique for your very own, use ½" pine and cut all pieces to shape, remembering that the back, sides, and front are cut full width or depth to allow for jointing.

After the back has been shaped and bored for the hanging hole, notch it to receive the sides. These will later be nailed into the back. Lay out and cut dovetails at the front corners. If you have never made this joint, this is a good place to learn because pine is soft and easy to work. The front is shorter than the sides by the thickness of the lid. Although the front slopes inward to the bottom, the dovetail joint is made as though the joint were to remain vertical. After sanding, assemble the front, back and sides with glue and nails. Check to see that the sides are square to the back and let dry.

Cut the bottom to size, then glue and nail into place. The spoon holders can also be applied at this time, nailing through the back.

The lid is the last piece to be added. It's rounded at the front and left to protrude over the edge to allow for ease of opening. The hinge mechanism is two dowels driven through the sides and into the lid as shown.

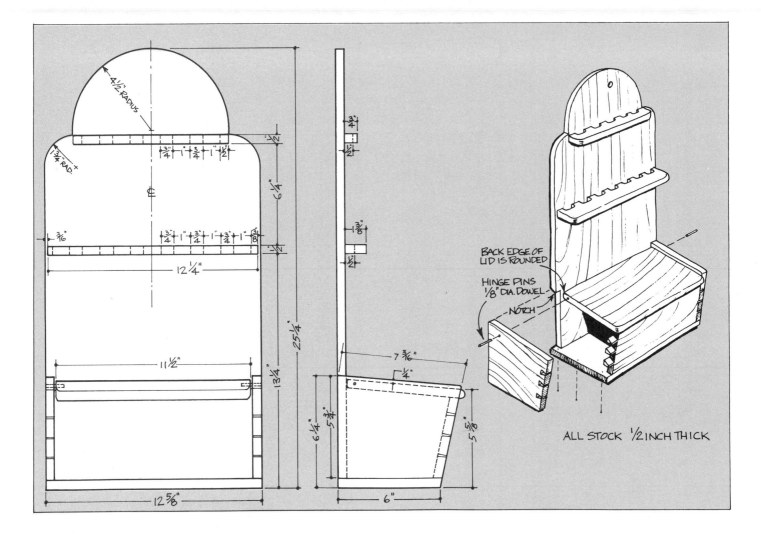

18th Century Sleigh Seat

Although not an exact reproduction, the overall design of this piece is based on a colonial original. Ours is used to display house plants in front of a sunny window, but it will also make a nice bench for a hall or den.

If you can't get 10″ wide boards it will be necessary to edge-join enough stock for the two sides and the seat. Boards cut 6 feet long will provide enough length for all three parts. For maximum glue strength, the gluing surfaces must be smooth and clean. If the edges look a bit rough or dirty, use the jointer or hand plane to clean them up. Keep knots away from the leg portion of the sides. A knot will weaken the strength of a leg.

After all parts have been cut to size and shape, give each one a thorough sanding. Assemble with glue and dowel pins as shown, using countersunk 1½ x #8 wood screws and glue to secure the aprons to the top.

Ours is finished with a coat of Minwax Special Walnut wood finish followed by two coats of Minwax Antique Oil finish.

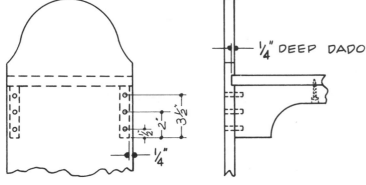

¼″ DEEP DADO

Bill of Materials (All Dimensions Actual)		
Part	Size	No. Req'd
Side	¾ x 10 x 20	2
Apron	¾ x 4 x 28½	2
Seat	¾ x 10 x 29	1

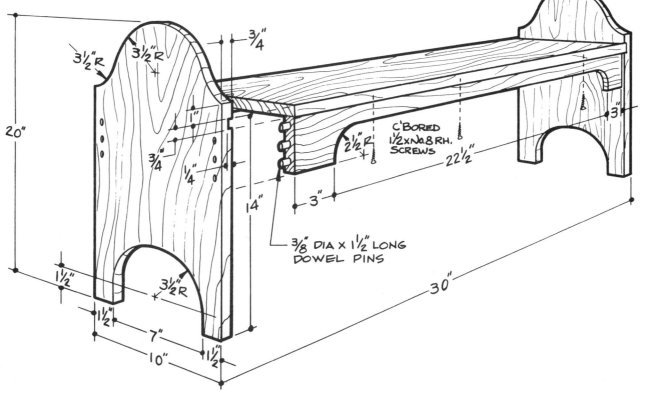

18th Century Chair Table

By and large, houses in colonial America were rather small, oftentimes just one or two tiny rooms. With small houses and small rooms, space was at a premium, so colonists had to be very practical when choosing furniture. The chair table is a good example of that practicality. It served two functions. At mealtime it was used as a table, right in the middle of a room. When the meal was over, it was opened as a chair and pushed out of the way against a wall.

The advantages of the chair table can still be enjoyed by many of us today. Anyone with a space problem can put it to use, particularly those with small homes or apartments. It truly is a timeless furniture style.

The sides (A) can be made first. If you can't get 10½" wide stock you'll have to edge-join two or more boards to get the needed width. Cut to width and length (including tenons), then lay out and mark tenons as shown in the details. Use the dado head in conjunction with a table or radial saw to cut the tenon cheeks. A back saw and sharp chisel will finish the job. Make all cuts with care. Also cut the ¼" deep x ¾" wide seat dado.

Arm rests (C) and feet (B) can be made next. Cut to overall length and width, then lay out mortise location. To cut mortises, drill a series of adjacent ¾" diameter x 1 9/16" deep holes. This removes most of the material. What's left can be cleaned up with the chisel. After mortises are completed, the curved profiles (as shown on the grid pattern) can be cut.

The back (D) is made from 1" (¾" actual) stock. As with the legs, you'll have to edge-join several boards to get the 16½" width. Note that it has a 1⅛" x 3½" notch at both upper corners, allowing the back to fit around arm rests (C). After completing both notches, the curved profile can be cut out.

The seat (E) can be cut next. If your local lumberyard carries 1" x 12" stock try to select a board that has a minimum of cup. If they only carry narrower stock, you'll once again have to join them.

Part (F), the cleats, are made from 1⅛" stock and cut to dimensions shown in both the side elevation and detail of the rear pivot hole location. Next, locate and drill the pivot and locking holes.

The 28" wide by 36" long top (G) can now be made. Edge-join boards as necessary, trim to length and width, then cut the corners to 30 degrees as shown.

At this point, before assembly, it's a good idea to give all components a thorough sanding job.

Assemble sides (A) to arm rests (C) and feet (B). Be sure to apply sufficient glue to both mortises and tenons.

Clamp securely and allow to dry overnight. When dry, drill ¼" dia. holes for dowel pins as shown. Cut pins a little long, then trim and sand flush.

The seat (E) is glued to the dado in side (A) and further secured with two countersunk woodscrews. The countersunk holes are then plugged and sanded flush. The back (D) can now be attached with glue and three countersunk and plugged woodscrews each end.

Each cleat is fixed to the top with three wood screws. Since the top will want to expand and contract in width due to seasonal humidity changes, it's best not to use glue here. The wood screws will allow some movement of the top and minimize the chance of cracking. Locate the cleat so that there is about ⅛" of "play" between the cleat and the arm rest.

Now, with the top resting in proper position on the arm rest, mark the location of the arm rest pivot and lock holes. After drilling holes, pegs can be made as shown in the detail.

Final sand all surfaces. Round off sharp corners, taking particular care to smooth curved edges. We stained our piece with 2 coats of Minwax Early American wood finish. After allowing the stain to thoroughly dry, we applied two coats of Minwax Antique Oil Finish. A light rub down with 0000 steel wool completed the project.

Chair Table

Bill of Materials
(All Dimensions Actual)

Part	Description	Size	No. Req'd.
A	Side Board	1⅛ x 10½ x 21 (Inc. tenons)	2
B	Foot	1⅛ x 5 x 20	2
C	Arm Rest	1⅛ x 4 x 14½	2
D	Back	¾ x 16½ x 28½	1
E	Seat	¾ x 11 x 26¾	1
F	Cleat	1⅛ x 1½ x 24¾	2
G	Top	¾ x 28 x 36	1
H	Pivot & Lock Pegs	See Detail	4

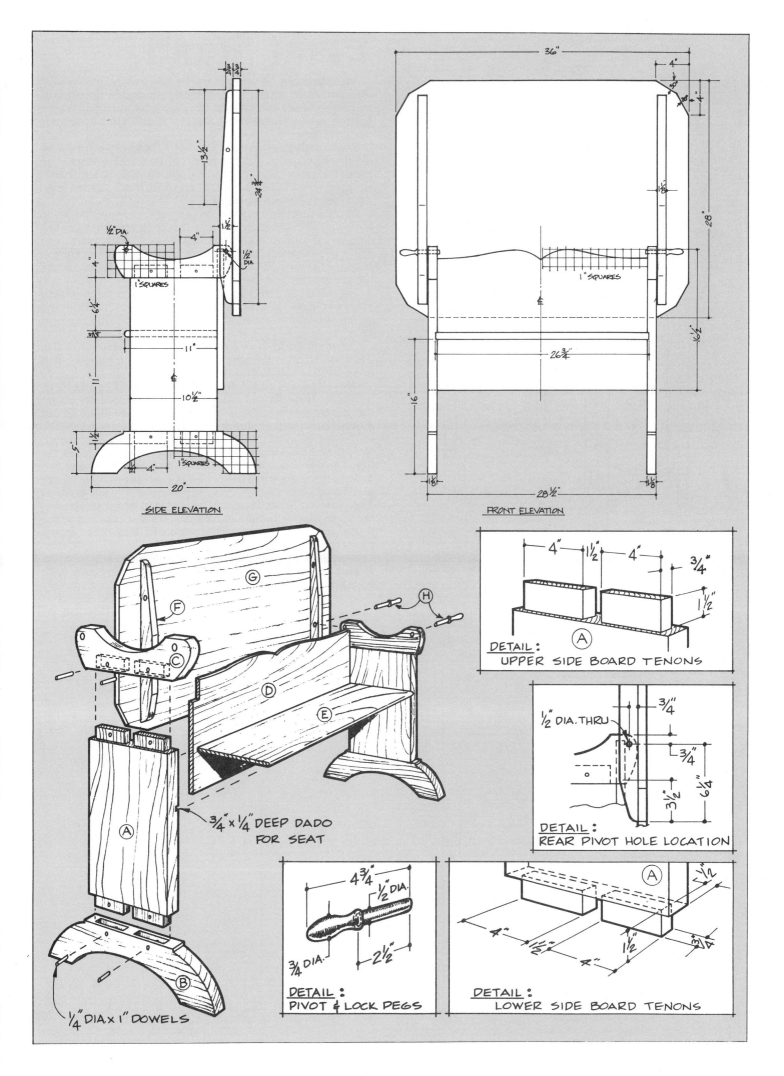

SIDE ELEVATION

FRONT ELEVATION

DETAIL:
UPPER SIDE BOARD TENONS
Ⓐ

DETAIL:
REAR PIVOT HOLE LOCATION

DETAIL:
PIVOT & LOCK PEGS

DETAIL:
LOWER SIDE BOARD TENONS
Ⓐ

½" DIA.

¼"DIA.x 1" DOWELS

¾"x ¼" DEEP DADO
FOR SEAT

1" SQUARES

1" SQUARES

½ DIA.THRU

Plant Stand

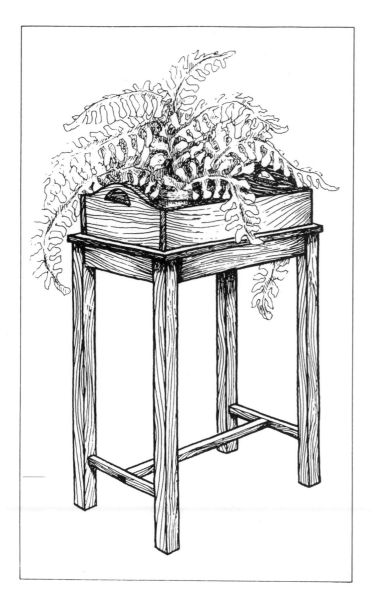

Just about any houseplant can be beautifully displayed in this attractive stand. It features a removable upper box, making it easier to transport the plants for such jobs as repotting or watering. Pine, maple, or oak are all suitable wood choices.

Begin with the legs (A). The 1½" thickness can best be obtained by face gluing two pieces of 1 x 8 x 23½" stock. Use enough clamps to insure good surface contact. After drying, rip the piece to 1½" widths to result in 1½" square legs. Also trim to a finish length of 23".

Cut the front and rear aprons (B) and side aprons (C) to size. The side stretcher (D) and the main stretcher (E) can also be cut and notched as shown. Now lay out, mark, and drill ⅜" dia. dowel holes for parts A, B, C, and D as shown. Note that aprons (B) & (C) are inset ⅛" while lower aprons (D) are centered on the leg.

The 12" wide top (F) will probably require edge joining narrower stock in order to gain enough width. Glue and clamp the boards overnight, then cut to a finish length of 19½".

Cut parts G, H, and I as per the Bill of Materials. Use freehand to trace the simple handle curve on part H, then use a band or saber saw to cut to shape.

Give all parts a complete sanding, then dry fit parts B, C, & D to A. If the fit up looks good, glue and securely clamp the joints, making sure everything is square. Part E can now be glued to D as shown.

The top is joined with four glue blocks (K), see detail. Note that the blocks are slotted to allow for movement of the top. The upper box, parts G and H, are joined with glue and dowel pins as shown. The ½ x ½ bottom support cleats are glued and screwed in place to support the plywood bottom. The plywood is not fastened, but instead drops in place to facilitate easy removal and cleaning. Dowel pins are glued to the top (F) as shown. These then fit into (but are not glued to) corresponding holes in part G.

Final sand all parts, rounding off any sharp edges. Stain to suit, apply 2 coats polyurethane, then rub down with 0000 steel wool.

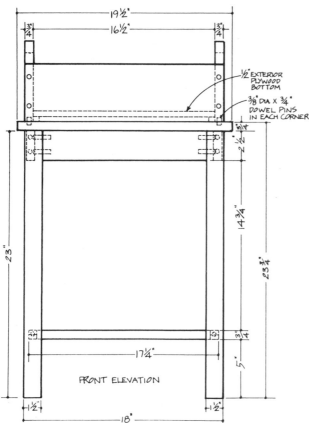

FRONT ELEVATION

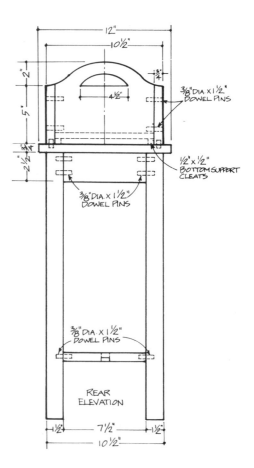

REAR ELEVATION

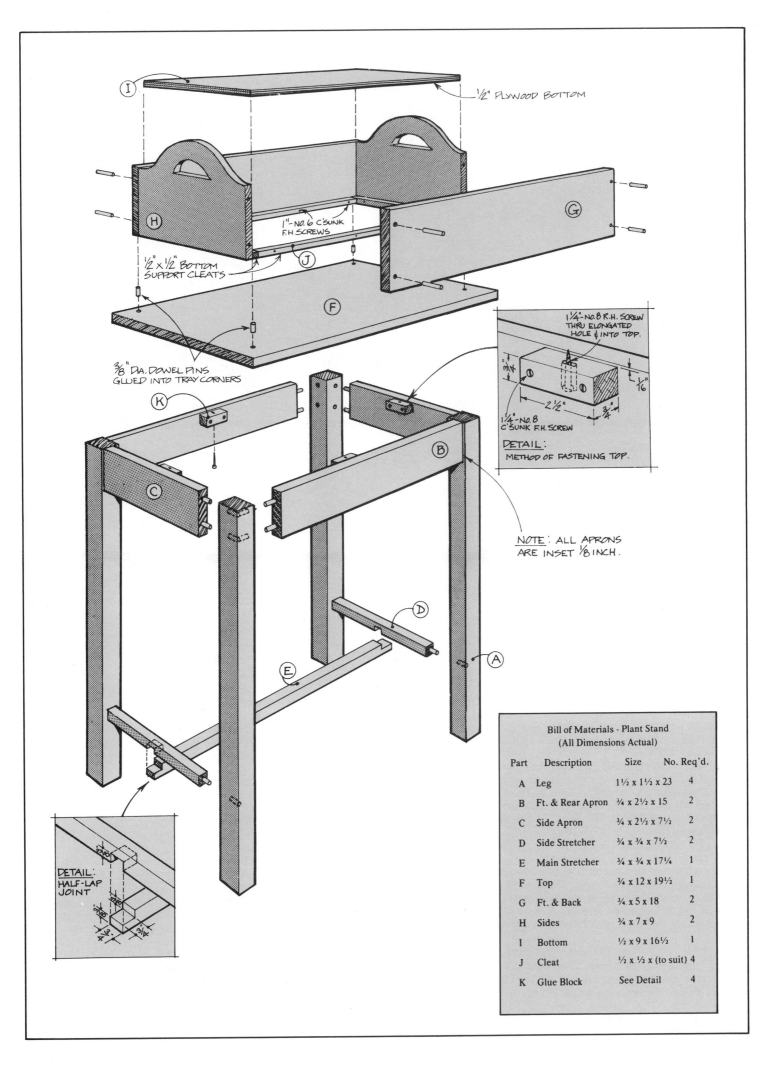

½" PLYWOOD BOTTOM

1" No.6 C'SUNK F.H. SCREWS

½" x ½" BOTTOM SUPPORT CLEATS

3/8" DIA. DOWEL PINS GLUED INTO TRAY CORNERS

1¼"- No.8 R.H. SCREW THRU ELONGATED HOLE & INTO TOP.

1¼"- No.8 C'SUNK F.H. SCREW

¾"

1/16"

2½"

¾"

DETAIL:
METHOD OF FASTENING TOP.

NOTE: ALL APRONS ARE INSET ⅛ INCH.

DETAIL:
HALF-LAP JOINT

Bill of Materials - Plant Stand
(All Dimensions Actual)

Part	Description	Size	No. Req'd.
A	Leg	1½ x 1½ x 23	4
B	Ft. & Rear Apron	¾ x 2½ x 15	2
C	Side Apron	¾ x 2½ x 7½	2
D	Side Stretcher	¾ x ¾ x 7½	2
E	Main Stretcher	¾ x ¾ x 17¼	1
F	Top	¾ x 12 x 19½	1
G	Ft. & Back	¾ x 5 x 18	2
H	Sides	¾ x 7 x 9	2
I	Bottom	½ x 9 x 16½	1
J	Cleat	½ x ½ x (to suit)	4
K	Glue Block	See Detail	4

Curio Shelves

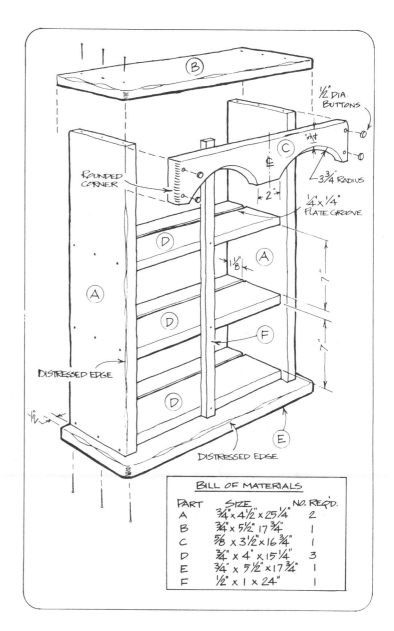

BILL OF MATERIALS		
PART	SIZE	NO. REQ'D.
A	3/4" x 4 1/2 x 25 1/4"	2
B	3/4" x 5 1/2" 17 3/4"	1
C	5/8 x 3 1/2"x16 3/4"	1
D	3/4" x 4" x15 1/4"	3
E	3/4" x 5 1/2"x17 3/4"	1
F	1/2" x 1 x 24"	1

If care is used in construction and finishing, this simple piece will look very attractive. It can be completed in a few hours by a novice woodworker using only hand tools. Units of this type can be mass-produced easily and are always popular gift items.

Ordinary knotty pine of ¾" thickness (actual) is used for all parts, although parts C and F will have to be planed down. If you use a handsaw, cut the parts slightly wide and plane the edges to the finished width. Remember to sand all parts before assembly and be sure to wipe all glue drips off with a damp rag.

Start by cutting sides A and the three shelves D to size. The plate grooves in the shelves are cut by clamping two straight strips to the shelves with just enough space between to run a handsaw blade. The saw is used to start a straight groove, then the strips are moved a very slight distance to start another groove. A ¼" chisel or gouge is then used to clean up and finish the groove to an equal depth.

Cut top B and bottom E to size. Coat ends of A with a thin layer of glue and allow to dry. Then spread on another layer and nail top and bottom to sides using 1½" finish nails. The shelves should be inserted when nailing to keep the sides evenly spaced. The top and bottom are nailed flush with

back edges of sides with an equal ½" overhang at the ends.

Mark locations of shelves and nail them in place making sure they are level and flush with the back edges of sides. Part C is then cut to size and planed down to ⅝" thickness. Lay out and make the circular cut-outs using a coping or saber saw.

Clamp part C to the edges of sides and butt tightly against the overhanging top. The center divider F is then cut and planed to ½" thickness. This is nailed to the center edge of each shelf and glued and clamped to the back of C. Bore holes in C to take decorative buttons or pieces of dowel to simulate pegs.

A half-round cabinet file is used to distress the outer edges of the unit as shown. Sand all surfaces again with 220 grit paper playing particular attention to smoothing the distressed edges. Stain unit with an oil type stain such as Minwax Early American. Apply stain with a disposable foam brush and use a rag to wipe and spread the stain evenly.

After at least 24 hours, apply two coats of satin finish urethane varnish. When the last coat is dry rub down all surfaces with 4/0 steel wool until an even soft luster is obtained, then polish with a soft cloth.

Early American Wall Shelf

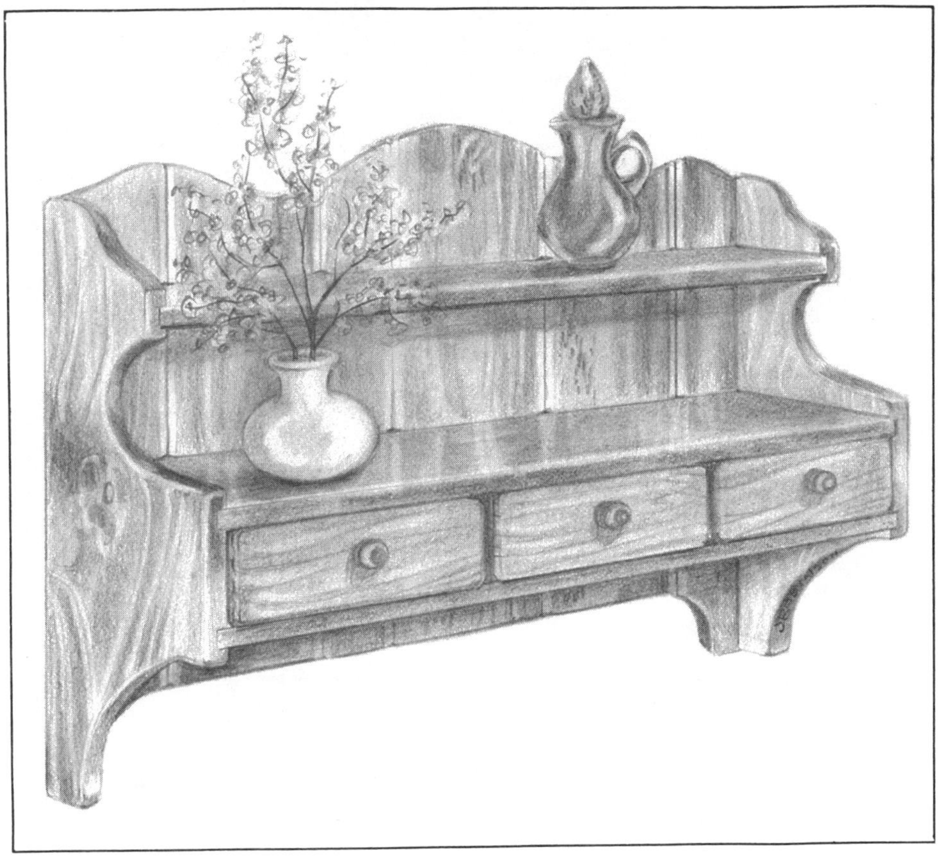

Wall shelves are always popular with our readers and this one should be no exception — especially if you enjoy the flavor of Early American.

Begin construction by cutting the two sides to length and width. Lay out and mark the location of the ¾″ wide x ¼″ dadoes, then use the dado head to cut out. This operation can also be done by making repeated passes with the saw blade. Now, referring to the grid pattern, lay out the profile shown, then cut out with the saber or band saw.

The back is made up of tongue-and-groove pine boards. First lay out the back stock, allowing ⅛″ space between the boards, clamp temporarily on a flat surface, transfer the illustrated grid and cut to shape (top & bottom). Later, the back boards will be screwed as shown to the shelf backs, maintaining the ⅛″ spacing to allow for wood movement.

Next, cut the three shelves and drawer dividers to size. Give all parts a complete sanding, then assemble with glue and finishing nails. Now add the back. The three drawers are then made as per the bill of materials and drawer detail shown. Note the sides and back are ½″ stock. A ⅜″ x ¾″ x 1″ drawer stop block is glued to the drawer support shelf. Center it just behind the drawer front.

Use a file to give all edges a good rounding before final sanding. Some well chosen distress marks will add a lot of old charm to new pine. Finish by staining with two coats of Minwax Early American stain followed by two coats of Minwax Antique Oil Finish.

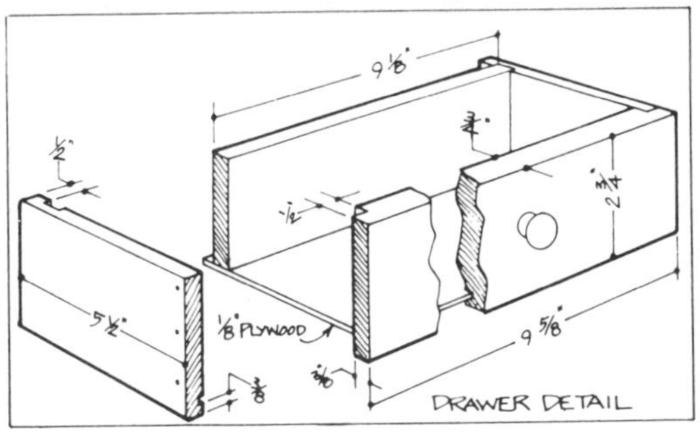
9⅛
½
2¼
5½
⅛ PLYWOOD
9 5/8
DRAWER DETAIL

Bill of Materials
(Dimensions in Inches)

		No. Req'd.
Side	¾ x 7 x 19⅜	2
Upper Shelf	¾ x 4½ x 31	1
Lower Shelf	¾ x 6¼ x 31	1
Drawer Support	¾ x 6¼ x 31	1
Drawer Divider	¾ x 2¾ x 6¼	2
Back	¾ x 22⅜ x 30½	1
Drawer Front	¾ x 2¾ x 9⅝	3
Drawer Side	½ x 2¾ x 5½	6
Drawer Back	½ x 2¼ x 9⅛	3
Drawer Bottom	⅛ x 5⅜ x 9⅛	3

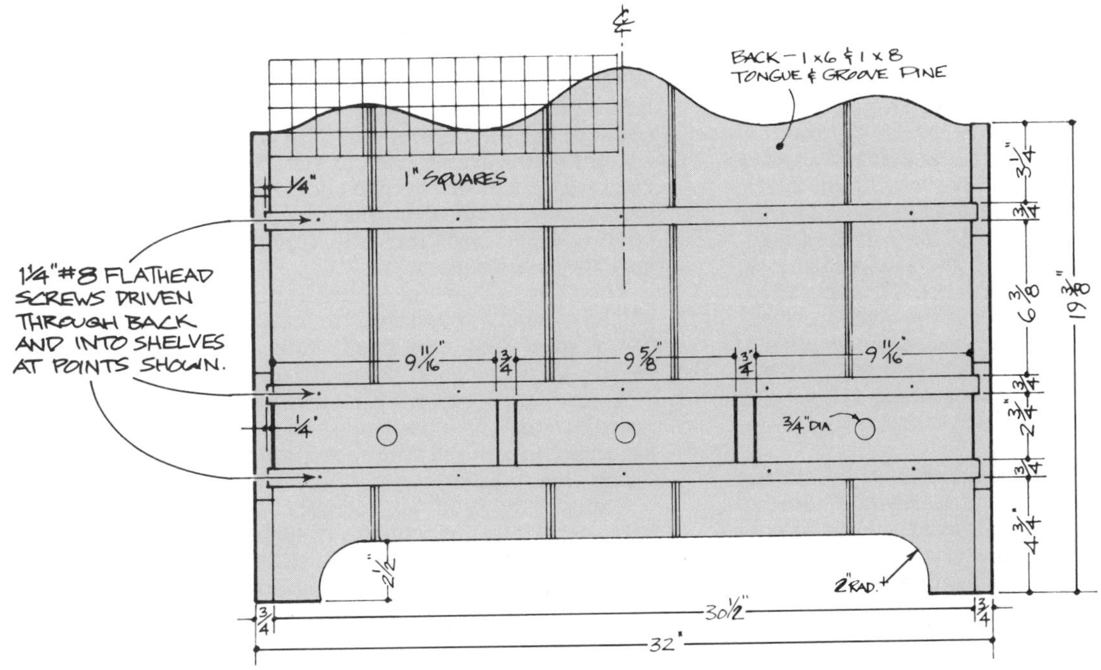
BACK – 1x6 & 1x8
TONGUE & GROOVE PINE
1" SQUARES
¼"
1¼" #8 FLATHEAD
SCREWS DRIVEN
THROUGH BACK
AND INTO SHELVES
AT POINTS SHOWN.
9 11/16"
9 5/8"
¾" DIA
2" RAD.
2½"
3¼"
6⅜
19⅜
2¾"
4¼"
30½"
32"

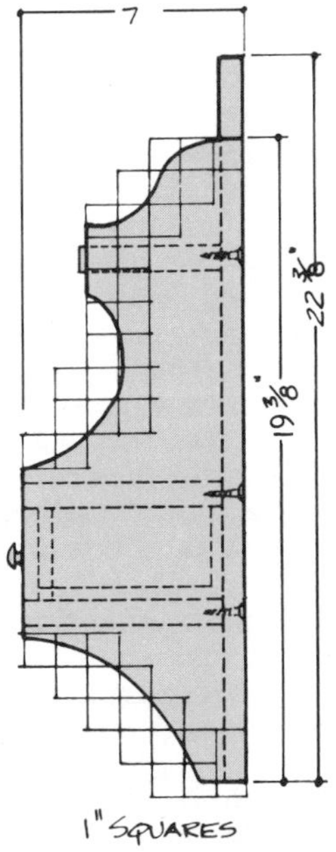
7
22⅜"
19⅜"
1" SQUARES

Kitchen Dish Rack

The dish rack is generally considered a purely utilitarian kitchen utensil - one that's just not expected to ever look like much. However, we think ours is an exception. Made from white ash, this rack is not only very attractive, it also folds flat so that it can be hung neatly on the kitchen wall.

The slats are made first. Begin by cutting two pieces of 1″ ash (13/16″ actual) stock to 1½″ wide by 38½″ long. Set the table saw rip fence for a ½″ wide cut and adjust the saw blade height to 13/16″. Now feed the stock, on edge, through the saw blade. (Note: be sure to use a pushstick and keep hands away from the blade.) This will produce a cut slightly more than halfway through the 1½″ wide stock. Next, flip the stock over and repeat the cut. This operation, called resawing, reduces the thickness of the stock from ¾″ to ½″. Now this ½″ thick x 1½″ wide stock can be ripped to ⅜″ widths, then cut to 7½″ lengths. This method of cutting will result in 30 slats (4 extra), each measuring ⅜″ x ½″ x 7½″. Also, at this time, cut the cup rack base (¾ x 1 x 17⅜) and back (2 pcs. ¼ x ⅜ x 17⅜).

Begin making the horizontal frame members by cutting ¾″ (actual) stock to 4½″ wide x 20″ long. At the middle of the board length (10″ from each end), mark the location of the center dado. Then, working out toward the ends, continue to mark the location of the remaining dadoes (6 on each side). This layout method assures that there will be room for the frame ends later on.

Now the dado head can be used to cut the thirteen, ⅜″ wide x ⅛″ deep dadoes across the 4½″ board width. Make several test cuts on scrap stock to make sure the slats fit snugly. If necessary, make adjustments in the dado width. When all 13 cuts have been made, the board can be ripped into 4 pieces, each 1″ wide. These pieces are longer than needed, but will be trimmed to fit when assembled.

Cut the four frame ends to size (¾ x 1 x 15), then cut the cup rack dadoes on the two short rack legs. Now lay out the location of the ⅜″ pivot pin hole. With each frame end pair edge-to-edge, drill the hole through both pieces. (Make sure the hole is square).

The slats can now be glued in place. Since the dish rack will have constant exposure to water, it's most important to use a glue that has good water resistance. Weldwood Plastic Resin is a good choice. Clamp firmly.

Assemble all other parts as shown. Always use water resistant glue and dowel pins where shown. The pivot pins are glued only to the long rack frame ends, leaving the short frame free to pivot.

Thoroughly sand all surfaces. A belt sander is useful here, especially on end grain surfaces. Slightly round all edges. No finish is necessary, since white ash is very suitable for applications that require regular washing and scrubbing.

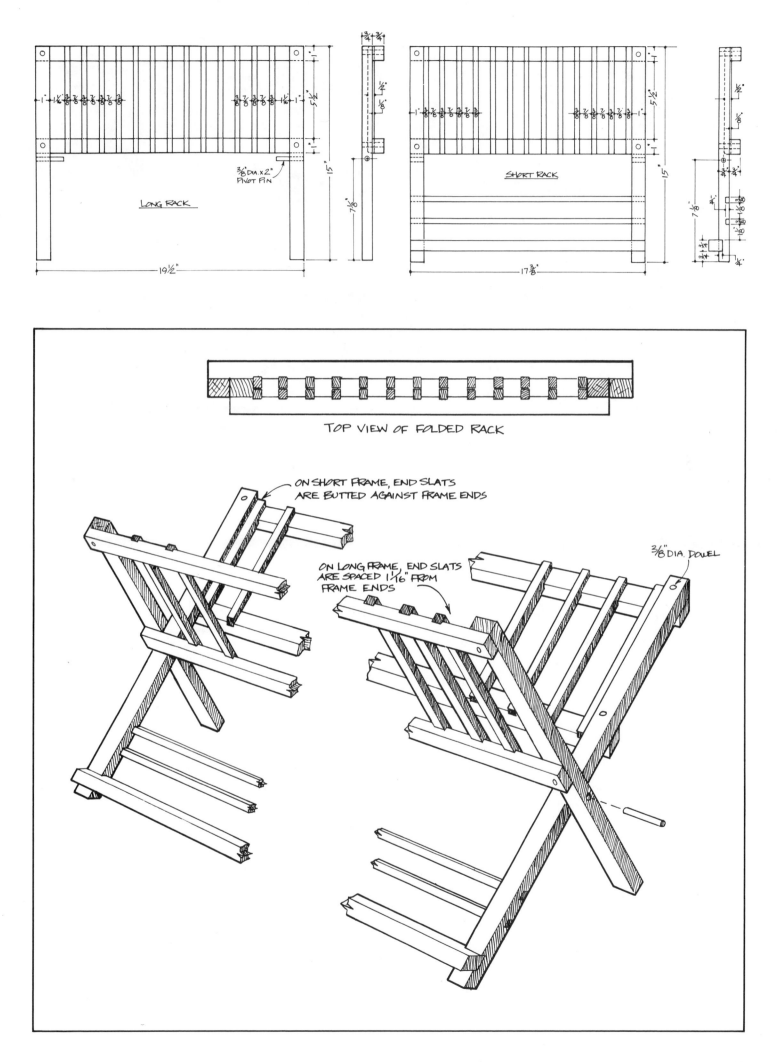

LONG RACK

3/8" DIA. x 2"
PIVOT PIN

SHORT RACK

TOP VIEW OF FOLDED RACK

ON SHORT FRAME, END SLATS
ARE BUTTED AGAINST FRAME ENDS

ON LONG FRAME, END SLATS
ARE SPACED 1 1/16" FROM
FRAME ENDS

3/8" DIA. DOWEL

18th Century Rudder Table

Space was at a premium in most early American homes, which perhaps explains why tables like this were so popular during that period. With the leaves folded down, the table took up little room when not in use. We think that feature was a good one, and that it can still be enjoyed today — especially for anyone with a small house or apartment.

A piece such as this is especially handsome in cherry or pine. The construction techniques are fairly straightforward and should not present any unusual difficulty.

Make the two sides (A) first. Standard 1 x 12 stock will provide enough width, or if necessary you can edge-join narrower stock. Cut to the length and width shown in the bill of materials, then lay out the location of the ⅜" thick x 2" wide x 1" long double tenons.

To make the tenons, equip the table saw with a dado head cutter and set it for a 3/16" depth of cut. With the stock held securely against the miter gauge, make a 3/16" x 1" rabbet cut on one end. Turn the stock over and repeat the cut. If you don't have a dado head, you can accomplish the same cut making repeated passes with a regular table saw blade. Since the stock is 2 feet long, you'll have a lot more control if you attach about an 18" length of scrap stock to the miter gauge. Make sure the scrap stock is straight. Now use a back saw to establish the 2" tenon width, then remove the remaining material with a sharp chisel.

The dado head cutter can also be used to cut the ⅜" x 2" notch for part C and the ⅜" x 6" notch for part D. Next, the 3½" high x 6" wide drawer opening can be located and marked on the stock. Drill one or two starting holes, then cut out with the saber saw. Note the drawer opening is located 1½" from the top and 1-1/16" from each side. Now transfer the grid pattern from the drawing and cut the profile to shape with the saber saw.

Cut the feet (B) to length and width, then lay out the location of the ⅜" x 2" x 1" mortises. It's a good idea to make the mortise a little deeper than 1" to allow for any excess glue. Use a ⅜" dia. drill bit to remove most of the stock, then use a chisel to square the corners and clean up waste stock. Transfer the grid pattern and cut to shape with the saber saw.

The stretchers (C) and aprons (D) can now be cut to length and width. Size the width for a good fit in the side (A) notches. The ⅜" x ¾" rabbets can be cut with the dado head on the table saw. Note that the stretcher (C) has a ⅜" dia. x ½" deep hole drilled to take the rudder (part E) tenon. Locate the hole halfway (14⅜") across the length and right in the center of the ¾" thickness.

Cut the rudder (E) to length and width. A ⅜" dia. x ¾" deep hole is drilled at a point ⅝" in from the side edge. Two holes are required, one at the top and one at the bottom. These holes must be located exactly in the center of the ¾" thickness in order for the rudder to operate properly. Now, transfer the grid pattern and cut to shape. Note that the rudder also has a slight notch with rounded corners. This is to insure that the rudder will clear the apron (D).

The top (H) can be made from standard 1" x 12" stock which measures 11¼" wide. Select stock that's flat and free of large knots or other imperfections. The ⅜" dia. x ½" deep hole for the rudder tenon is drilled on the underside of H. Locate the hole halfway across the length and ½" in from the edge. If you think the drill bit point might break through the other side, make the hole just ⅜" deep and shorten the rudder tenon to fit. The leaves (I) can also be made from standard 1" x 12" stock. Cut these parts slightly longer than necessary, then butt together and scribe a 33¾" dia. circle. Cut out with the saber saw.

Before assembly, give all parts a complete sanding. Take extra care with the curved edges so they look clean and smooth. Cut ⅜" dia. x 1¼" long dowel stock and glue in place for the rudder tenons. Assemble parts A and B using glue and clamps. When dry, parts C

and D can be joined to the leg, again using glue and clamps. Parts F and G can then be cut, sanded, and glued together (see detail), then joined to fit the apron (D).

Attach the four hinges, then assemble the top to the base using four fastening blocks (see detail part J). When installing, it's not necessary to overtighten the screw — just enough so the top contacts part D. The two drawers (K) are made as shown.

Our table was finished with two coats of Deft Pumpkin wood stain followed by two coats of Deftco (Deft) Danish Oil finish.

Bill of Materials (All Dimensions Actual)		
Part	Size	No. Req'd
A	¾ x 11 x 24 (inc. tenons)	2
B	1½ x 2 x 19	2
C	¾ x 2 x 28¾	2
D	¾ x 6 x 28¾	2
E	¾ x 11¼ x 20½	2
F	¾ x 1½ x 27¼	2
G	¹¹⁄₁₆ x ¾ x 27¼	2
H	¾ x 11¼ x 33¾	1
I	¾ x 11¼ x 33½	2
J	¾ x 1 x 2½	4
K	See Drawing	2

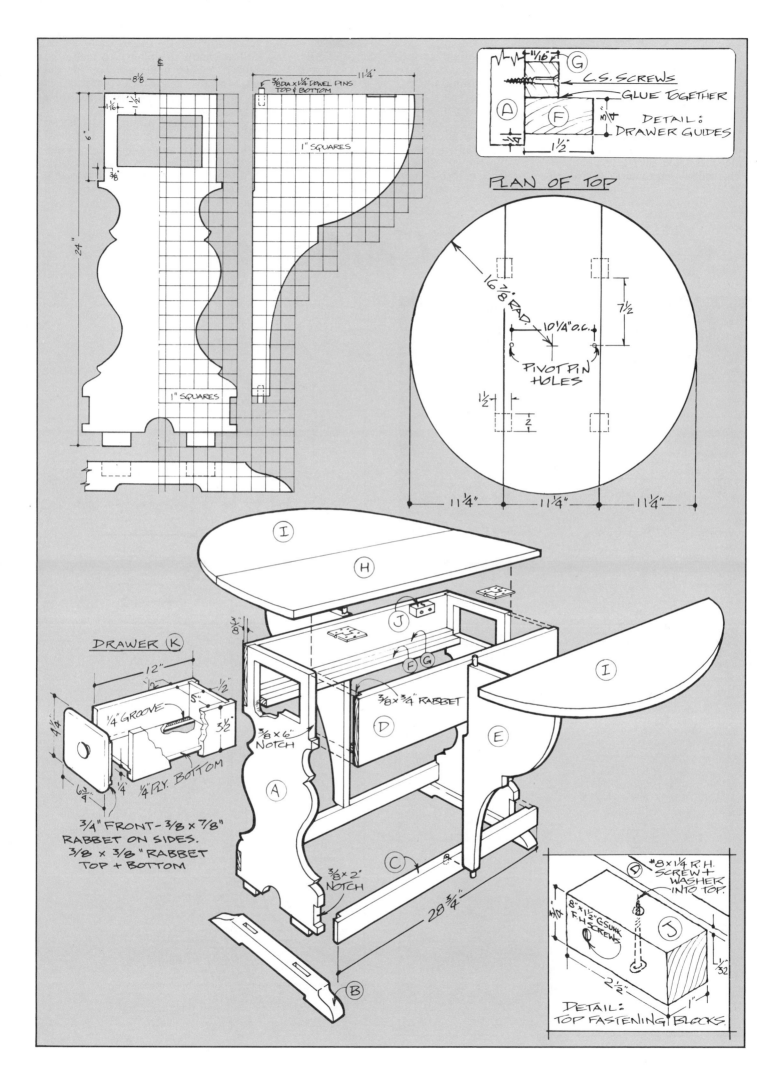

Top-left patterns
8⅛

1 7/16 · 1/2

6"

24"

3/8

1" SQUARES

1" SQUARES

3/8" DIA. x 1/4" DOWEL PINS TOP & BOTTOM

11¼"

1" SQUARES

Detail: Drawer Guides (top right)
11/16"

G

C.S. SCREWS

GLUE TOGETHER

A   F

3/4

DETAIL:
DRAWER GUIDES

1½"

PLAN OF TOP
16⅞" RAD.

7½

10¼" O.C.

PIVOT PIN HOLES

1½

2

11¼"   11¼"   11¼"

Drawer detail
DRAWER K

12"

1½

1/2

5"

1/2

¼" GROOVE

3½

4¼

6¾

¼

¼ PLY. BOTTOM

3/4" FRONT - 3/8 x 7/8"
RABBET ON SIDES.
3/8 x 3/8" RABBET
TOP + BOTTOM

Exploded view labels
I

H

I

J

F G

3/8 x 3/4" RABBET

D

E

A

3/8 x 6"
NOTCH

3/8 x 2"
NOTCH

C

28 ¾"

B

3/8

Detail: Top Fastening Blocks (bottom right)
#8 x 1¼" R.H.
SCREW +
WASHER
INTO TOP.

8" x 1½" CSUNK
F.H. SCREWS

J

1/32

2½"

1"

DETAIL:
TOP FASTENING BLOCKS

An attractive pair of wooden candlesticks always makes a nice gift item. Colonial homes depended on them for precious table light, especially on cold winter evenings. While not the necessity they once were, we still enjoy them today for the warmth and charm they add to the family dining table. We made ours from maple (stained), but birch, walnut, and cherry can also be used.

To minimize waste, the candlestick is made in two parts. Part A is a spindle turning and part B is a faceplate turning.

Make part A from a 2″ square turning block. Start with a length of about 9″. Rough out the stock to a 2″ diameter cylinder, then cut to the profile shown. Thoroughly sand all surfaces before removing from the lathe. The top should be slightly dished-in to collect candle drippings. To make the tapered candle hole, grind or file the edges of a ⅞″ spade bit so that it tapers to ¾″ at the end. Use this bit to drill a 1″ deep hole.

After faceplate turning, part B can be joined to part A with a 1½″ x #8 woodscrew, countersunk ¼″. Final sand all surfaces, then stain if desired. We used a walnut stain on our maple set. Two coats of Watco Danish Oil completes the project.

Colonial Candlesticks

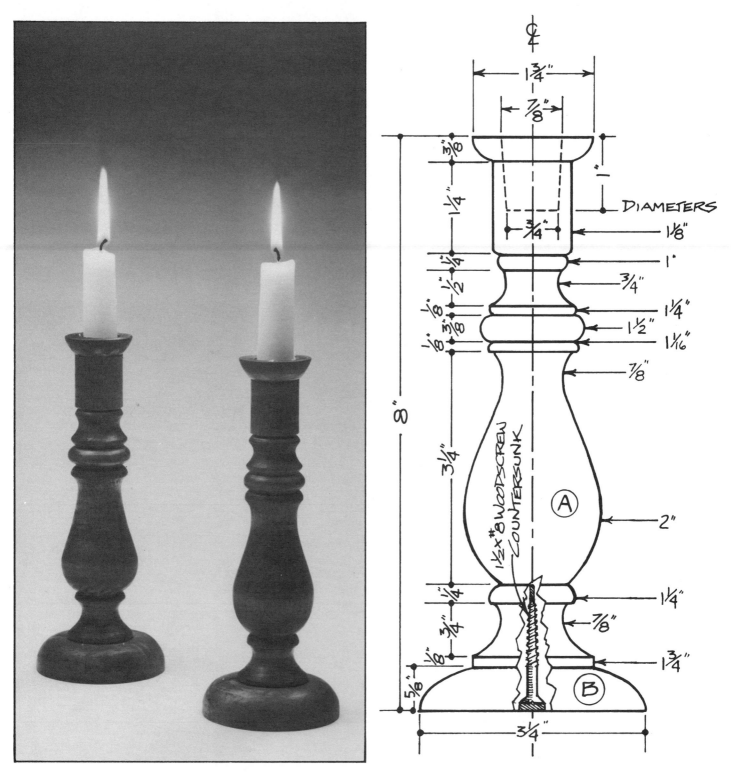

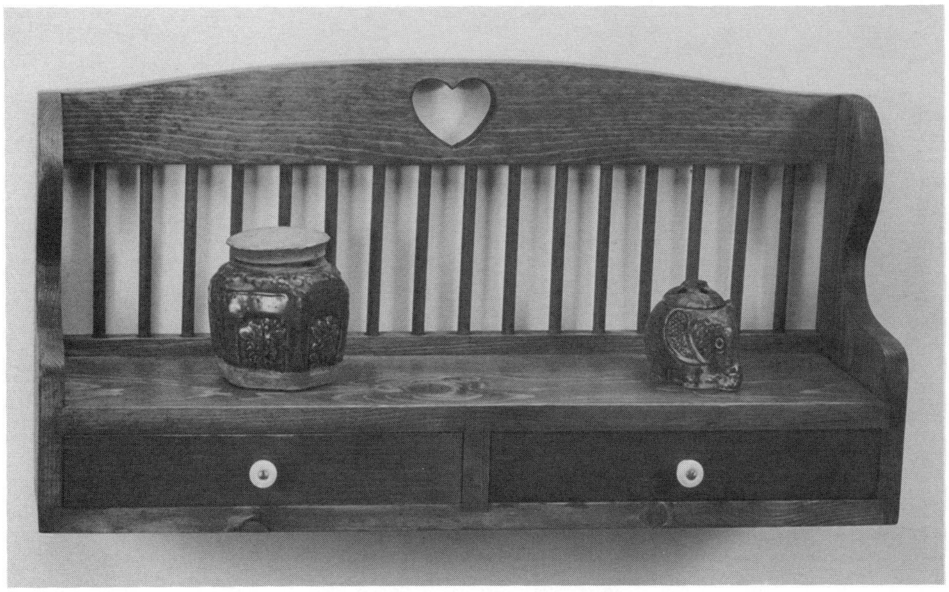

Deacon's Wall Shelf

Resembling an old-fashioned Deacon's bench, this attractive wall unit will add a bit of charm to most any room.

Begin by cutting the sides (A) to length and width. Lay out and mark the location of the ¼" deep dado and lower rabbet, then make the cut with a dado head cutter, or make repeated passes using the table or radial arm saw. Cut the rabbet and dado slightly narrower than the mating parts (E & F). Then, when parts E and F are sanded, the fit will be just right. The back notches can be cut using the same method. Next, using the grid pattern shown, lay out, mark, and cut the curved profile.

Parts E and F can now be cut to size. Note each one has a ¼" deep dado to take part G. Cut part G so that its end grain goes into the dadoes rather than showing in front.

After parts B and C are cut to size, lay out and mark the location of the sixteen dowels. Use a ⅜" dia. bit to drill each hole to a depth of ⅜". If you have one, use a countersink bit to apply a slight (1/16") chamfer to each hole. It's a small detail, but one that shows that care and concern went into the piece.

Sand all parts thoroughly, then assemble using glue and finishing nails. Since the shelf is fairly heavy and is hung from part B, be sure to glue each dowel for added strength. Assemble the drawers as shown. A ¼" by 1" notch is cut in the bottom of part K to permit the drawer to fit over part H.

Our shelf is finished with one coat of Deft Pumpkin wood stain followed by two coats of Deftco (Deft) Danish Oil Finish. Two angled holes drilled through part B and into part A permit the shelf to be hung on a pair of finishing nails.

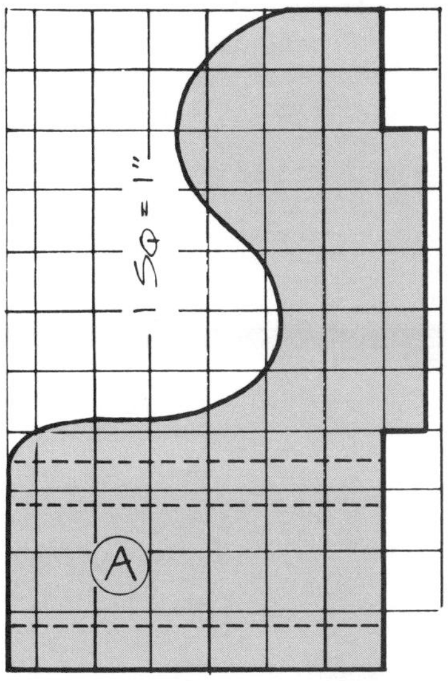

Bill of Materials
(All Dimensions Actual)

Part	Description	Size	No. Req'd
A	Side	¾ x 7¼ x 11	2
B	Upper Back	¾ x 3 x 24½	1
C	Lower Back	¾ x 4 x 24½	1
D	Dowel	⅜ dia. x 5¾	16
E	Bottom	¾ x 6½ x 23½	1
F	Shelf	¾ x 6½ x 23½	1
G	Divider	¾ x 6½ x 2½	1
H	Drawer Stop	¼ x ¾ x 1	2
I	Drawer Front	¾ x 2 x 11⅛	2
J	Drawer Side	½ x 2 x 5⅝	4
K	Drawer Back	½ x 2 x 10⅝	2
L	Drawer Bottom	¼ x 4 15/16 x 10 9/16	2

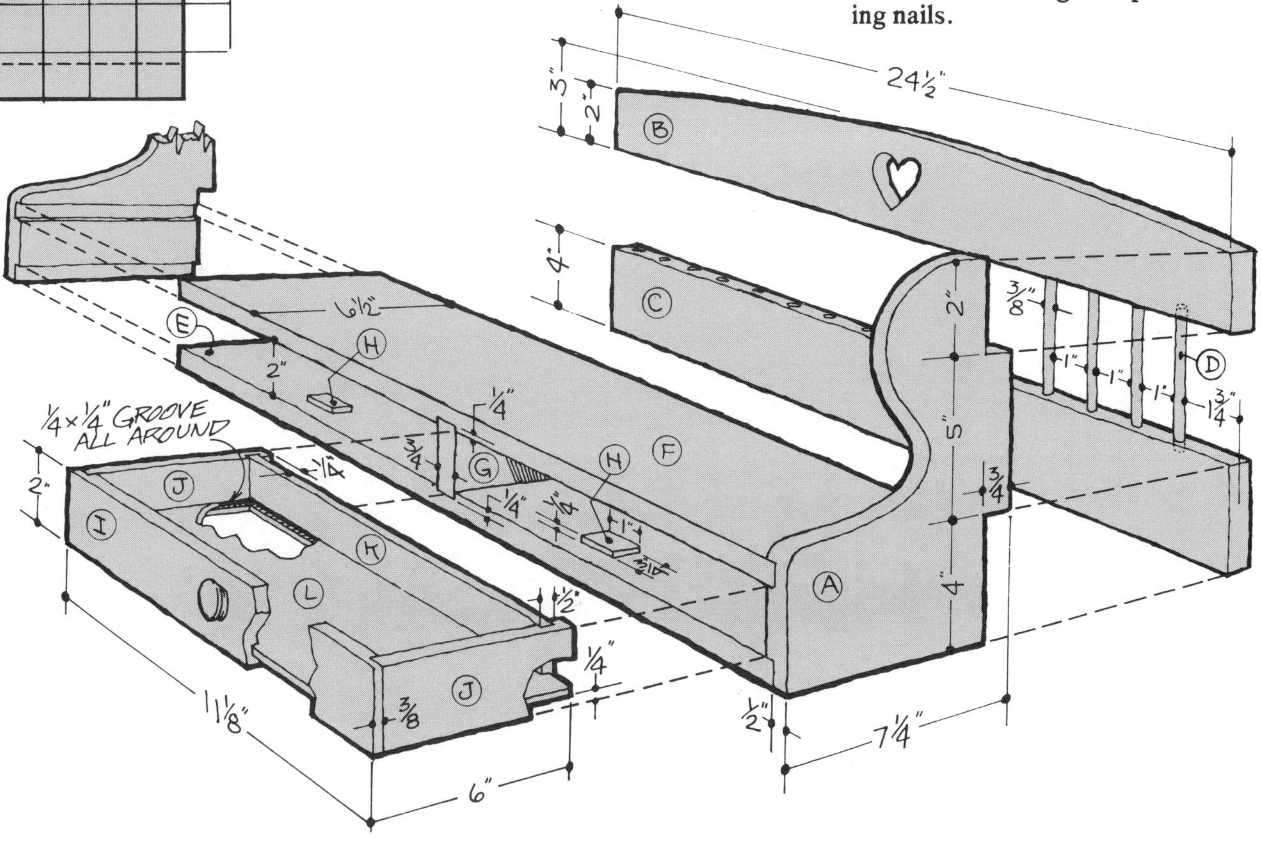

This sled from the 1880's is a bit of pure nostalgia and the perfect vehicle for a toddler's first winter snow ride. Unscrew the seat portion and bigger kids can have a lot of fun with it too, once they learn the knack of steering with body English.

Hardwood such as oak or maple should be used for the main parts. The runners (A) can be cut from 8″ wide boards, but it's less expensive to use 5½″ wide boards and simply glue and dowel on pieces of 2½″ x 6″ stock to form the horns at the front. A saber saw will do a nice job of cutting the curves. Lay out the hand slots and drill the ends with a ¾″ auger; then cut between the holes. Also bore ⅜″ deep sockets for the 1″ birch dowel.

Steel strap, available at hardware stores is bent to form a loop over each runner horn and drilled and countersunk at 4″ intervals. Fasten the steel "shoes" with ⅝″ x No. 6 flathead wood screws and trim the shoes flush with the back ends of the runners.

The bed (B) is made of two or three edge-joined ¾″ boards (or a piece of plywood). Lay out and cut the curves at each end and the notches which are centered on the runner slots. Screw the cleats (C) to the underside using 1½″ x No. 8 roundhead wood screws.

The seat parts are cut next. Note that the seat back is tilted and fits into a ¼″ rabbet in the sides. Join these parts with six 1½″ x No. 6 flathead wood screws and glue and bevel off the bottom edge of the back. Sand all parts carefully,

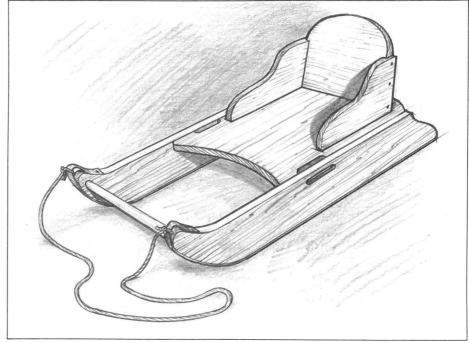

Old-Time Sled

putting a generous radius on all upper edges.

Scribe a line 1¼″ below the top edge of each runner to serve as a guide for locating the corner braces which are fastened with ¾″ x No. 6 flathead wood screws. Turn the sled upside down, add the front dowel and with pipe clamps holding the bed between the runners, screw the corner brackets to the bed.

The seat is fastened centered on the bed and about 4″ from the back edge using 1½″ x No. 6 roundhead wood screws.

Many of these sleds were gaily decorated with bright colors and gold striping, but this easily wears away unless heavily coated with varnish. The sled looks fine if left natural and just given two or three coats of urethane varnish.

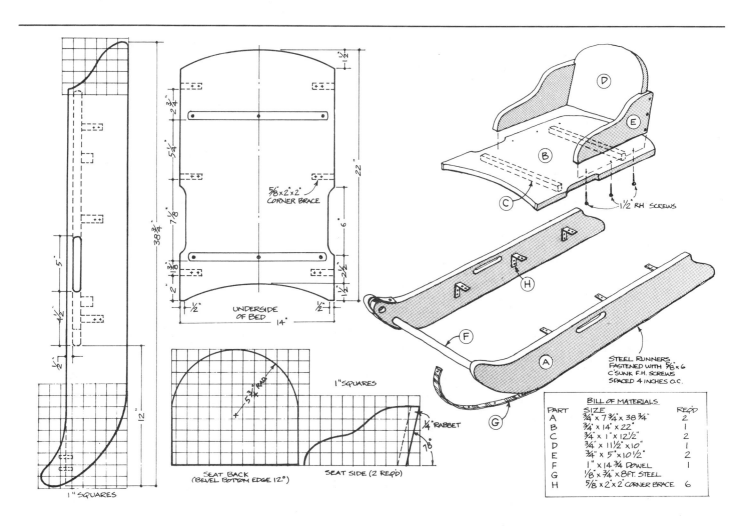

UNDERSIDE OF BED

SEAT BACK (BEVEL BOTTOM EDGE 12°)

SEAT SIDE (2 REQ'D)

1″ SQUARES

BILL OF MATERIALS		
PART	SIZE	REQ'D
A	¾″ x 7¾″ x 38¾″	2
B	¾″ x 14″ x 22″	1
C	¾″ x 1″ x 12½″	2
D	¾″ x 11½″ x 10″	1
E	¾″ x 5″ x 10½″	2
F	1″ x 14¾″ DOWEL	1
G	⅛″ x ¾″ x 8 FT. STEEL	
H	⅝″ x 2″ x 2″ CORNER BRACE	6

Antique Knife Tray

In times past, the knife tray was used as a means to store and carry the household table knives. We found this fine example of an early knife tray at the Gunn Historical Museum in Washington, Connecticut. The museum was kind enough to let us take photographs and some actual measurements.

This well-proportioned tray owes its graceful appearance to the sloping sides and ends, and the use of thin stock throughout. The divider incorporates a sensitively shaped dowel which is fastened to the top for a handle.

Referring to the drawing, make all parts as shown. Assemble with glue and finishing nails. Note that the handle bottom is planed flat before attaching with angled dowels and glue. Sand thoroughly, stain and final finish with two coats of Minwax Antique Oil Finish.

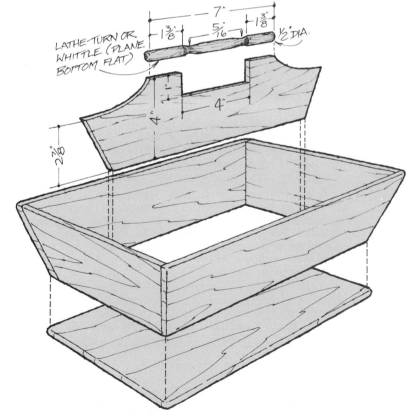

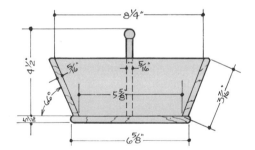

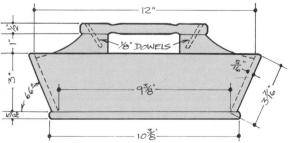

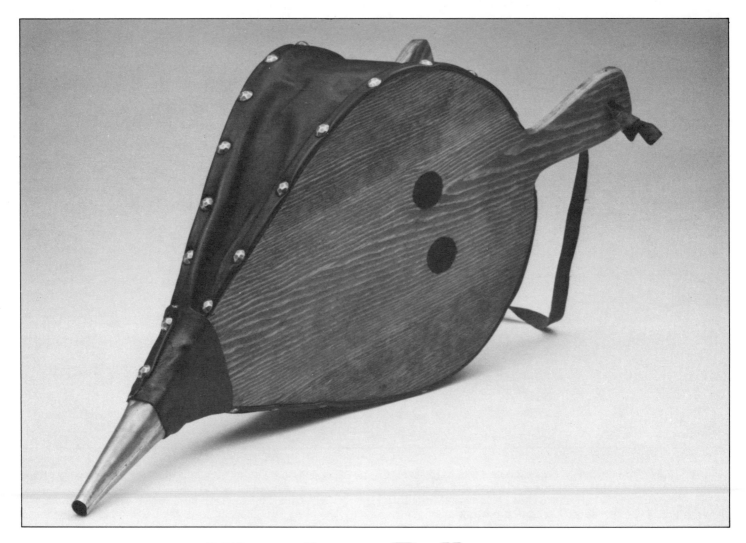

Fireplace Bellows

In addition to woodworking, this old style bellows requires a little metalwork and leatherwork. None of it is very difficult though, and the whole project can be completed in just a few evenings in the workshop. The one shown is made of pine, but any good cabinet wood is suitable.

Make the wooden halves first. If ½" thick stock is not available in your area, you'll have to hand plane thicker stock. To do this, edge-join two pieces of 1" (¾" actual) thick stock by 6" (5½" actual) wide by 37" long stock. This extra length and width is good to have in case some edges splinter as you plane. If you use dowels when edge-joining, make sure you locate them where they will not show when the bellows is cut to shape. Also, planing is much easier if the grain of both boards runs in the same direction.

Clamp the edge-glued board to your bench so that you can plane without interference from your clamps. A sharp jack plane will remove most of the material. Finish up with a smooth plane.

Cut the board into two pieces, each one 9" wide by 18" long, then transfer the profile for the grid pattern and cut to shape on the band saw. Clamp both halves together and drill a ½" diameter by 3" long hole in the center of the nozzle end. Cut off 1½ inches of the tip of one board and glue and clamp this piece to the other board as shown. Also, in one board, drill two 1" dia. valve holes.

Next, make the metal tip, using copper (or brass) sheet, about .030-inch thick. We used copper flashing purchased locally. Lay out a pattern as shown and cut with metal shears. Roll the sheet into a cone, lapping the edges ⅛ inch and soldering the seam. When the solder has set, shape the

large end of the cone into a square. The end of the bellows is fitted into the square end of the metal tip, the end first being shaped carefully with a carving knife to fit the square snugly, and so the metal laps the wood by ½ inch. Use epoxy to secure the metal tip to the bellows end. All the wood parts are then sanded, and finished with stain, varnish or paint. We chose to finish ours with a coat of walnut stain followed by two coats of satin polyurethane varnish. To minimize chances of warping, it is necessary to finish both sides of the boards in the same way. Allow to thoroughly dry before proceeding with assembly.

A leather "web" is cut from a 36-inch length of soft hide to the dimensions shown in the drawing. From the scrap material left from shaping the web, cut two small leather squares, 2 by 2 inches. These are the flapper valves for the air intake holes. Stretch each square tightly on the inner face of the bellows, one over each hole, and tack it in place with one carpet tack at each corner.

Attach the web, starting at the center, between the handles of the bellows. Fold the leather over ½-inch all along the edge so that a double thickness takes the ornamental brass upholsterer's tacks. The tacks are placed at 1¼-inch intervals. No tacks are necessary where the leather crosses near the handles, but the leather should be stretched tightly across this unfastened area.

Referring to the pattern, cut a piece of leather to wrap around the tip of the bellows - wide enough to cover the end of the cone and to extend up the bellows 1½ inches past the hinge. This leather piece is glued to the metal cone and ornamented with upholsterer's tacks.

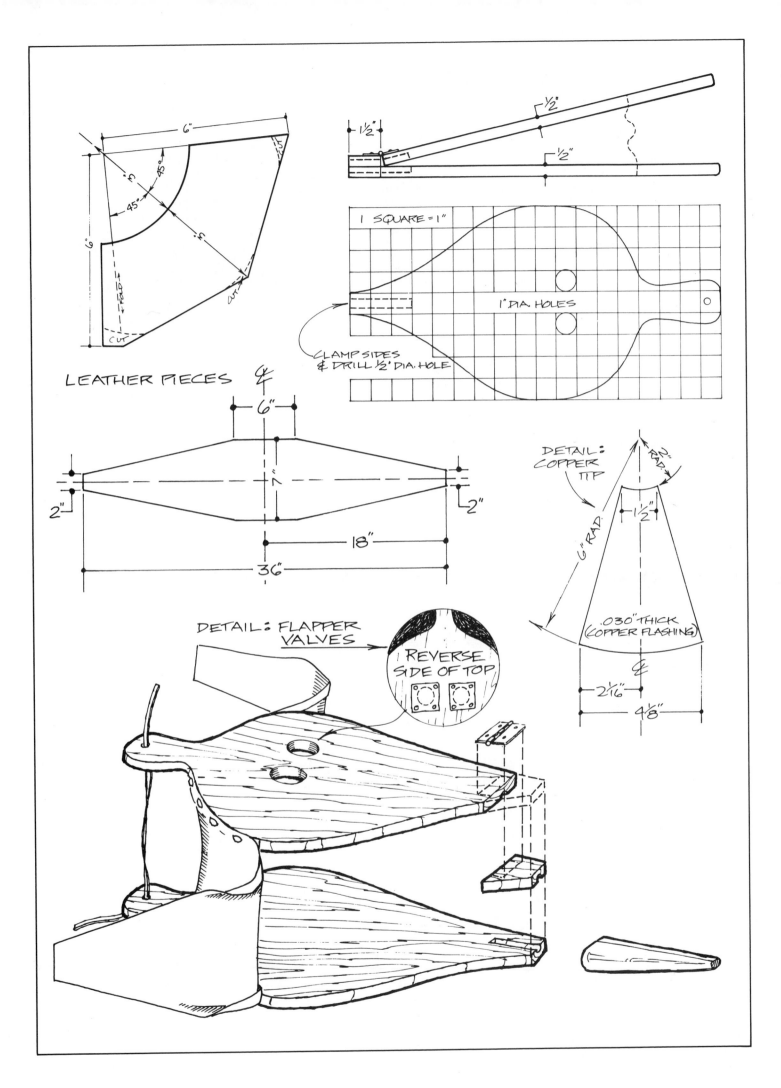

6"

45°
45°
5"
45°
5"
6"

FOLD

CUT

CUT

LEATHER PIECES

1½"

½"

½"

1 SQUARE = 1"

1" DIA HOLES

CLAMP SIDES
& DRILL ½" DIA. HOLE

℄

6"

7"

2"

2"

18"

36"

DETAIL:
COPPER
TIP

2" RAD.

1½"

6" RAD.

.030" THICK
(COPPER FLASHING)

℄

2 1/16"

4 1/8"

DETAIL: FLAPPER
VALVES

REVERSE
SIDE OF TOP

Candle Box

Thanks to Thomas Edison, the candle box has been obsolete in most American homes for the better part of a century. But by "obsolete," we mean that it is no longer needed for its original purpose. It is still a very handy and attractive accent piece, a perfect place to store the electric bill and other incoming mail until we have the time and money to respond.

The candle box shown here is not a reproduction of any surviving, Colonial original; rather, it has been designed and sized for its modern use. But, at a glance, an 18th century American would certainly experience a sense of familiarity.

Assemble as shown using glue and pegs. Stain to suit and final finish with two coats of polyurethane varnish.

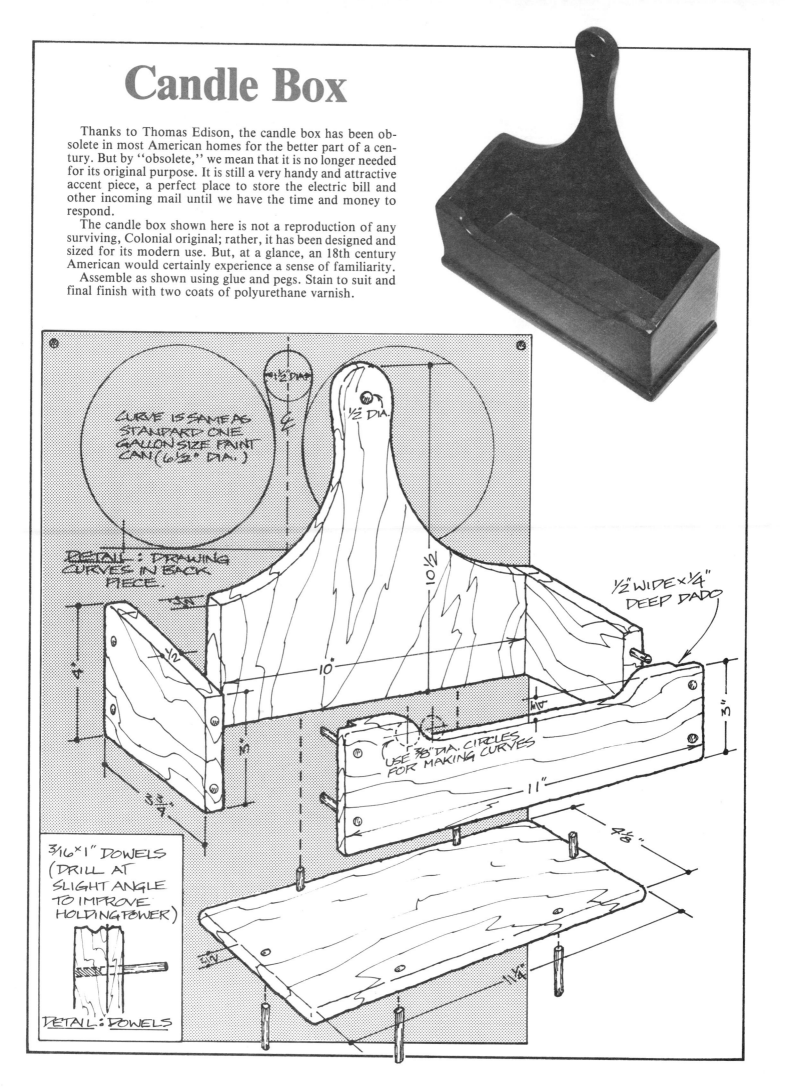

CURVE IS SAME AS STANDARD ONE GALLON SIZE PAINT CAN (6½" DIA.)

1½ DIA.

½ DIA.

DETAIL: DRAWING CURVES IN BACK PIECE.

3⅜"

10½"

½"

4"

3⅛"

½"WIDE x ¼" DEEP DADO

10"

½"

½"

3"

11"

USE ⅜"DIA. CIRCLES FOR MAKING CURVES

4⅝"

1¼"

3/16 x 1" DOWELS (DRILL AT SLIGHT ANGLE TO IMPROVE HOLDING POWER)

DETAIL: DOWELS

This reproduction of an antique hutch is so simple in design that it can be made with a minimum of tools. Since it's made of number 2 common pine with no elaborate hardware, it can be built at a cost appreciably under $100.00 and will be an attractive addition to any Early American setting.

Begin by gluing up 1" pine lumber (actually ¾" thick) to make the sides (A). A 7¼" wide board slightly longer than 6 feet is glued and clamped to a 7½" wide x 36½" long board. If both boards are carefully jointed and glued, no dowels should be necessary to reinforce the joint. Make up two sides (A) and trim them to finish width and length. The dadoes for the shelves and rabbet for the top (C) can be cut with the radial arm, table saw or portable router and straight bit.

After completing the sides cut the shelves to size (parts B, D and E) and the top (C). Note that parts B and D have grooves for plates. These are made by running the lumber over a table saw blade set at 45 degrees and then at 90 degrees. The grooves need only be about ¼" deep.

The two shelves (E), differ in that one has a 20½" long by ¼" deep notch cut into it and the other has a ¼" x ¼" rabbet. These modifications follow the original while all else is ¾" thick with the exception of the ⅜" door panel.

The door is next. The stiles, parts K, L, and M, are cut from full 1 inch thick pine and joined together with mortises and tenons. The panel for the door, part N, is glued up from ½" thick stock and planed down to ⅜". An alternate door assembly would use ¾" thick (actual) pine for the stiles and rails and, if available, pine veneered plywood of ¼" thickness could be used for the door panel. If this method is used, the rail tenons and corresponding grooves should be cut ¼" wide rather than ⅜".

The original door panel molding was shaped with a molding plane but most lumberyards carry a suitable small panel molding similar to the molding P shown in the detail. This molding is mitered and attached to the door rails and, stiles with glue and small brads. Do not glue the molding to a door panel made from solid stock. The back of the panel may be left as is or dressed up with a small quarter-round molding.

Secure the shelves with counterbored 1" x #10 fh wood screws that are plugged with ⅜" dia. dowels before sanding the assembled hutch. The top (C) is secured with finishing nails.

The hutch back consists of three wide ¾" thick boards joined together with tongues and grooves or a ship lap joint. The back boards are held to the sides and shelves with finishing nails. If sufficiently wide boards cannot be secured, narrower boards can be used to avoid gluing up wide boards. The matching tongues and grooves can be

Stepped-Back Hutch

Part	Description	Size	No. Req'd	Part	Description	Size	No. Req'd
			Bill of Materials (All Dimensions Actual)				
A	Side	¾ x 14¾ x 72	2	I	Bottom Stile	¾ x 8 x 33	2
B	Counter	¾ x 15¼ x 37½	1	J	Back Board	¾ x as req'd x 71¼	As Req'd
C	Top	¾ x 7 x 35¾	1	K	Door Stile	1 x 3¼ x 33	2
D	Upper Shelf	¾ x 6¼ x 35½	2	L	Upper Door Rail	1 x 3¼ x 14¾	1
E	Lower Shelf	¾ x 14 x 35½	2	M	Lower Door Rail	1 x 5¾ x 14¾	1
F	Top Rail	¾ x 5¼ x 36½	1	N	Door Panel	⅜ x 14⅝ x 24⅝	1
G	Top Stile	¾ x 4½ x 29¾	2	O	Top Molding	(See Detail)	5 Ft.
H	Bottom Rail	¾ x 3¼ x 36½	1	P	Door Molding	(See Detail)	7 Ft.

safely cut with a portable router.

Parts F, G, H and I are next cut to size and attached to the sides and shelves with counterbored and plugged 1″ x #10 fh screws.

The door hinges, brass or black steel, are mortised into the door. Black, flush-mounted "H" hinges can be substituted and will also look authentic. The turnbutton, or latch is cut from a piece of scrap and mounted with a 1″ x #10 black round-head wood screw. The 1¼″ diameter door knob is of the standard turned wood type found in most hardware stores.

The upper molding, part O, consists of two pieces of ¼″ pine and ¾″ cove.

These pieces can be individually mitered and fastened with small finishing nails.

Before putting on the finish, plug all screw holes with ⅜″ dowel plugs and sand them flush. Screws may also be covered with plugs cut from face grain of pine scrap using a ⅜″ plug cutter in an electric drill. Plugs of this type will not be very noticeable which you may or may not prefer. They do sand down flush easier than birch dowel plugs.

After sanding, the choice of stains to be used will depend on your individual preferences. The choices are all attractive and include light and dark browns, reddish browns or honey tones.

Pigmented oil stains are readily available and easy to apply evenly with brush and rag.

Two or three coats of a satin finish varnish should be applied to all visible surfaces. The final coat is rubbed down with 4/0 steel wool to achieve a uniform low sheen. To minimize warping, don't forget to varnish both sides of all parts including the shelves. An easier finishing method is to apply a number of coats of one of the modern penetrating oils such as Watco Danish Oil. Initial coats penetrate and help stabilize the wood. Additional coats will enhance the color and build up an attractive low luster surface finish.

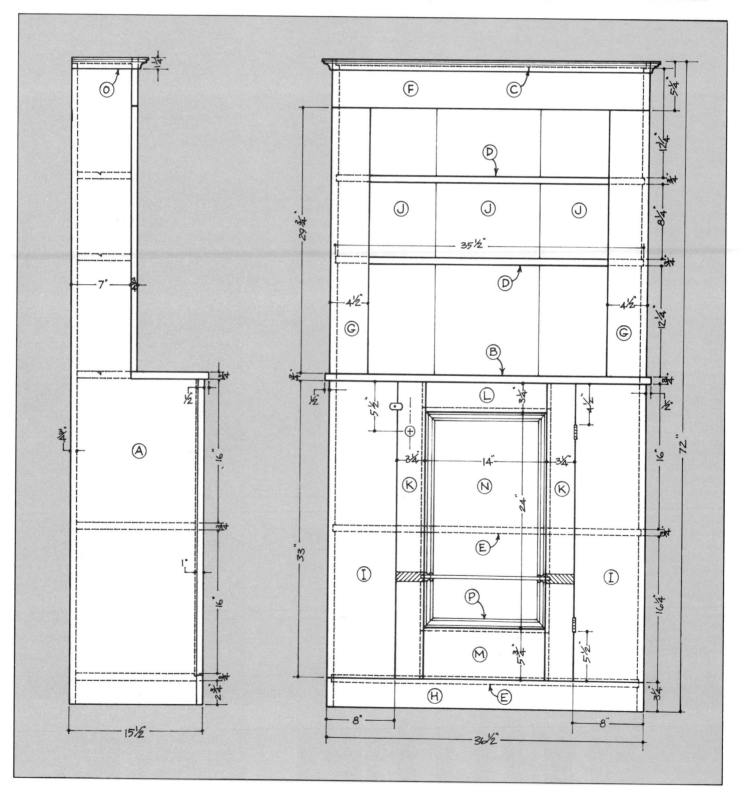

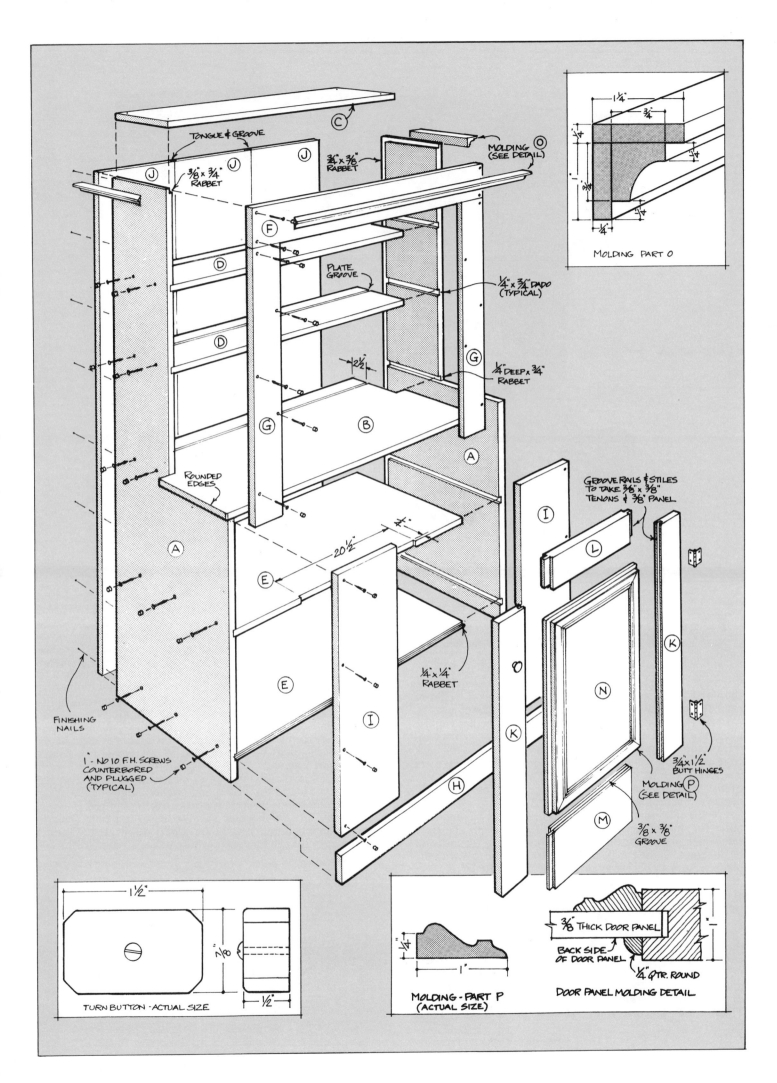

TONGUE & GROOVE

C

MOLDING O
(SEE DETAIL)

¾" x ⅜"
RABBET

3/8 x 3/4
RABBET

J J J

PLATE
GROOVE

F

D

D

2½"

¼" x ¾" DADO
(TYPICAL)

G

¼" DEEP x ¾"
RABBET

G

B

A

ROUNDED
EDGES

GROOVE RAILS & STILES
TO TAKE ⅜" x ⅜"
TENONS & ⅜" PANEL

I

A

L

E

20½"

¼" x ¼"
RABBET

I

E

O

N

K

FINISHING
NAILS

K

1" - No 10 F.H. SCREWS
COUNTERBORED
AND PLUGGED
(TYPICAL)

I

H

M

⅜ x ⅜
GROOVE

3/4" x 1½"
BUTT HINGES

MOLDING P
(SEE DETAIL)

MOLDING PART O

1¼"
¾"
¼"
¼"
¾"
¼"
¼"

MOLDING PART O

1½"

7/8"

½"

TURN BUTTON - ACTUAL SIZE

¼"

1"

MOLDING - PART P
(ACTUAL SIZE)

⅜ THICK DOOR PANEL

BACK SIDE
OF DOOR PANEL

¼" QTR. ROUND

DOOR PANEL MOLDING DETAIL

Buckboard Seat

This antique buckboard seat was discovered in an antique shop and for those who enjoy a bit of nostalgia it would be perfect in a child's room, a hallway, or as a window seat.

Begin the project with the seat (part A). Whether you use glued-up boards or a single piece of 1 inch (¾ inch actual) thick lumber, you'll have to miter cut the sides and the back edge at a 10-degree angle. Note that on the side edges, there is a stop cut to be made to allow for a molding on the edge of the seat. Also note that this stop cut is beveled at 10 degrees to accept the front edge of part C.

For the sides (parts C), you'll have to make a compound miter for the back edges. Note that there's a left and right side which are mirror images of each other, so the cuts will be different. These can be done on a radial-arm saw with the blade set at a 44-degree angle and the arm at 10 degrees. On the table saw, set the blade at 44 degrees and the miter gauge at 10 degrees. The top and bottom edges will also have to be ripped at 10 degrees. Round the front corner with a saber or band saw, or use a wood rasp.

The back of the seat (part B) can now be cut to size, using the same compound miter procedure. Make the cuts accurately for a good fit with the sides (C) and seat (A). Parts D, the corner blocks, will also have to be compound mitered. These hold the sides and back together with the aid of 1¼ x #10 flat head screws that are plugged with dowels. These screws are driven into D through the sides (C) and back (B).

The legs (part E) with their shoe-foot backs come next.

On the original, these were made from solid pine boards, but I would recommend gluing-up narrower stock. Note the direction of grain. The cloverleaf design can be done with a 1¼ inch spade bit as shown in the detail. The legs are attached to the underside of the seat with ⅜ inch diameter x 2 inch long dowels. The steel straps that are attached to the inside of the legs are very important and should not be excluded. They stiffen them and will keep them from splitting along the grain. The brackets on the underside prevent lateral movement of the seat. To make them, clamp ⅛ inch thick x ¾ inch wide steel flat stock (available in most hardware stores) in a vise and bend to 45 degrees at two points as shown.

Lengths of ⅜ inch thick by ¾ inch wide pine molding act as a trim around the inside and outside edges of the seat. Compound miters at the corners are again required.

Almost any finish would seem to do, even paint. The original has a patina that could be closely duplicated by using Minwax's Puritan Pine stain with a satin varnish finish.

Bill of Materials (All Dimensions Actual)			
Part	Description	Size	No. Req'd
A	Seat	¾ x 13 x 37½	1
B	Back	¾ x 6½ x 39¼	1
C	Side	¾ x 6½ x 13¼	2
D	Corner Blocks	1 x 1 x 6	2
E	Leg	¾ x 13¾ x 14¾	2
F	Outside Molding	⅜ x ¾	As Req'd
G	Inside Molding	⅜ x ¾	As Req'd

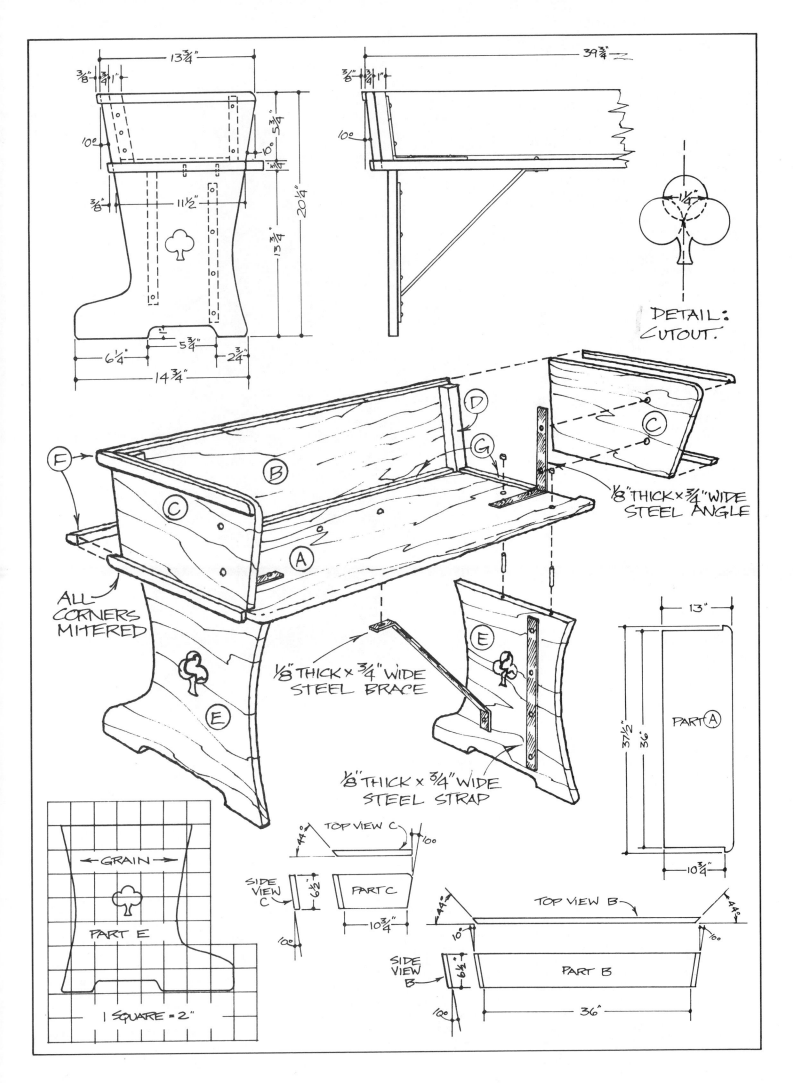

13¾"

⅜" ¾"1"

10°

3⅞"

11½"

5¾"

10°

3¾"

13¾"

20¼"

6¼"

5¾"

2¾"

14¾"

39¾"

⅜" ¾"1"

10°

10°

¾"

1¼"

DETAIL: CUTOUT.

F

B

D

C

A

G

C

⅛" THICK × ¾" WIDE
STEEL ANGLE

ALL CORNERS MITERED

⅛" THICK × ¾" WIDE
STEEL BRACE

E

E

⅛" THICK × ¾" WIDE
STEEL STRAP

13"

37½"

36"

PART A

10¾"

←GRAIN→

PART E

1 SQUARE = 2"

44°

TOP VIEW C

10°

SIDE
VIEW
C

6½"

PART C

10¾"

10°

44°

TOP VIEW B

44°

10°

10°

SIDE
VIEW
B

4½"

PART B

10°

36°

18th Century Corner Shelf

The bowed front of this small corner shelf provides a nice detail, and no doubt, many woodworkers will find this an interesting challenge. There's nothing overwhelming about any of the procedure though, so if time and care is taken, even a novice will be able to build this piece and be pleased with the results.

It seemed appropriate for us to choose mahogany for ours, since early shelves of this style often used that wood. In many ways mahogany is an ideal wood for woodworking. It's hard enough to resist denting and splintering, but not so hard that it becomes burdensome to work with when using hand or power tools. Mahogany is usually straight grained and free of knots, so it planes well.

The two sides can be made first. Use ½ inch thick stock for both parts. Note that one side measures 7¾ inches wide while the other is 7⅜ inches. Cut each side to a 22 inch length, then use a dado head cutter to cut the ⅛ inch deep by ½ inch wide rabbet in the 7¾ inch wide board. Next, transfer the profile to each board, then cut out with a band or saber saw.

In order to make the lower shelf and the bottom you'll need a means to mark the 13¾ inch radius. There are a variety of ways to do it, but perhaps the easiest is to take a strip of scrap stock that measures about ⅛ inch thick and 15 inches long. Drill a small hole for a brad in one end, then measure 13¾ inches and drill a second hole big enough to fit a pencil point. Using the brad as a pivot point, scribe the radius on a piece of ½ inch stock. The piece will look best if the grain runs as shown in the sketch, so try to keep this in mind when you orient the radius on the stock. After scribing both pieces, use a band or saber saw to cut out. Make sure the two back legs meet at 90 degrees or the two sides won't be square when they're glued-up later on.

To make the bowed front, we used a piece of 5/4 inch (1-1/16 - 1-1/8 inch actual) solid mahogany, but it would also be suitable to use 5/4 inch pine and add a mahogany veneer front later on.

Cut the stock to a width of 4 inches and a length of 10 inches. Using the lower shelf or bottom as a template, scribe the 13¾ inch radius on both the top and bottom edge of the stock. If you don't have a band saw to make this cut, clamp the stock securely and use a sharp smooth plane to cut the curve roughly to shape. A belt sander is then used to remove any roughness and further smooth the radius. Hand sanding will finish the job. This technique may sound tedious, but we did it this

way and found it was surprisingly easy. If you plan to veneer, it can be added now. The veneer can run either vertically or horizontally, although in fine cabinetwork it usually runs vertically.

The table or radial arm saw can be used to cut the 45 degree corners as shown. Also, at this time, the front is cut into three separate pieces. Use care here to get a square cut.

The lower shelf, bottom, and bowed front halves can now be assembled (see sketch). A 1⅛ inch square corner block is cut to a length of 4 inches, then the two halves are inset so that their outside ends are flush with the edges of shelf and bottom. Use glue and clipped brads as shown, then clamp securely.

When dry, this sub-assembly is attached to the two sides with glue and finishing nails driven from the back. The upper shelf is cut to size and joined in the same manner. The drawer is made to the dimensions shown using resawn stock. If pine is used for the drawer parts you may want to stain them to match the mahogany. Two drawer guides are also added.

Sand all surfaces thoroughly, especially the edges of the curved sides. Remove all scratched and sharp edges. For a final finish we used Deft's Danish Oil (Natural #1114). This is a penetrating oil that's easy to apply and results in a lovely satin finish. A ⅝ inch diameter brass cabinet knob completes the project.

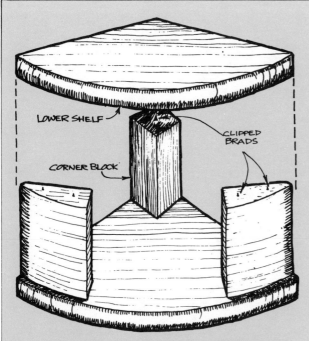

LOWER SHELF

CLIPPED BRADS

CORNER BLOCK

BOWED FRONT PARTS AND CORNER BLOCK ARE GLUED & CLAMPED BETWEEN BOTTOM AND LOWER SHELF. BRADS PREVENT SKIDDING UNDER CLAMP PRESSURE.

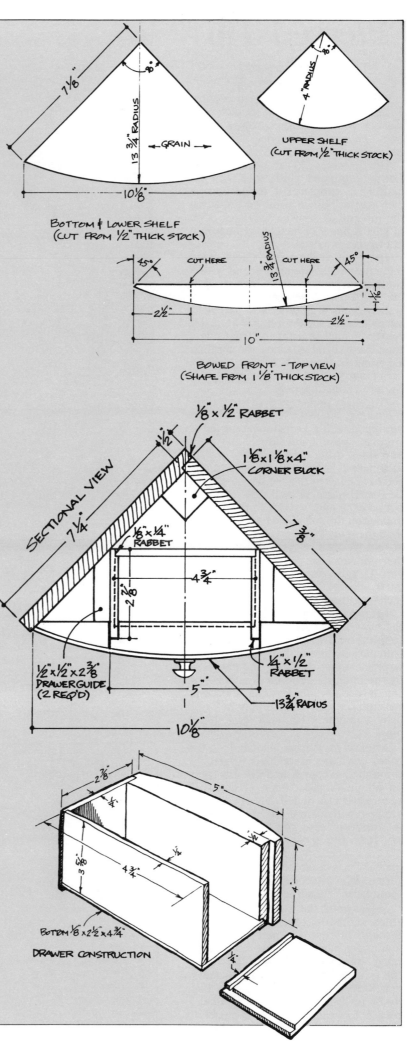

7⅛"

90°

13 ¾" RADIUS

←— GRAIN —→

10⅛"

BOTTOM & LOWER SHELF
(CUT FROM ½" THICK STOCK)

4" RADIUS

UPPER SHELF
(CUT FROM ½" THICK STOCK)

45°   CUT HERE   13¾" RADIUS   CUT HERE   45°

2½"   10"   2½"

1/16"

BOWED FRONT – TOP VIEW
(SHAPE FROM 1⅛" THICK STOCK)

⅛" × ½" RABBET

½

SECTIONAL VIEW
7¼"

⅛" × ⅛" × 4"
CORNER BLOCK

⅛" × ¼"
RABBET

4¾"

2⅛"

7³⁄₁₆"

½" × ½" × 2⅜"
DRAWER GUIDE
(2 REQ'D)

¼" × ½"
RABBET

5"

1

13¾" RADIUS

10⅛"

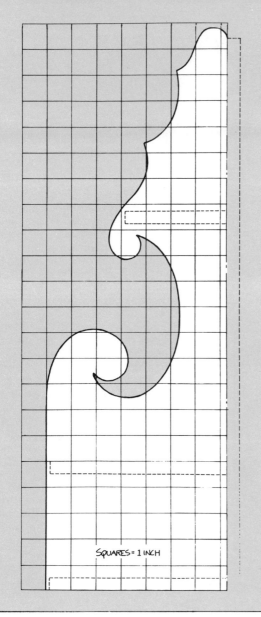

SQUARES = 1 INCH

2⅛"   5"

3⅝"   4¾"   ½"   ¼"

4"

¼"

BOTTOM ⅛" × 2½" × 4¾"

DRAWER CONSTRUCTION

49

Pierced Tin Cabinet

Based on an authentic 18th century design, this sturdy wall cabinet will make a lovely addition to any home that enjoys the style of Early American.

The two sides (A) can be made first. Cut to length and width, then with the dado head cutter set to a depth of ⅜ inch, cut a ¾ inch wide rabbet along the top end as shown. The back edge of part A has a ⅜ inch by ¼ inch rabbet to accept part G.

The ¼ inch deep by ⅜ inch wide dado for part D can best be cut with a router equipped with a ⅜ inch straight bit. With part A secured to the workbench, clamp a guidestrip to part A to act as a fence for the router. Stop the router ½ inch short of the front edge, then use a chisel to square the corners. To complete work on part A, drill ¼ inch diameter by ½ inch deep holes for the shelf adjusting pegs.

The base, part B, is made to the dimensions shown, then a router equipped with a ½ inch beading bit is used to apply a molding to the front and sides. After cutting part C to size, a ¼ inch x ⅜ inch rabbet is cut along the back edge to receive the back, part G. Part D has a ¼ inch x ⅜ inch rabbet on each end in order to fit into the dadoes on the sides, part A. Also, note that the two front corners of part D have a ¼ inch x ½ inch notch. The door divider, part I, is tenoned into part D and part F, so both of these parts will require a ⅜ inch wide x 1 inch long through tenon.

Temporarily join the bottom (B) to the two sides (A) using 1½" x #8 counterbored wood screws as shown. Add part D, holding it in place with bar or pipe clamps. After cutting part H to fit the opening between B and D, locate it in it's proper position, then drill through from the top and bottom for ⅜ inch diameter x 1½ inch long dowel pins.

After all parts have been sanded the case can be assembled (parts A through I, except E and G). Use glue on all joints. The wood screws will secure parts A and B, all other parts are held with clamps. Be sure the case is square or else you'll have lots of problems fitting the door frames and drawers. The crown and cove molding (part J) is available at most lumberyards. It's attached with glue and countersunk finishing nails.

Select good flat stock for the door stiles and rails (parts K and L). The through mortise for part K and the tenons for part L are best cut using a table saw tenon jig. Glue and clamp the frame, then check for squareness. When dry use a router with a ⅜ inch by ⅜ inch piloted rabbet bit to cut a recess for part M. Use a chisel to square the corners.

Tin panels, measuring 11" x 14", can be purchased via mail-order from Country Accents, P.O. Box 437, Montoursville, PA 17754. To give the tin an "antique" look use very fine (220 grit) garnet or aluminum oxide paper and give the sheet a thorough sanding.

Bill of Materials
(All Dimensions Actual)

Part	Description	Size	No. Req'd
A	Side	¾ x 6½ x 22½	2
B	Bottom	¾ x 7½ x 31	1
C	Top	¾ x 6½ x 28¼	1
D	Lower Shelf	¾ x 6¼ x 28	1
E	Upper Shelf	¾ x 5½ x 27⅜	1
F	Rail	¾ x 2 x 27½	1
G	Back	¼ x 28¼ x 22⅛	1
H	Drawer Divider	¾ x 6¼ x 4	1
I	Door Divider	¾ x 1 x 17¾	1
J	Molding	See Detail	As Req'd
K	Door Stiles	¾ x 1½ x 16¼	4
L	Door Rails	¾ x 1½ x 13¼	4
M	Tin Panel	See Detail	2
N	Molding	¼" quarter round	As Req'd
O	Drawer Front	¾ x 4 x 13⅜	1/Dwr.
P	Drawer Side	½ x 4 x 5⅞	2/Dwr.
Q	Drawer Back	½ x 3½ x 12⅝	1/Dwr.
R	Drawer Bottom	¼ x 5½ x 12⅞	1/Dwr.

Work in one direction only while maintaining even pressure. Wash the tin and dry completely, then place in a shallow non-metallic container - a glass baking dish or plastic dish pan will do just fine. Add vinegar to the container until the panel is covered with about ¼" of vinegar. Do only one piece at a time. Soak for 6 - 8 hours, then remove, wash and dry.

Transfer the pattern to the tin, then place the panel on a scrap board for piercing. Nailsets, awls, screwdrivers, square flooring nails, etc. have all been used for piercing tin, each tool producing its own distinctive mark when struck with a hammer. For this project we used a round punch of about ⅛ inch diameter.

After making the drawers and adding the molding, ours was painted with a coat of Williamsburg Powell Waller Red, one of the colonial colors sold by Williamsburg Paint. The piece will also look good if stained and oiled with Minwax's Antique Oil Finish.

The shelf can now be added and the back secured with small common nails. The tin panels are held in place with ¼ inch quarter round molding tacked in place.

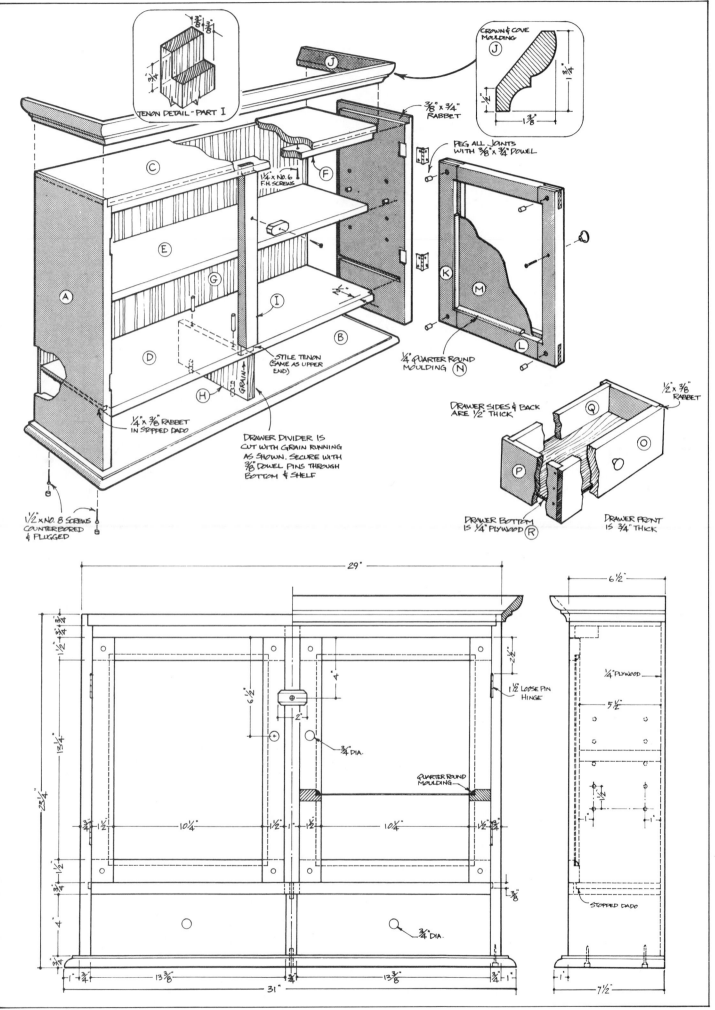

TENON DETAIL - PART I

CROWN & COVE MOULDING

⅜" x ¾" RABBET

PEG ALL JOINTS WITH ⅜" x ¾" DOWEL

1¼" x NO. 6 F.H. SCREWS

¼" QUARTER ROUND MOULDING Ⓝ

STILE TENON (SAME AS UPPER END)

¼" x ⅜" RABBET IN STOPPED DADO

DRAWER DIVIDER IS CUT WITH GRAIN RUNNING AS SHOWN. SECURE WITH ⅜" DOWEL PINS THROUGH BOTTOM & SHELF

1½" x NO. 8 SCREWS COUNTERBORED & PLUGGED

DRAWER SIDES & BACK ARE ½" THICK

½" x ⅜" RABBET

DRAWER BOTTOM IS ¼" PLYWOOD Ⓡ

DRAWER FRONT IS ¾" THICK

29"

6½"

1½ LOOSE PIN HINGE

¼" PLYWOOD

5½"

¾ DIA.

QUARTER ROUND MOULDING

10¼"

10¼"

STOPPED DADO

23¾"

13¼"

¾ DIA.

31"

13⅜"

13⅜"

7½"

(continued on next page)

I SQUARE = 1"

PATTERN FOR TIN PANELS

Hutch Clock

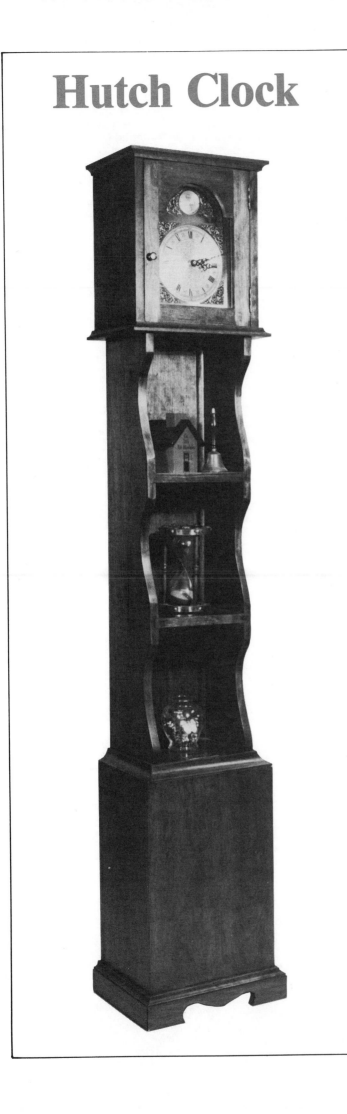

This handsome hutch clock can make an attractive addition to a hallway, den or just about any small area in your home. With three good-sized shelves, there's plenty of room for knickknacks and curios. The clock shown is made of cherry, though almost any hardwood, or even pine, will give beautiful results.

The project should be started by cutting to size the two hutch sides (A) and the three shelves (B). The scalloped edges for parts A are transferred from the grid pattern to the stock, then cut out with a jig or band saw. Full dadoes for the shelves are cut into part A with a table or radial arm saw. A router with a ½ inch rabbet bit can cut the ½ inch by ½ inch rabbets on the back edges. Note that two inches of the rabbeted edge will have to be cut flush to allow for the back panel that widens for the lower section of the clock. A backsaw or dovetail saw can be used for this job.

After sanding, parts A&B can be assembled by gluing and clamping. Make sure the shelves are square to the sides. Next, parts C&D can be cut to size. Part D will require a ¾ inch wide by ½ inch deep rabbet on its outer edges. Also, a ½ inch x ½ inch rabbet is cut on the inside back edge of part C. The two parts F, which are 1 inch square and made of hardwood such as maple, hold C and D together with screws as shown.

Parts E are made next. These are spacers that separate the middle and lower sections. They too should be made of a hardwood. Because of the confined space between the sides A, it might be best to attach parts E to A before the shelves are glued into place and the drill holes made on the insides of A. When the middle and lower sections are joined, a push drill can start the holes in part C.

For the back, part G, I used a ½ inch piece of wide stock instead of a ¼ inch panel, giving the clock a solid look and feel to it. Where it widens for the lower section, 1¼ inch pieces were added on. The back is then attached with 1 inch wood screws countersunk ¼ inch. These are covered with wood plugs that are sanded flush.

(continued on next page)

Bill of Materials (All Dimensions Actual)			
Part	Description	Size	No. Req'd
A	Hutch Side	¾ x 8¼ x 37⅝	2
B	Shelf	¾ x 7¾ x 9	3
C	End	¾ x 9¼ x 20	2
D	Front	¾ x 12½ x 20	1
E	Spacer	½ x 2 x 7¾	2
F	Cleat	1 x 1 x 18	2
G	Back	½ x 12 x 55⅝	1
H	Top & Bottom	¾ x 8¼ x 11½	2
I	Clock Side	¾ x 8¼ x 13	2
J	Lower Dial Frame	¾ x 1½ x 7	1
K	Upper Dial Frame	¾ x 4¼ x 7	1
L	Side Dial Frame	¾ x 1⅞ x 13	2
M	Lower Door Frame	1 x 1½ x 7	1
N	Upper Door Frame	1 x 4¼ x 7	1
O	Side Door Frame	1 x 1½ x 13	2
P	Clock Back	¼ x 10¾ x 13	1
Q	Molding	See Detail	
R	Molding	¾ x 2 x 10¼	2
S	Molding	¾ x 2 x 14	1
T	Molding	See Detail	
U	Movement		

Work can begin on the top and bottom by cutting to size parts H. The lower part H is attached to parts A with wood screws that are located behind where the groove (in part I) for the dial frame will be. Next, make parts I. These will require a ⅜ inch by ⅜ inch groove for the dial frame 1 inch in from the front edges. The back edges will require a ¼ inch deep by ⅜ inch wide rabbet for the back panel, part P, which is made from ¼ inch plywood.

Construct the dial frame by cutting to size parts J, K, and L, doweling, gluing and clamping them together. Once the glue has set, a router with a ½ inch rabbet bit will cut out a groove ⅜ inch deep for the dial.

Now glue and clamp together parts I and the dial frame and attach the back panel with ½ inch brass screws. Turn the assembly over and drill ⅜ inch diameter holes 1 inch deep for the dowel pins, located where they will not be over the screws that hold H to A, but behind the dial frame. Insert dowel centers into the holes and center the assembly on H. Then, ½ʺ deep holes are drilled into H and dowels are inserted with glue to hold together parts I and H. The same procedure can be used for the upper part H.

The door frame (parts M, N, & O) can now be assembled using dowels and glue. This will also have a rabbet, ⅜ inch deep by ⅜ inch wide, to hold the glass. The door is held with 2 inch brass hinges that are mortised into the door side and

screwed flat on the case side. A button magnet catch recessed into the dial frame holds the door closed.

The moldings, parts Q and T, can be bought at most lumber companies as standard cove molding. If you make them as I did, a ½ inch cove bit run along the edge of a ¾ inch board that is ripped ¾ inches wide will make molding T. You'll need about 10 feet. Molding Q can be made on a table saw by running a wide board at an angle over the blade and ripping to shape. All molding, including R, is attached with countersunk nails that are covered with wood filler.

The bow dial and battery movement are both available from the mail-order company Armor Products, Box 445, East Northport, NY 11731. I used their solid brass dial (part no. 30008), however a brass-plated alternate dial (part no. 30007) can be obtained for about one-half the price of the solid brass version. Both dials look exactly alike. I used Armor's part no. 22201 movement, with their part no. 00804 black hands, which are provided with the movement at no extra charge.

The button magnet catch, brass door knob and flexible molding to hold the glass in the door can also be purchased from Armor Products.

I finished the clock with Minwax Jacobean stain followed by several coats of tung oil.

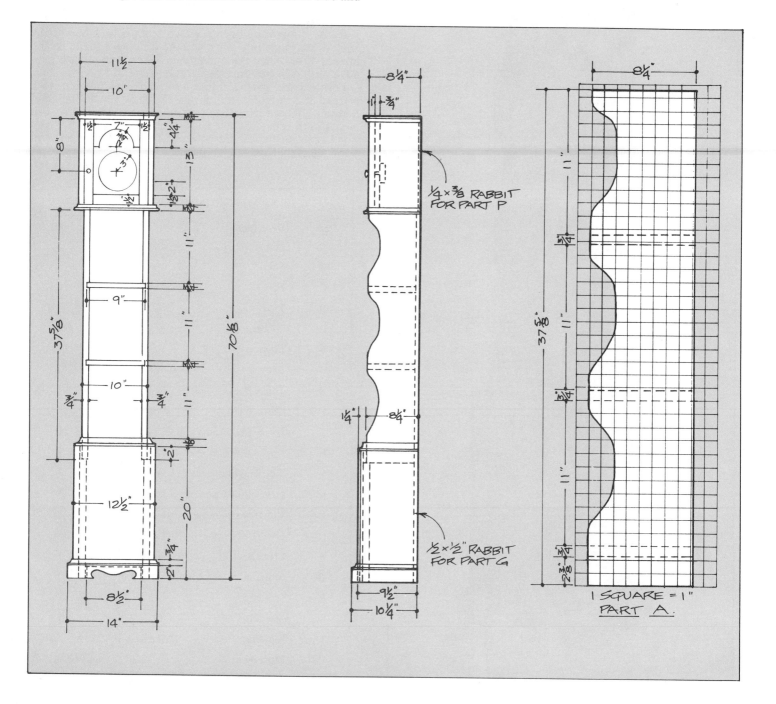

DETAIL:
DIAL + FRAME
ASSEMBLY USING
FLEXIBLE
MOLDING

½" WIDE × ⅜"
DEEP RABBIT
ALL AROUND

BACK OF BOW DIAL

REAR VIEW OF DIAL FRAME

DETAIL:
SEPARATOR BLOCK BE-
TWEEN CLOCK FACE AND
MOVEMENT.

3/16"
2"
2"

⅜ × ⅜ GROOVE
FOR DIAL FRAME

⅜ × 1½" DOWELS

DETAIL: RABBIT IN
REAR OF I

⅜"
¼"

1½" #8 C'SUNK
F.H. SCREWS

⅜ × 1½" DOWELS

1" STOCK

DETAIL: HINGES
MORTISED ON
DOOR ONLY

⅜ × ⅜ RABBIT FOR GLASS

9½"

35 ⅝"

55 ⅝"

20"

1¼"   1¼"

DETAIL: RABBIT IN REAR OF A

½"
¼"

¾" WIDE × ¼"
DEEP DADO

12"

½ × 2" NOTCH

2"   8½"   2"

DETAIL: MOLDINGS

¾
¾
½
⅛
½"   ¼"

SEPARA-TOR BLOCK

GLASS

SEPARATOR BLOCK

MOVEMENT
BOW DIAL

SIDE SECTIONAL VIEW

Country Kitchen Cabinet

This handy wall unit serves a variety of uses in our kitchen. Behind the glass door we keep a collection of sugar bowls and creamers. In the drawer is a recipe card file and the pigeon holes provide room for bills, letters, coupons, etc. The towel holder is handy for dishtowels, while on top we keep glass canisters for spaghetti, rice, popcorn and the like.

Make the two sides (A) first. Cut to overall length and width, then lay out and mark the location of the ¼ inch deep by ¾ inch wide dadoes. The left side of part A has three dadoes, the right side has two. Stop the dadoes ½ inch short of the front edge. The dado can be cut with a router or on a table or radial arm saw using the dado head cutter. Transfer the profile from the drawing (note that the top profile is different than the bottom), then cut to shape with a band or jig saw.

Cut the top shelf (part B) to overall length and width, then cut a ¼ inch wide by ¼ inch deep groove for plates. Locate the groove about 1¾ inches from the back edge of part B. Also, cut a ¼ inch by ⅜ inch notch on the two front corners. Part B also has three, ¼ inch deep by ½ inch wide by 7¼ inches long, stopped dadoes cut in the bottom.

The bottom shelf (C) is made next, requiring only that it be cut to length and width. Notches are not needed on the two front corners because part G is inset and will cover the dado end.

Cut the divider (D) to size, then lay out the location of the ¼ inch deep by ¾ inch wide dado. Like the dadoes in the side (A) this one is stopped ½ inch short of the front edge.

Parts F, G, and N can be made next. Transfer the grid pattern to the stock before cutting out with a band or saber saw.

The pigeon hole base (part H) has three, ¼ inch deep by ½ inch wide by 7¼ inch long, stopped dadoes. The drawing shows their locations. Also, the two front corners have a ¼ inch by ⅜ inch notch.

The door rail (P) and stile (Q) are made as shown in the door joint detail. Cut the tenon for a smooth fit in the open mortise. Dry fit the frame for squareness and if all looks okay, add glue and clamp. Double check for squareness before setting aside to dry. When dry, a router equipped with a piloted ¼ inch rabbet bit is used to cut a ¼ x ¼ rabbet on the back. A chisel is used to square the corners. Now the decorative cross-hatch (R) is cut to size, half-lapped at the center, and notched at the ends, then glued to the frame.

The five spindles (I) can be turned to the dimensions shown or a very similar spindle can be purchased from Woodworks, 4013-A Clay Ave., Ft. Worth, TX 76117. Order part no. BS-1010. The rail (O) is simply ¾ inch square stock with a ⅛ inch groove as shown in the detail. The towel holder (part S) is lathe turned to the dimensions shown, or if you don't have a lathe, substitute ⅝ or ¾ inch diameter dowelstock.

The drawer (parts J, K, L, and T) are made to the dimensions shown in the bill of materials. Part K has a ⅜ inch deep by ½ inch wide rabbet cut on each end to accept the side (J), and also a ⅜ inch deep by ¾ inch wide decorative dado down the front. A ⅛ inch wide by 3/16 inch deep groove is cut around the inside of parts J, K, and L to accept the hardboard drawer bottom (T). Locate this groove ¼ inch from the bottom edge of the drawer parts.

Assemble as shown in the drawing. Part D is joined to B & C with glue and three countersunk wood screws. This unit is then joined to the sides in the same manner. Glue is added to the ends of H & M before sliding them in from the back. Add the other parts as shown, then plug the screw holes and sand flush.

Stain to suit, then add two coats of polyurethane satin varnish. When dry, apply a coat of good paste wax.

Pewter knobs were used on the door and drawer, but porcelain will also look good.

Bill of Materials
(All Dimensions Actual)

Part	Description	Size	No. Req'd	Part	Description	Size	No. Req'd
A	Side	¾ x 10 x 30	2	L	Drawer Back	½ x 5 x 11	1
B	Top Shelf	¾ x 9⅞ x 23	1	M	Pigeon Hole Dividers	½ x 7¼ x 8¼	3
C	Bottom Shelf	¾ x 9⅛ x 23	1	N	Upper Scroll	¾ x 1½ x 12	1
D	Divider	¾ x 9⅞ x 13½	1	O	Rail	¾ x ¾ x 20	1
E	Adjustable Shelf	¾ x 7½ x 9½	1	P	Door Rail	¾ x 1½ x 9¾	2
F	Back Board	¾ x 6 x 22½	1	Q	Door Stiles	¾ x 1½ x 13½	2
G	Lower Scroll	¾ x 3¼ x 22½	1	R	Cross-Hatch	½ x ¾ x 12½	2
H	Pigeon Hole Base	¾ x 9⅞ x 12½	1	S	Towel Holder	See Detail	1
I	Spindle	See Detail	5	T	Drawer Bottom	⅛ x 11⅜ x 8⅝	1
J	Drawer Side	½ x 5 x 9⅛	2	U	Drawer Stop	¼ x ¼ x 12	1
K	Drawer Front	¾ x 5 x 12	1				

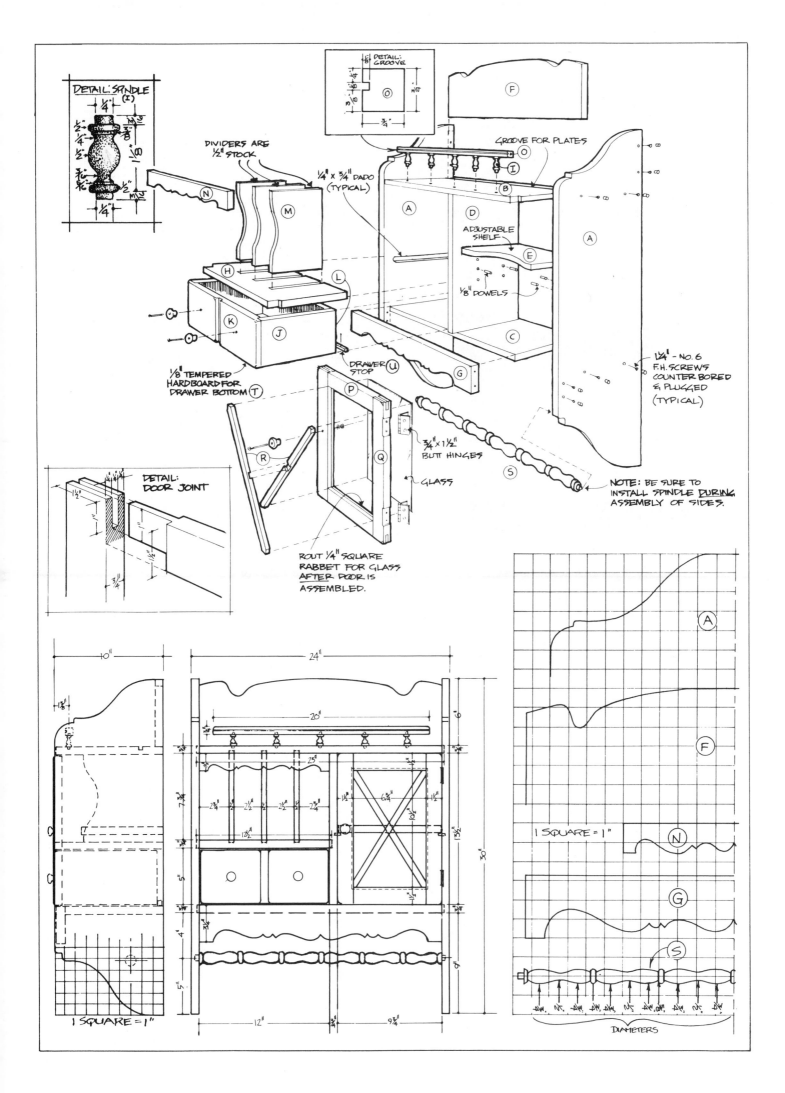

DETAIL: SPINDLE (I)

DETAIL: GROOVE

DIVIDERS ARE 1/2" STOCK

1/4" X 3/4" DADO (TYPICAL)

GROOVE FOR PLATES

ADJUSTABLE SHELF

1/8" DOWELS

1 1/4" - NO. 6 F.H. SCREWS COUNTER BORED & PLUGGED (TYPICAL)

1/8" TEMPERED HARDBOARD FOR DRAWER BOTTOM T

DRAWER STOP

DETAIL: DOOR JOINT

3/4" X 1 1/2" BUTT HINGES

GLASS

ROUT 1/4" SQUARE RABBET FOR GLASS AFTER DOOR IS ASSEMBLED.

NOTE: BE SURE TO INSTALL SPINDLE DURING ASSEMBLY OF SIDES.

1 SQUARE = 1"

1 SQUARE = 1"

DIAMETERS

Rough-Sawn Cedar Clock

Rough-sawn cedar is gaining in popularity as interior paneling, wainscoting and trim. Here's the perfect accessory for a room that's been remodeled with rough cedar. It's basically a simplified version of the old standard school clock built out of rough-sawn 1 x 4 nominal (¾ x 3½ actual) cedar fence boards.

Start by cutting the octagonal front (A). Set your tablesaw miter gauge to make a 22½ degree angle and cut the eight pieces needed. Add glue to the miters, then assemble the octagon, securing with a web clamp. When the glue is dry, use a jig saw or coping saw to cut the circular opening for the clock dial. A router is then used to cut a ¼ x ¼ rabbet for the dial board (O) and also to chamfer the front edge of the opening.

Next rip the ¼ x 1 edging (B) that goes around the octagon front (A). When cutting an edge that will be exposed, use the coarsest blade available in order to give it the rough-sawn look. Cut the edging to length with the miter set for a 22½ degree angle. Make sure you make the cuts so that the original rough-sawn face of the edging will be on the outside. Using the web clamp again, glue the edging to the outside of the octagon.

Construction of the case (parts I, J, K, and L) is straightforward enough. The only complication is clamping the 22½ degree miter joints at the bottom. Probably the easiest way to do it is to cut a piece of ¾ inch plywood the exact size and shape of the inside of the case, then clamp the case around the plywood with a web clamp. The door (parts D, E, F, and G) to the pendulum case is made by resawing the cedar to ¼ inch thickness and gluing it to the ¼ inch plywood door back (H). This makes a strong door while using simple miter joints. Part H is cut smaller than the door to form the door lip, and the hole in the center is ½ inch larger to make a ¼ inch rabbet for the glass (see detail). The door is attached with two small brass hinges (R).

If you want to simplify construction, you can make a non-opening door. Cut parts E, F, and G from ¾" thick cedar and cut a ¾" x ½" rabbet on the outside edge. Part D is cut the same except do not cut the ¾" x ½" rabbet. Omit the ¼" x ¼" stopped rabbet on part J and the front rabbet on parts K and L. (See the alternate cross-sections on plan). Attach this door to the case with glue and small finish nails.

Any nails used on the door and elsewhere on the case can be effectively hidden with natural color plastic wood dough. Apply the wood dough with the tip of a small screwdriver in order to avoid getting it on the surrounding wood. Leave the surface of the dough rough and it will blend right in with the rough-sawn wood.

The paper clock dial (available from the Mason and Sullivan Co., 586 Higgins Crowell Rd., West Yarmouth, MA 02673; order part no. 2820P, specify 8½ inch diameter time ring) is attached to a ¼ inch hardboard dial board (O). The Mason and Sullivan dial will have Roman numerals, not the Arabic style shown. After the paper dial has been attached to part O, glue it into the rabbet in the octagonal front (A).

The octagon front (A) is attached to the case by means of screws through the corner braces (P) and the case divider (C). The clock shown uses a battery operated quartz pendulum movement (Q) also available from the Mason and Sullivan Co. Order part no. 3722X. However, if you prefer, you can substitute a non-pendulum movement, Mason and Sullivan part no. 3723X. If you choose a pendulum movement, install the clear glass (N) in the pendulum door and put the back (M) on the case. If you choose a movement without a pendulum, you can install a mirror in place of the glass and a decorative decal can be placed on the mirror. If you choose the latter method, the alternative door can be used and the back of the case (M) can be omitted. In either case, the glass or mirror is held in place with glazier's points. It's a good idea to cover the back of the mirror with cardboard before installing the glazier's points to protect the silvered back.

No finish is necessary, but a thin coat of clear sealer will help keep that fresh-cut look.

Bill of Materials (All Dimensions Actual)			No.
Part	Description	Size	Req'd
A	Front	¾ x 2¾ x 5⁵⁄₁₆	8
B	Edging	¼ x 1 x 5¼	8
C	Divider	¾ x 3½ x 8⅞	1
D	Door Top	¼ x 2¼ x 8⅞	1
E	Door Sides	¼ x 2¼ x 6¼	2
F	Door Corners	¼ x 2¼ x 3¹¹⁄₁₆	2
G	Door Bottom	¼ x 2¼ x 3¹¹⁄₁₆	1
H	Door Back	See Detail	1
I	Case Top	¾ x 2½ x 7⅞	1
J	Case Side	See Detail	2
K	Case Corners	¾ x 2¼ x 3¹¹⁄₁₆	2
L	Case Bottom	¾ x 2¼ x 3¹¹⁄₁₆	1
M	Case Back	¼ x 7⅞ x 21⅛	1
N	Glass		4
O	Dial Board	¼ x 9½ Diameter	1
P	Corner Brace	¾ x 1½ x 1½	2
Q	Movement w/Pendulum		1
R	Brass Hinges		2
S	Brass Hook		1

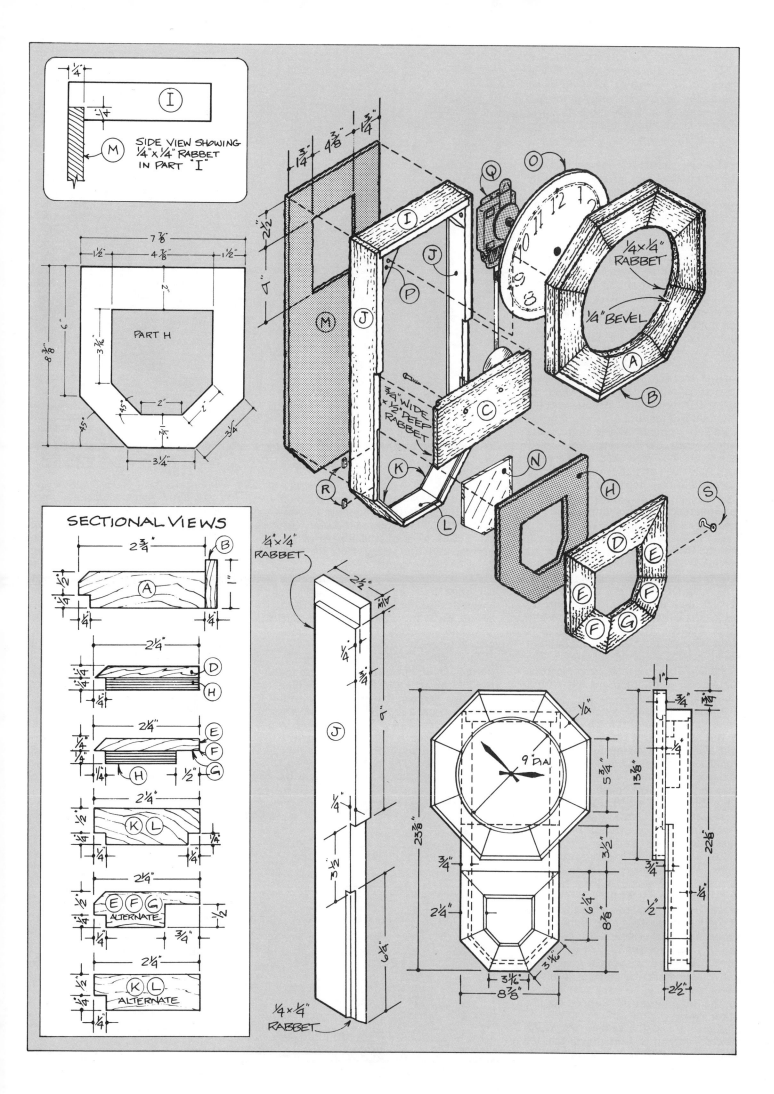

SIDE VIEW SHOWING ¼" x ¼" RABBET IN PART "I"

PART H

SECTIONAL VIEWS

ALTERNATE

ALTERNATE

¼ x ¼ RABBET

¾" WIDE x ½" DEEP RABBET

¼ x ¼ RABBET

9 DIA

19th Century Step-Chair

Here's a project that we think will prove to be a useful item to have around the house, especially in the kitchen near those high cabinets. And when it's not being used as a step stool, it functions very nicely as a chair.

The one shown was made in Denmark sometime around 1890, probably by a country cabinetmaker. Although this one was made from hard pine, we recommend oak in order to insure adequate strength.

Before starting, all 1 inch nominal stock (13/16 inch actual) should be surface planed to ¾ inch actual thickness. Make the step unit (parts A, B, C, D, and E) first. Cut part A to overall width and length, then lay out and cut the tenons and the notch for part E. Refer to the drawing for dimensions to make the remaining cuts.

Cut parts B and C to size, then lay out the location of the dovetails (see dovetail layout on drawing). Make all cuts with care so that a strong, neat fitting joint will result.

Part D is made to the dimensions shown, then the ¾ inch wide by 2 inch long by ¾ inch deep mortises are cut. Sand all parts thoroughly before assembling the step unit as shown. Use glue and clamp securely. Check for squareness before setting aside to dry.

The chair unit is made next. Part F and the two upper steps (parts G & H) are made and assembled in the same manner as parts A, B, and C.

The leg (K) is made from 5/4 stock (1-1/16 inch thick actual). Be sure to select stock that's free of knots or any other defects. Transfer the profile to the stock, then cut out with a band or saber saw. Lay out the location of the ⅜ inch wide by ⅞ inch deep mortises for parts L & M, then cut out with a sharp chisel.

A framing square is used to determine the location of the leg in relation to the seat (I). Cut the seat to length and width, then clamp in your workbench so that the seat end is flush with the workbench top. Lay the framing square on the workbench so that one edge butts against the seat bottom (see Detail A). Locate the square so that its other edge extends 1½ inches past the back edge of the seat. Now, place the leg on the framing square as shown (15¾ inches from the bottom of the seat and 2¼ inches from the corner of the frame). With the leg held in place, use a pencil to scribe the curve of the leg on the seat end. Repeat this procedure on the other end. Now cut the ½ inch deep by ¾ inch wide rabbet on each end of the seat, then with the remaining scribe mark as a guide, use a sharp chisel to cut a notch equal to the leg thickness. Repeat on the other side.

Again clamp the seat in the workbench, only this time have the leg notch flush with the bench top. Locate the framing square as before, then insert the leg into the notch in its proper position in relation to the seat. Use this set-up to mark the length of the half-lap joint on the leg. Note the half-lap is ¾ inches deep.

After giving all parts a thorough sanding, the seat (I) can now be assembled to the leg (K). Parts L & M are added at the same time. Use glue and clamp securely. Check for squareness before setting aside to dry.

The sub-assembly consisting of parts F, G, and H is now fitted into the rabbet on part I and secured with glue and two screws driven through the half-lap of each leg. Note that the two front corners of part F are rounded to allow clearance as the unit is pivoted.

Part J is cut to size and its ends rounded over. The part of J that extends beyond part F should have its thickness reduced about 1/16 inch. This will allow some slight clearance as the units are pivoted.

Lay out the pivot pin location on J (see Detail), then drill a ¼ inch diameter by ¾ inch deep hole. Also, at this time locate the pivot pin location on the step-unit. Make this hole ¼ inch diameter by 9/16 inch deep. Cut ¼ inch diameter steel rod to a length of 1¼ inches, then epoxy it into the step unit pivot hole. Fit part J on the pivot pin, then secure it to the chair unit with four countersunk wood screws as shown. Check for a smooth pivoting action. The countersunk holes can be filled with wood plugs.

Give the project a final sanding, taking care to round-off sharp edges. Finish up with 220 grit paper. Generally, we feel that a project like this looks best with just a clear finish, so we would suggest a penetrating oil such as Watco or Deftco Danish oil.

Bill of Materials (All Dimensions Actual)

Part	Description	Size	No. Req'd
A	Step Unit End	¾ x 8⅝ x 17	2
B	First Step	¾ x 4 3/16 x 13½	1
C	Second Step	¾ x 4-5/16 x 14	1
D	Foot	1 x 1¾ x 15½	2
E	Step Unit Stretcher	½ x 1⅛ x 14	1
F	Chair Unit End	¾ x 8⅝ x 16¼	2
G	Third Step	¾ x 4-5/16 x 13½	1
H	Fourth Step	¾ x 4-5/16 x 13½	1
I	Seat	¾ x 9 x 14	1
J	Cleat	1 x 1¾ x 12¾	2
K	Leg	See Detail	2
L	Inside Stretcher	⅝ x 1 x 13⅝	1
M	Outside Stretcher	⅝ x 1½ x 13⅝	1

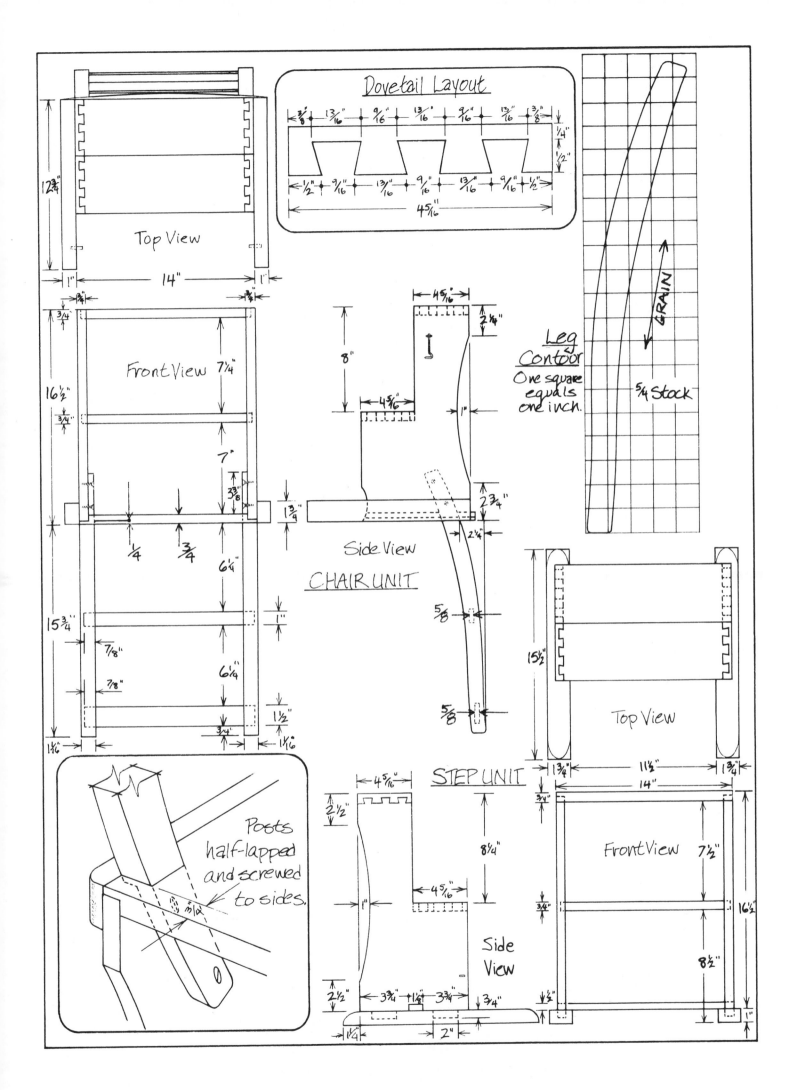

Top View

Dovetail Layout

Front View 7¼"

Leg Contour
One square equals one inch.

⁵⁄₄ Stock

GRAIN

Side View
CHAIR UNIT

Top View

STEP UNIT

Front View 7½"

Posts half-lapped and screwed to sides.

Side View

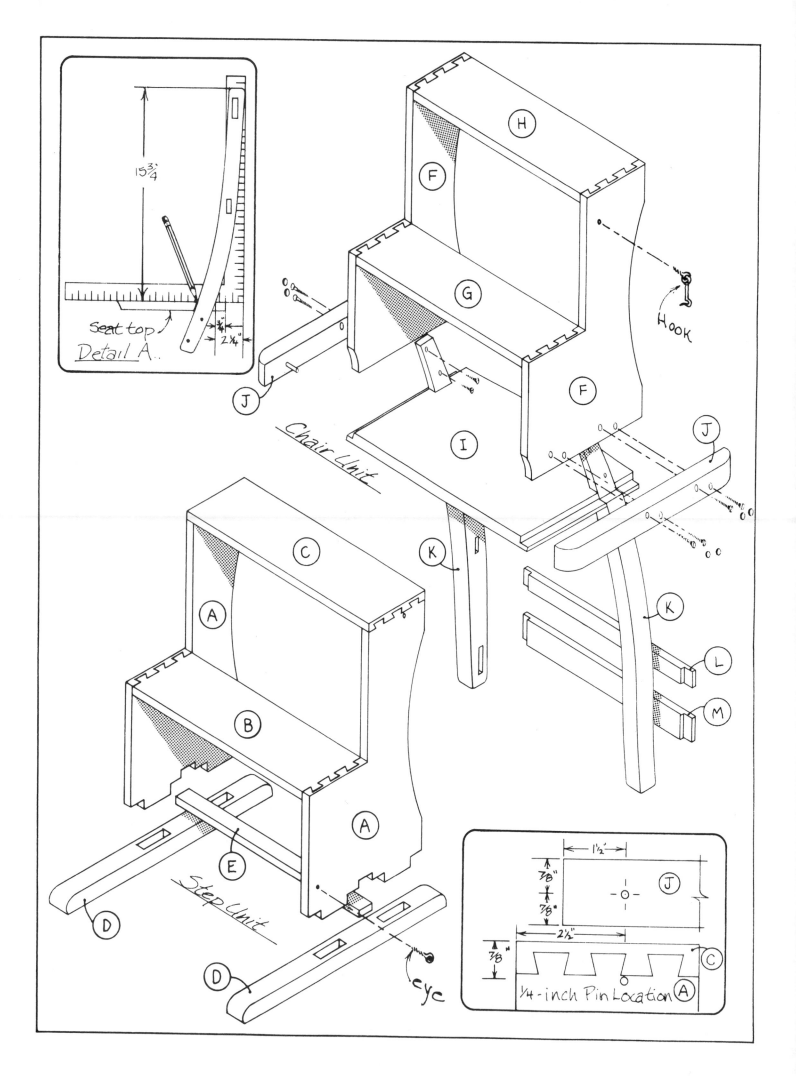

Detail A.

$15\frac{3}{4}$"

seat top

$2\frac{1}{4}$"

Chair Unit

Hook

H

F

G

F

I

J

J

K

K

L

M

C

A

B

A

E

Step Unit

D

D

eye

$1\frac{1}{2}$"

$\frac{7}{8}$"

$\frac{7}{8}$"

J

$2\frac{1}{2}$"

$\frac{7}{8}$"

C

$\frac{1}{4}$-inch Pin Location

A

Sailing Ship Weather Vane

We think you'll agree that this is an uncommonly handsome weather vane. With her mainsail set, this replica of an early 19th century U.S. revenue cutter will keep her bows facing into the wind and safely ride out the summer squalls and winter gales of many years. Construction is simple and all materials should be readily available at building supply and hardware stores.

Start by enlarging the grid pattern for the hull (not including the keel) and transfer the pattern to a piece of ¾" clear pine (1¹⁄₁₆" actual thickness) as shown in Fig. 1. Tack two pieces of ¾" stock together and bandsaw the shape as shown in Figs. 1 and 2. If no bandsaw is available cut the sides separately, then clamp them together and sand them so they are identical. Bow and stern cuts can be planed and filed.

Fig. 3 shows how the two thick hull sides are glued to a central ½" x 6" x 24" pine board so that the top edges are flush. Be sure to use a water resistant glue such as Weldwood plastic resin or resorcinal.

Before cutting the keel and rudder to shape, lay out the mast locations. The ⅜" diameter holes are best drilled with a drill press while either the assembly or the table is tilted at 5 degrees. Lacking a drill press, use a simple bored block as a doweling jig. Take care that the holes are drilled in the same planes. The masts must rake at the same angle and line up when viewed from fore and aft.

The sheerline can now be bandsawn or shaped by hand. A compass or steel washer can be used as shown to mark a cutting line around the bow stem and along the keel (Fig. 4).

The hull is now carved using the photo and Figs. 5 and 6 as a guide. The stern section is hollowed with a gouge or round rasp until the stern presents a "wineglass" shape. About 4 inches forward of the stern, this hollow section is faired into the slightly rounded section amidships. The bow should be tapered smoothly to the stern and down to the keel. Don't fret over the hull shape too much because after it is painted and mounted high on your roof it will look fine.

The various spars are cut from dowel as indicated on the drawing. Mast tops and the ends of the yards are tapered only for a short distance using a block plane and sandpaper. File flat sections on masts and their tops and join them with quick setting epoxy, then wrap the joints with windings of 20 gauge cop-

per wire. Tuck the free ends into small holes drilled through the masts. The bowsprit and jib boom are joined in a similar manner.

Before gluing masts and bowsprit into place, drill them and the other spars with small holes to take the 20 gauge copper rigging wire. Where the shrouds pass through the masts drill ⅛" diameter holes.

Pad the hull and lock it in the bench vise. Glue masts and bowsprit in place with quick setting epoxy. Four small copper or galvanized nails are driven into the hull on each side just behind each mast. These anchor the shrouds which are led up one side, through the ⅛" holes in the masts and down to the opposite side. Pull the shrouds as taut

as possible without bending the masts.

The double back stays supporting the foremast are paired like the shrouds and terminate at a nail on each side of the deck. The stays from the foremast to the bowsprit are next added along with the bowsprit rigging and bobstay which is anchored to the stem with a nail.

Join gaff and main boom to the mizzenmast with copper strips as shown in the detail. The yards are then added and rigged with a continuous length of wire running from a nail on deck, up through the yard tip to the mast and down to the opposite side of the deck.

After the mizzenmast has been rigged and the gaff and boom are firmly

(continued on next page)

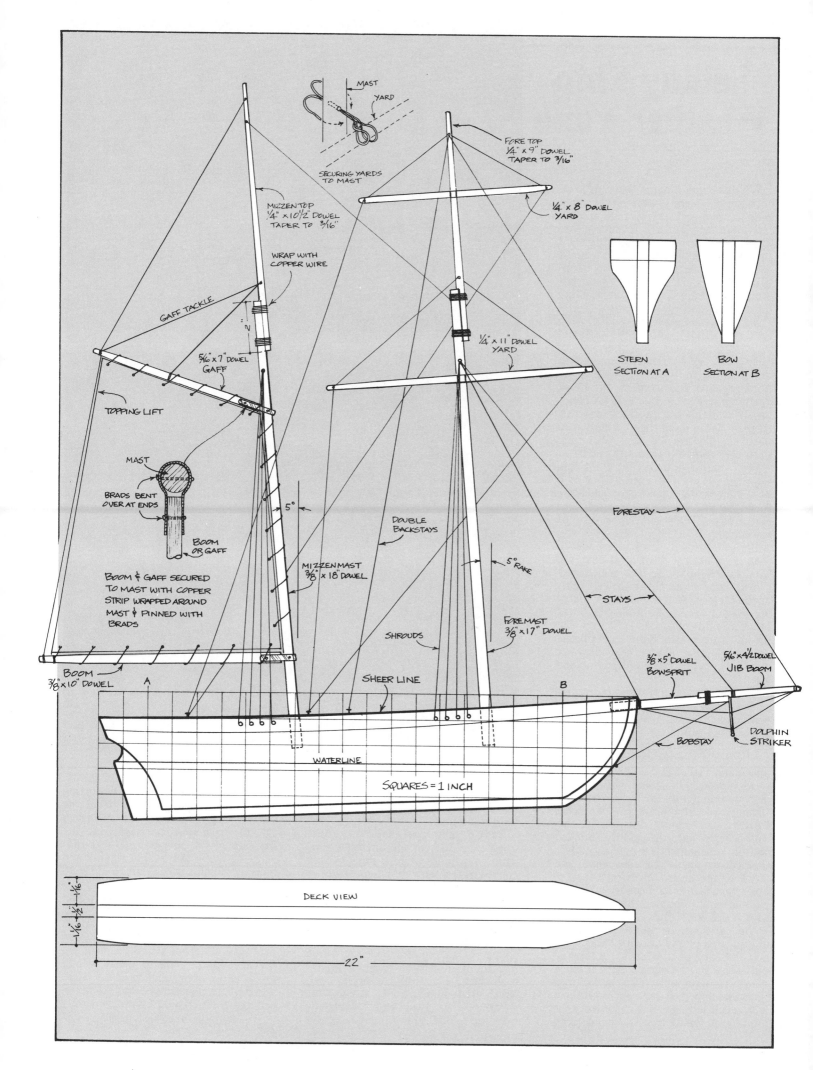

MAST

YARD

SECURING YARDS TO MAST

FORE TOP
¼" × 9" DOWEL
TAPER TO 3/16"

MIZZEN TOP
¼" × 10½" DOWEL
TAPER TO 3/16"

¼" × 8" DOWEL
YARD

WRAP WITH
COPPER WIRE

GAFF TACKLE

5/16" × 7" DOWEL
GAFF

¼" × 11" DOWEL
YARD

TOPPING LIFT

STERN
SECTION AT A

BOW
SECTION AT B

MAST

BRADS BENT
OVER AT ENDS

BOOM
OR GAFF

5°

FORESTAY

BOOM & GAFF SECURED
TO MAST WITH COPPER
STRIP WRAPPED AROUND
MAST & PINNED WITH
BRADS

DOUBLE
BACKSTAYS

MIZZEN MAST
3/8" × 18" DOWEL

5° RAKE

STAYS

FOREMAST
3/8" × 17" DOWEL

SHROUDS

BOOM
3/8" × 10" DOWEL

A

SHEER LINE

B

3/8" × 5" DOWEL
BOWSPRIT

5/16" × 4½" DOWEL
JIB BOOM

BOBSTAY

DOLPHIN
STRIKER

WATERLINE

SQUARES = 1 INCH

1/16
½
1/16

DECK VIEW

22"

64

in place, cut a sheet copper sail to fill the area between these spars. We used ordinary copper chimney flashing though thin galvanized steel can also be used. Holes are punched in the edges of the sail as shown and it is laced to the spars with rigging wire.

The ship is finished by applying two coats of spar varnish to the deck and all spars. The hull is given two coats of flat black and white enamel using masking tape to assure a neat job of edging at the waterline and gunwales. The copper sail can be polished and varnished or left to weather naturally.

Lay the completed ship on the workbench with the masts hanging over the edge and find the balance point with a short length of dowel. This should be somewhere near the mizzenmast. Drill up into the keel with a ½" bit to a depth of 2 inches and perpendicular to the waterline. A solid ½" diameter x 34" steel rod is inserted in the hole and locked in place by drilling through the hull and rod a hole sufficiently large enough to drive a steel pin cut from a nail.

The staff that supports the steel rod consists of a 30" length of standard ½" galvanized pipe threaded on one end to take a pipe cap. Cut a 1" thick x 3¼" square piece of hardwood and scribe intersecting lines from the center of each side to mark locations of the holes which will hold the letters representing the four points of the compass. Drill ¼" holes in each side to a depth of about 1 inch, then scribe a 3" dia. circle and cut the disc or mount it on a face plate and lathe-turn it.

A central hole is bored through the disc for a snug fit over the galvanized pipe. A ¾" spade bit is used after which the hole should be carefully reamed until the disc just slips over the pipe. Later it will be locked in place on the pipe, after you've determined the proper orientation of the north, south, east and west arms.

The ¼" steel rods which fit the disc are cut to 12" lengths and a slot is hacksawed in one end for the letters which are cut with aviation snips and soldered or epoxied to the rods. Spread some epoxy in the disc holes and drive in the rods.

By carefully hacksawing four lengthwise slits in the unthreaded end

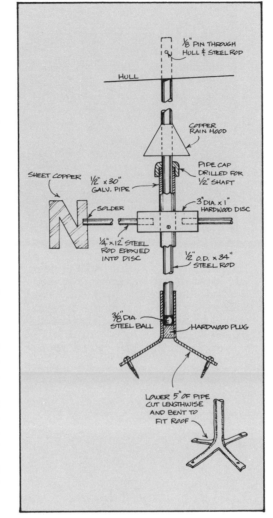

of the galvanized pipe, as shown, you can bend the four resulting strips out to conform to your roof. Two strips ride the ridge while the other two fit the slope on either side. Drill through these feet to take long galvanized screws which are driven into ridge and rafters.

After bending the mounting feet cut a hardwood plug to fit tightly in the pipe bottom. Epoxy this plug in place and also seal its bottom face with epoxy. Center-drill the pipe cap with a ½" bit and screw the cap on the galvanized pipe.

Lock the galvanized pipe in the vise and drop a steel ball of about ⅜" diameter down into the pipe. Now place the steel rod with the ship attached into the hole in the pipe cap and let it rest on the ball bearing. A small copper rain hood is then cut and soldered to the solid rod just far enough above the pipe cap to prevent water from entering and without interfering with the movement of the weather vane. For better visibility against the sky, the entire assembly can be given a couple of coats of black enamel.

To mount the weather vane it will be necessary to use a hand compass to determine the direction of magnetic north. If you're a sailor you'll know that this isn't likely to be true north but it's close enough for our purposes. The galvanized staff should be fastened to the roof, applying caulking under the feet where the screws are driven into the roof. The disc with the four direction arms is located about 5" below the pipe cap and rotated to the proper orientation. Hold it in place while you drill a pilot hole for a screw through the disc and into the pipe without touching the inner rotating rod. A bit of motor oil poured down through the pipe cap will keep the ball bearing well lubricated and operating smoothly for years. Be prepared to take orders for this weather vane when your friends see it.

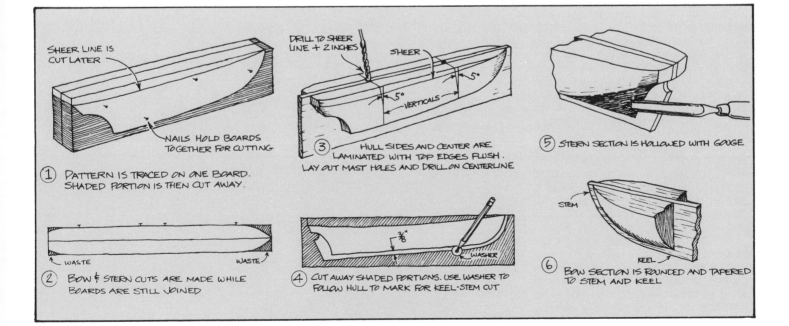

Dovetailed Footstool

If you've never done dovetail work, yet would like to give it a try, why not consider this small footstool for your next project. There are few joints that can match its attractive appearance and even fewer that have such inherent strength. This particular type of dovetail joint, called a through dovetail, is not as difficult to make as you might think, and the process goes pretty quickly once you get started.

Before beginning though, give your chisel a good sharpening. Trying to cut dovetails with a dull chisel is just asking for aggravation. Also, it's helpful to have a fine-tooth dovetail or back saw. You just won't get a good clean cut if you try to cut them with a coarse sawblade.

At this point, it's also worth pointing out some basic dovetail terminology. A dovetail joint consists of mating segments cut on the ends of the two boards to be joined. Each segment on one board is cut in the shape of the tail of a dove, and appropriately called the dovetail, or sometimes just the tail. The other board is cut to receive the dovetails and the resulting segments are called pins. Referring to the drawing, the dovetails are cut in the top (part A) and the pins are cut in the sides (part B). Also, a single dovetail is cut on the end of the stretcher (C).

Begin by laying out the dovetails on the ends of part A, referring to the drawing for all dimensions. Ideally, the length of the tail should be equal to the thickness of part B, plus about 1/32 inch. Later, when the joint is assembled, the tails will stick out 1/32 inch, allowing them to be sanded perfectly flush with the side. As you lay out the dovetail locations, work accurately, and use a hard sharp pencil.

Once the tails have been laid out, mark the waste material between dovetails with an "x" to avoid confusion. Scribe the tail location not only on the face surface of the board, but also on the end grain. Secure the top (A) in a vise and use the fine-tooth saw to make the angled cuts. Work carefully, cutting on the waste side of the line, just grazing but not removing it.

Bring the cuts almost, but not quite to the scribed bottom line. A coping saw can now be used to cut across the grain, removing the waste. Remove the workpiece from the vise and clamp it flat on the bench over a scrap board, then use the chisel to dress the sides and bottom of the cutouts.

The pins on the sides (part B) can best be laid out and scribed by using the finished dovetails as a template. To do this, clamp part B in the vise, end up. Lay the dovetailed top (A), in its proper position, on part B and trace

the dovetails with a sharp knife or pencil. Use a square to carry the scribed lines to the face of the board. For reasons mentioned earlier, this distance should be equal to the thickness of A, plus 1/32 inch.

Once again, mark the waste portions with an "x", then cut out in the manner used to cut the dovetails. A well fitted joint should go together with only light tapping from a mallet and scrap block. If needed, trim further with the chisel. When the fit is good, apply glue to all surfaces and clamp securely.

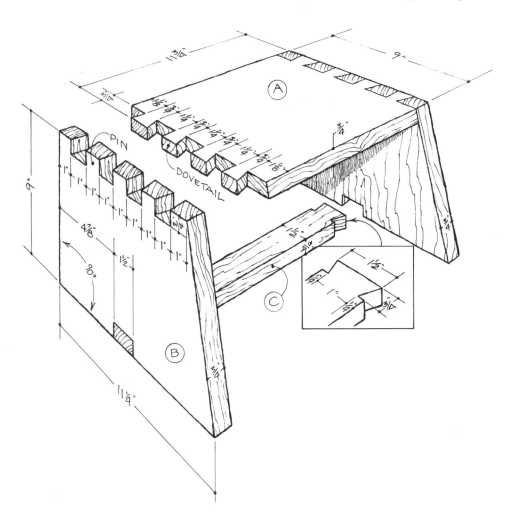

Plant Stand

Plant stands are always popular with our readers, and this one should have a special appeal to those who enjoy the style of Early American. It could also serve as a small night stand for a lamp, perhaps in a bedroom or hallway.

Using 1 inch nominal stock (¾ inch actual), make the two sides first. Since they measure a full 12 inches wide at the bottom it will be necessary to edge glue two narrower boards. Glue and clamp firmly, then allow to dry overnight. When dry, rip to a width of 12 inches, then set the table saw blade for a 3 degree angle. Now, using the miter gauge, crosscut the sides to length.

Next, lay out the location of the shelf dadoes and replace the regular sawblade with a dado head cutter (the angle should still be set at 3 degrees). Set the dado head gauge to cut the dado as shown in the drawing.

The sides taper from 12 inches at the bottom to 9 inches (before cutting the notch) at the top. To cut the taper, clamp the two sides together, then mark the taper with a straight-edge and pencil. A sharp plane will cut to the taper line in short order.

To complete work on the sides, lay out the apron notches and the curved bottom profile. A back saw will cut out the notches while a band or saber saw will remove the bottom curve.

Cut the two aprons to size (¾ x 2 x 11), then lay out and cut the curved profile.

The top can be cut from a piece of 1 x 12 (¾ x 11¼ actual) but the shelf, which is 12 inches wide, will require edge-gluing. Cut both parts to length as shown.

Assemble all parts as shown using glue and 1½ x #8 wood screws, countersunk and plugged. Sand all parts thoroughly and round edges to simulate years of wear. Ours was finished with one coat of Minwax Special Walnut followed by two coats of Minwax Antique Oil Finish.

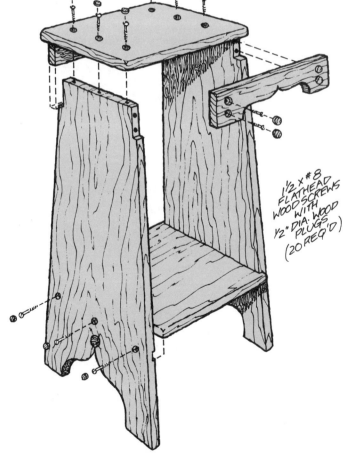

1½ x #8 FLATHEAD WOOD SCREWS WITH ½" DIA. WOOD PLUGS (20 REQ'D)

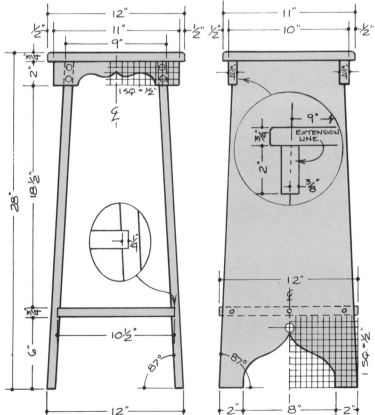

Blanket Chest

The attractive traditional design and simple construction of this chest make it an ideal project, even for a novice woodworker. A table saw, router, sabersaw, and drill are the only power tools required.

While the chest shown was made from pine, a hardwood such as cherry or walnut, or an aromatic cedar (a softwood), would be excellent alternate selections.

We opted to include a pair of friction lid supports, which will hold the lid open in the desired position, providing easy access to the chest. A lock might also be added, if you prefer. Both the friction lid supports (order part no. 75J87L, and 75J87R) and the chest lock are available from: Constantine's, 2050 Eastchester Rd., Bronx, NY 10461. Note that you will need two lid supports; a left-hand and a right-hand version.

Make the front (A), two sides (B), and back (C) first. Standard 1 x 12 (¾ x 11¼ actual) pine will provide the necessary width, but if 1 x 12 is not available, you'll have to edge-join narrower stock.

Note that part A has a ¾ inch wide by ½ inch deep rabbet on each end, while part B has a ¾ inch wide by ⅜ inch deep rabbet on one end. These rabbets are best cut using a dado head cutter, although they can also be done by making repeated passes over a regular sawblade.

Parts A, B, and C can now be assembled. Use glue and clamp securely with pipe or bar clamps. Some short pieces of scrap stock should be used to protect the worksurface from clamp marks.

It's most important that this box be square. If it isn't, loosen the clamps and make adjustments before setting aside to dry overnight.

The plywood bottom (D) is made next. Cut it slightly wider and longer than the box (parts A, B, & C), then attach it to the bottom with glue and finishing nails. When dry, use a plane to remove the overhanging edges. This results in a flush edge all around.

The two lid supports (G) are cut to fit snugly between parts A and C. Add glue to the ends and the edge that contacts part B, then clamp in place. Make sure it's flush with the top edges of the box.

The spacers (part O) can now be cut to size and glued to the underside of part G. Secure in place with a clamp until dry.

Cut the two lid frame ends (I) and lid frame back (J) to size. Fasten in place with glue and 1¼" x #8 flat head wood screws. Slightly countersink the screw heads.

The two top sides (L) and the top back (M) are cut to overall length and width, then the corners are spline mitered as shown. The spline groove is cut ⅛ inch wide (or the width of your table or radial arm sawblade kerf). In order to have maximum strength the spline should be cut so that its grain runs in the same direction as parts L and M, or another alternative is to use plywood as the spline material. After cutting the spline, transfer the curved profile from the grid pattern to the stock. Use a band saw or saber saw to cut to shape. Parts L and M can now be assembled to the box using blind dowels as shown. The dowel spacing isn't critical, just be sure to avoid the screwholes.

The top (H) will require that two or more boards be edge-joined in order to get adequate width. After the stock has been edge-glued and allowed to dry it can be cut to overall width and length. Since wide boards have a tendency to warp, it's a good idea to add the two cleats (N). Secure with a screw at the center, and one about one inch from each end of the cleat, screwing up and into the top (H). The cleat should not prevent the top from moving due to changes in humidity — if it does the top might crack. Don't use glue here. Also, it helps if the screw hole on each end of the cleat is slotted, thereby allowing unrestrained movement of the top.

Next, make the base front and back (E) and the base ends (F). Cut a little on the long side, then cut the miters to fit the exact dimensions of the box. The ⅛ inch by 1 inch notch can be cut with the dado head or with a regular sawblade. After cutting the 45 degree bevel and the curved profile, add glue to the notch and the mitered end, then secure to the box with pipe or bar clamps. Allow to dry overnight.

Cut and fit glue block (K) for added strength, then give all surfaces a thorough final sanding. Give corners a liberal rounding. Add 2 inch brass butt hinges and friction lid supports as shown.

Ours was finished with a coat of Minwax Special Walnut stain followed by two coats of Minwax Antique Oil Finish. After drying, the friction lid supports were adjusted to support the lid in any position.

Bill of Materials (All Dimensions Actual)			
Part	Description	Size	No. Req'd
A	Front	¾ x 11¼ x 44	1
B	Side	¾ x 11¼ x 16¾	2
C	Back	¾ x 11¼ x 43¼	1
D	Bottom	½ x 17 x 44	1
E	Base Front & Back	¾ x 4 x 45¼	2
F	Base Ends	¾ x 4 x 18¼	2
G	Lid Support	¾ x 3 x 15½	2
H	Lid	¾ x 14¾ x 38	1
I	Lid Frame End	¾ x 3¾ x 14¾	1
J	Lid Frame Back	¾ x 3¾ x 45½	1
K	Glue Block	1 x 1 x 2¾	4
L	Top Sides	¾ x 4¾ x 16¾	2
M	Top Back	¾ x 6½ x 44	1
N	Cleat	¾ x 1½ x 12	2
O	Spacer	¾ x 3 x 4	2

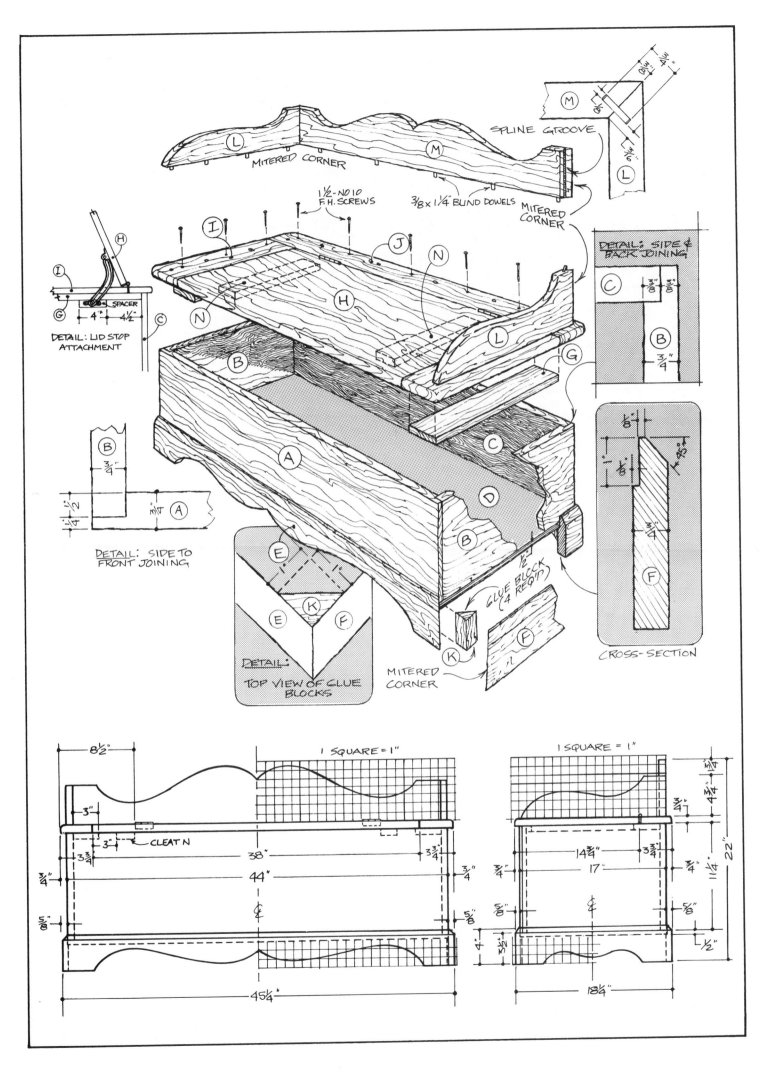

SPLINE GROOVE

Ⓜ ⅓" ¾"
Ⓛ ⁶⁄₁₆"

MITERED CORNER

1½-NO10
F.H. SCREWS

⅜ x 1¼" BLIND DOWELS

MITERED
CORNER

Ⓘ
Ⓘ

Ⓙ

Ⓝ

Ⓗ

Ⓛ

Ⓝ

Ⓗ

DETAIL: SIDE &
BACK JOINING

Ⓒ ⅜" ⅜"

Ⓑ ¾"

Ⓗ
Ⓘ
SPACER
4" 4½"
Ⓖ
Ⓒ

DETAIL: LID STOP
ATTACHMENT

Ⓑ

Ⓑ
¾"

½"
¼"

Ⓐ

DETAIL: SIDE TO
FRONT JOINING

Ⓑ

Ⓐ

Ⓓ

Ⓒ

Ⓛ

Ⓖ

⅛"
-25°
1"
¾"

Ⓕ

CROSS-SECTION

Ⓔ

Ⓔ Ⓚ Ⓕ

DETAIL:
TOP VIEW OF GLUE
BLOCKS

½"
GLUE BLOCK
(4 REQ'D)

Ⓚ

Ⓚ

MITERED
CORNER

Ⓕ

8½"

1 SQUARE = 1"

1 SQUARE = 1"

3"

3" CLEAT N

3¾"

38"

3¾"

¾"
¾"

44"

¢

⅝"

⅝"

45¼"

¾"
¾"

14¾"
17"

3¾"

¾"

¢

⅝"

3½"
4"

18¼"

¾"
4¾"
11¼"
22"

½"

69

18th Century Lawyer's Case

Originally used by lawyers to store files, abstracts, and titles, this handsome case will find modern use as a place to keep books and magazines handy. This one is made from cherry, but walnut or mahogany would also be good choices.

If wide stock is not available you'll need to edge-join two or more narrower boards. If you are able to select your own hardwood stock, do it with care. Try to choose boards that have a pleasing grain pattern (a better word to describe grain pattern is "figure"). The boards should also be flat and free of any splits, cracks, or other obvious defects.

While dowel pins were once commonly used in edge-joining, from a strength standpoint they actually reduce the glue surface, and thereby the strength in a good long grain-to-long grain joint. However, they do provide a very useful service by keeping the mating boards in line when clamp pressure is applied. This is especially helpful when working with long boards.

Perhaps most important to the success of an edge-joint is a clean, smooth surface on both mating parts. This allows close contact between both surfaces resulting in maximum glue strength. Ripping to width on the table or radial arm saw will usually leave a fairly rough edge, so it's best to smooth it out with a sharp plane. Take several light cuts, don't try to do it in one pass, and of course, plane with the direction of the grain. When planing, it's important that the edge remain square to the face of the board. Check for this by using a square.

After edge-joining, parts A and B can be cut to overall length and width. Note that part B is ¼ inch narrower than part A. Also, part B has three, ¼ inch deep by ⅜ inch wide stopped dadoes. These are best cut with a router equipped with a ⅜ inch diameter bit. Lay out the location of the dadoes, then securely clamp a fence (made from a piece of scrap stock) to serve as a guide for the router. Stop the dado at a point 5½ inches from the back edge, then cut the corners square with a chisel.

Part A has a ¼ x ¼ rabbet cut along the entire length of the inside back edge. This can be cut on the table or radial arm saw or with a router equipped with a piloted ¼ inch rabbet bit.

Next, cut part C to overall length and width, then lay out the location of the ¼ inch deep by ⅜ inch wide dadoes. Except for the fact that these are stopped on both ends, the method for cutting them is the same as for part B. After cutting the dadoes, use the router and a piloted ¼ inch radius cove bit to apply a cove to all four edges.

Parts E and F are identical. Cut to length and width, then use a piloted 5/32 inch Roman ogee bit to rout a molding around all four edges.

The dividers, part D, are made from ⅜ inch thick stock. If you have fairly narrow pieces of heavier stock (1½ - 2 inches wide) they can be resawn on the table saw. These resawn boards can then be edge-glued to form the wide divider panels. Of course, if you have a band saw you'll be able to resaw much wider stock. Perhaps the easiest way to get ⅜ inch stock is to hand plane ¾ inch stock. It doesn't take very long, and besides, most woodworkers agree that hand planing a piece of wood is one of the most pleasurable aspects of this hobby.

Once you have stock for the dividers, transfer the profile from the grid pattern shown. Use a saber saw or band saw to cut out, then sand the edges of the curves to remove all rough spots.

For the back (G), ¼ inch hardwood plywood should be used.

Sand all parts, then assemble as shown using glue and wood screws, countersunk and plugged. Allow glue to dry before giving the project a thorough final sanding. Lightly round all corners and sharp edges. Finish to suit. The one shown, made of cherry, was not stained. Instead it was simply finished with two coats of Watco Danish Oil.

Bill of Materials
(All Dimensions Actual)

Part	Description	Size	No. Req'd
A	End	¾ x 8½ x 12	2
B	Top	¾ x 8¼ x 15⅜	1
C	Bottom	¾ x 9½ x 17⅞	1
D	Partition	⅜ x 7¾ x 11¾	3
E	Crown	¾ x 10½ x 18⅞	1
F	Base	¾ x 10½ x 18⅞	1
G	Back	¼ x 15⅞ x 12	1

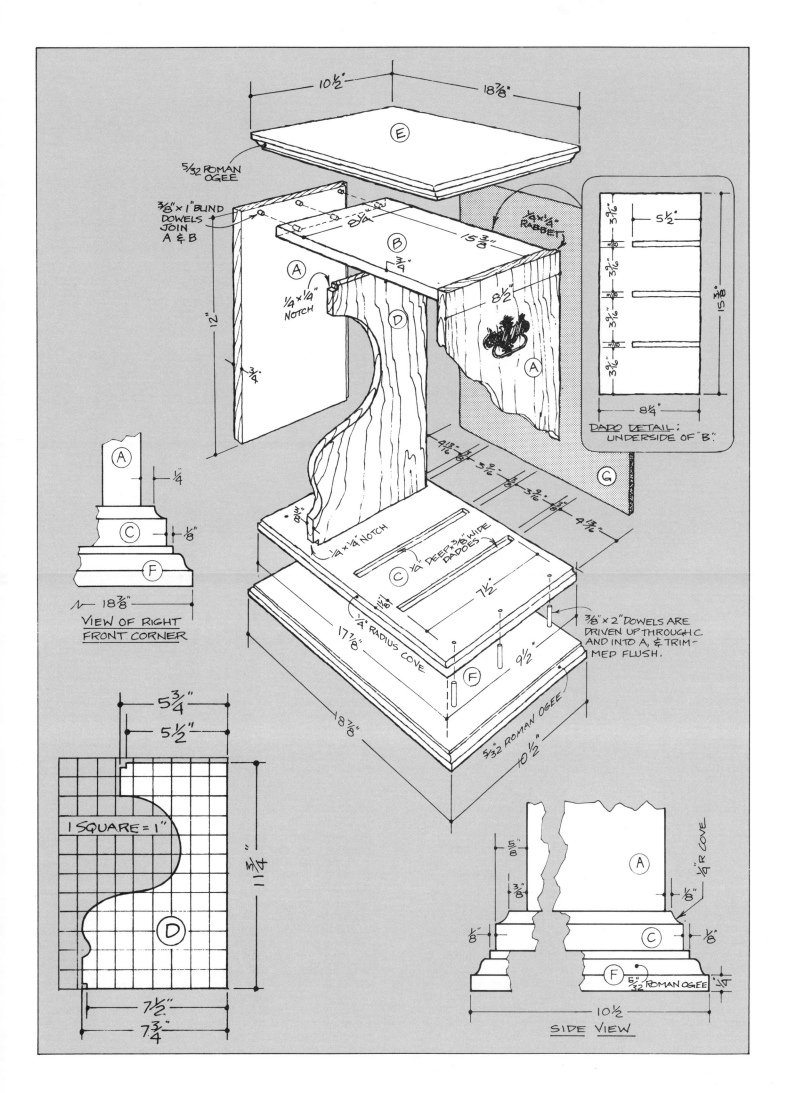

10½"

18⅞"

E

5/32 ROMAN OGEE

⅜"×1" BLIND DOWELS JOIN A & B

8¼"

¼"×¼" RABBET

15⅜"

B

¾"

A

¼×¼" NOTCH

12"

¾"

D

8½"

A

DADO DETAIL: UNDERSIDE OF "B"

3/16"

5½"

3/16"

3/16"

3/16"

3/16"

3/16"

8¼"

15⅜"

A

C

¼"

¼"

⅛"

F

18⅞"

VIEW OF RIGHT FRONT CORNER

G

4 13/16"

5 9/16"

3 9/16"

4 3/16"

¼"×¼" NOTCH

¼" DEEP×⅜" WIDE DADOES

C

7½"

⅛"

¼" RADIUS COVE

17⅞"

F

9½"

⅜"×2" DOWELS ARE DRIVEN UP THROUGH C AND INTO A, & TRIMMED FLUSH.

5/32 ROMAN OGEE

10½"

18⅞"

5¾"

5½"

1 SQUARE = 1"

D

11¼"

7½"

7¾"

⅝"

⅜"

A

¼"R COVE

⅛"

⅛"

C

⅛"

F

5/32 ROMAN OGEE

10½"

SIDE VIEW

19th Century Danish Washstand

Nowadays we all wash-up at the bathroom sink, but before the advent of modern plumbing, it was the washstand that served this function. The bowl was filled from a pitcher, and here one would wash away the dirt and sweat of a long hard day's work.

Built in the late 1800's, this well-constructed washstand was obviously the work of a skilled country craftsman. The liberal use of rabbets and dadoes, along with the dovetail and mortise and tenon joints, is evidence that it was built to last — not just for a dozen years, but rather a dozen generations. And last it did, for in spite of the many years of daily use, it remains basically a sound and functional piece of furniture.

Like most pieces of American or European country furniture, it was made from pine. Of course, most any wood can be used for a reproduction, but pine would probably be your best choice. Look for stock with a minimum of warp and reasonably free of knots.

The two sides (part A) can be made first. Since 13½ inch wide boards are a rarity these days, you'll have to edge-glue two or more narrower boards in order to get enough width. There's an assortment of dadoes and grooves cut on part A. Refer to the exploded view and the detail drawing for locations and dimensions of each groove. These cuts can best be made with a router equipped with a straight bit. Use guidestrips and stop blocks to control the router. Next, transfer the curved profile from the grid pattern and cut out with a band or saber saw.

After cutting part B to size, the half-dovetails can be laid out and cut. Make the cuts with care to insure a good fit.

The bottom (C), center shelf (D), and base shelf (E) are identical and can be made next. Refer to the detail for the dimensions of the ¼ inch by ⅜ inch rabbet on each end. This cut can be made by making repeated passes with the table or radial arm saw, or with a router and piloted ⅜ inch rabbet bit. When cutting the rabbets, try to make them slightly thicker than the dadoes. Then, when the rabbeted board is sanded, it will result in a good snug fit.

The plinth (part F) can be cut to overall length and width as shown. Make repeated passes on the table or radial arm saw to form the ⅜ by ⅜ inch tongue on each end. Transfer the curved pattern from the grid before cutting out with the band or saber saw.

Part G, the front, can now be cut to size. Since this piece shows prominently, try to select stock with an attractive figure. Note the detail drawing showing the ⅜ inch by ⅜ inch rabbet on each end. This rabbet can be cut in the same manner as the shelf rabbets were.

The back cleat (part H) is made from 5/4 nominal stock (1⅛ inch actual). As shown in the detail, a ¼ inch wide by ⅜ inch deep groove is cut along its length. A couple of passes over the table saw will cut this groove in short order. The 45 degree bevel serves to make the cleat less noticeable after the project has been assembled.

The two side cleats, part I, are cut to a 10½ inch length. Later, when installed, this length will allow a slight gap between the back cleat(H) and the front (G). It's a good idea to have this gap because as the sides (A) tend to shrink during

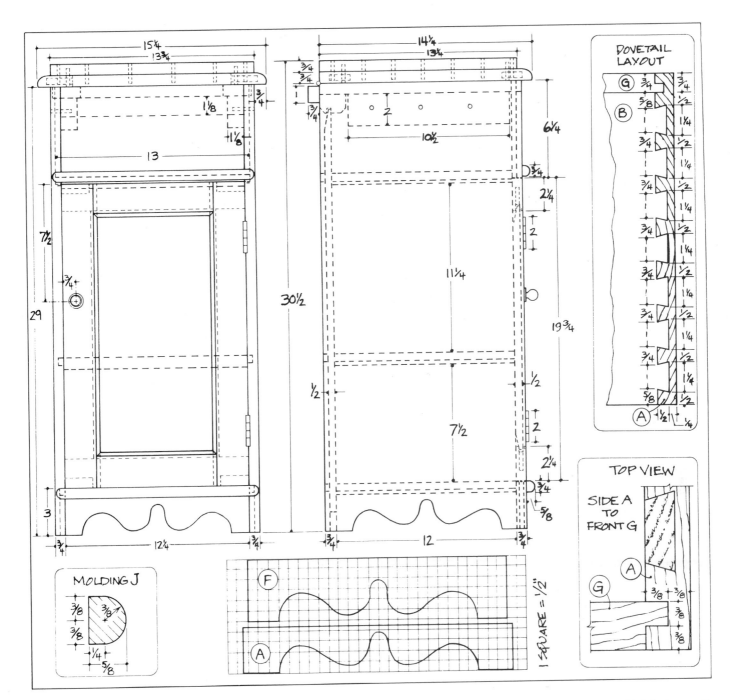

the winter, part H and part G will move closer together. Cutting the cleat (I) a little short allows this movement without putting any stress on part G or part H.

Parts J, the two molding strips, are made from ¾ inch stock. The dimensions are shown in the detail. Probably the easiest way to duplicate the ⅜ inch radius is to cut a piece of wide (around 1½ inches or so) stock to a length of 27½ inches, then clamp it in a vise. Mark the radius on each end, then use a sharp hand plane to round the edges. Finish rounding with coarse, then smooth, sandpaper. Now use the table or radial arm saw to rip the molding to a ⅜ inch width, then cut to 13½ inch lengths and round the ends.

The back (K) is made of edge-glued ½ inch thick stock. The beveled edge (on the sides and top only) can best be cut by setting the table saw blade to an angle of 17 degrees, then running the stock (as it's held against the rip-fence) through the blade on edge. The location of the rip-fence and the height of the blade must be carefully adjusted before making the cut.

The door assembly (parts L, M, and N) can now be made. Referring to the detail, note that the door rails and stiles have a bevel around their inside edges. The procedure for making these parts is shown in the step by step drawing on page 75. As can be seen, the joint can be cut with a table saw. Mortises are drilled out and cleaned up with a mortis-

ing chisel. It's usually best to cut tenons slightly larger than necessary and allow them to protrude to be later trimmed flush with the stiles. When allowing for extra tenon length remember that the critical rail dimension is the distance between tenon shoulders.

The bevels on the rails are coped or cut at an angle to fit against the stile bevels giving the appearance of a mitered corner. After completing step 8, the corner joint should fit together perfectly without further trimming. Tenon haunches can be quickly cut with a dovetail or small backsaw or by using the miter gauge and making repeated passes over the table saw blade.

The top frame (parts O and P) is joined with mortise and tenon joints. All dimensions are shown in the detail. Note that the inside edges of parts O and P have a curved radius. These curves were applied to allow the frame to fit over the lip of the washbowl. Even if you don't plan to use this as a washstand, the curves are a nice detail and worth including.

Before assembly give all parts a complete sanding. Check all joints for proper fit-up, then assemble as shown. Glue and clamp, then add the ¼ inch diameter dowel pins where shown. Do not glue the back (K) and door panel (N). However, part K should be joined to parts C, D, and E, with a single dowel at the center (measuring across the back) of each shelf. Two blocks (R) to support the open top are glued

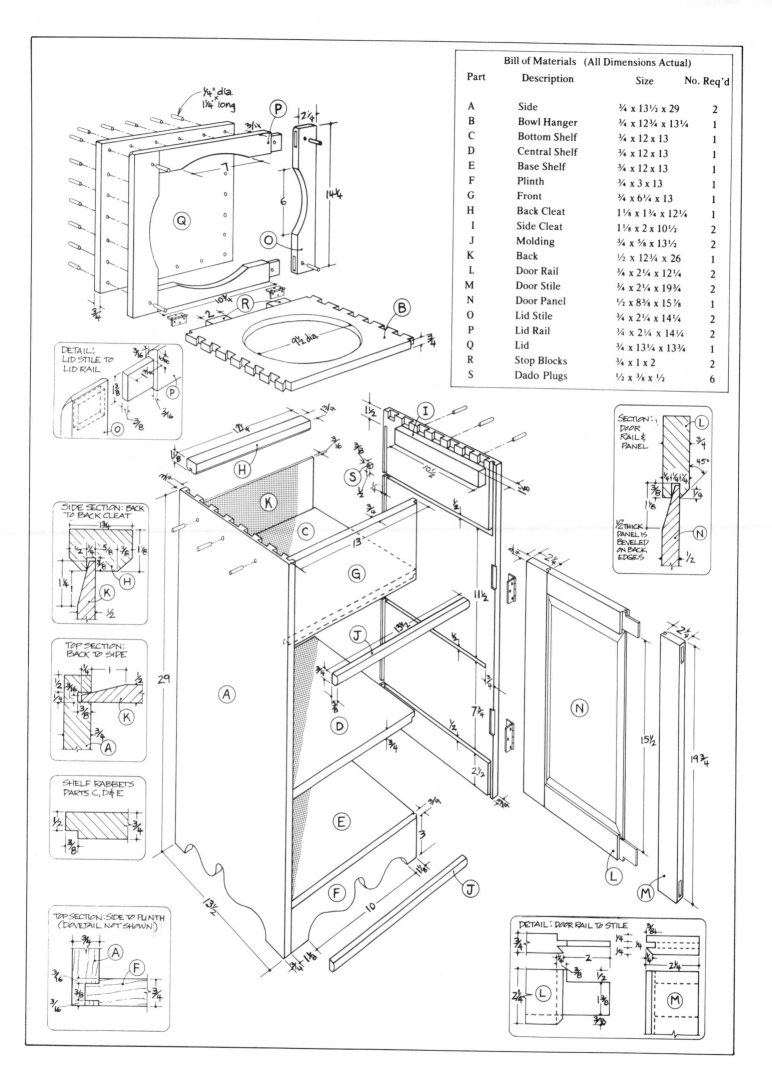

Bill of Materials (All Dimensions Actual)

Part	Description	Size	No. Req'd
A	Side	¾ x 13½ x 29	2
B	Bowl Hanger	¾ x 12¾ x 13¼	1
C	Bottom Shelf	¾ x 12 x 13	1
D	Central Shelf	¾ x 12 x 13	1
E	Base Shelf	¾ x 12 x 13	1
F	Plinth	¾ x 3 x 13	1
G	Front	¾ x 6¼ x 13	1
H	Back Cleat	1⅛ x 1¾ x 12¼	1
I	Side Cleat	1⅛ x 2 x 10½	2
J	Molding	¾ x ⅝ x 13½	2
K	Back	½ x 12¾ x 26	1
L	Door Rail	¾ x 2¼ x 12¼	2
M	Door Stile	¾ x 2¼ x 19¾	2
N	Door Panel	½ x 8⅜ x 15⅞	1
O	Lid Stile	¾ x 2¼ x 14¼	2
P	Lid Rail	¾ x 2¼ x 14¼	2
Q	Lid	¾ x 13¼ x 13¾	1
R	Stop Blocks	¾ x 1 x 2	2
S	Dado Plugs	½ x ⅜ x ½	6

DETAIL: LID STILE TO LID RAIL

SIDE SECTION: BACK TO BACK CLEAT

TOP SECTION: BACK TO SIDE

SHELF RABBETS PARTS C, D & E

TOP SECTION: SIDE TO PLINTH (DOVETAIL NOT SHOWN)

SECTION: DOOR RAIL & PANEL

½" THICK PANEL IS BEVELED ON BACK EDGES

DETAIL: DOOR RAIL TO STILE

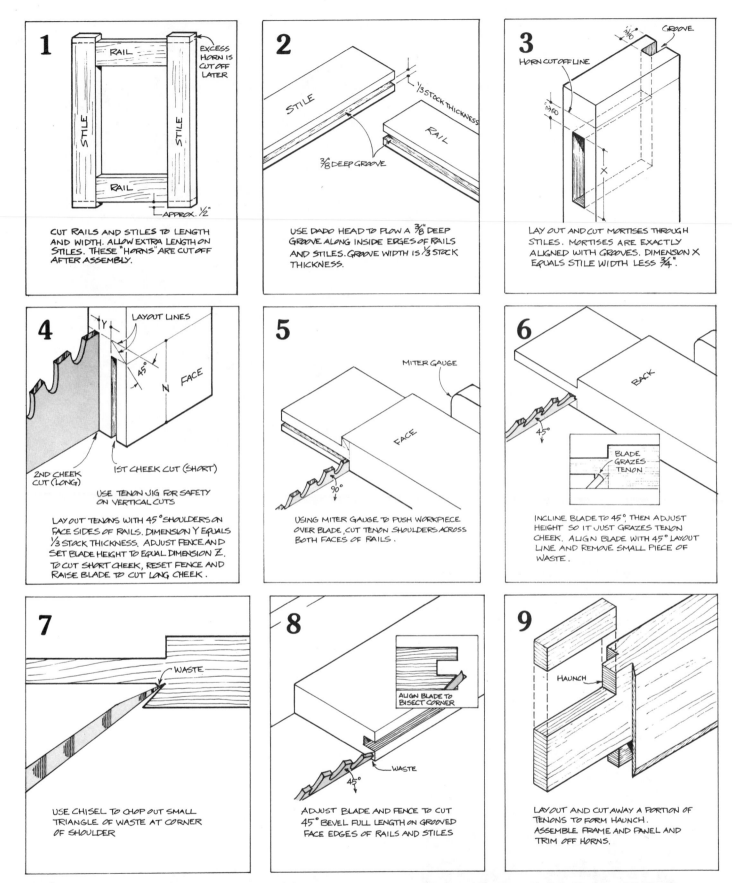

1

CUT RAILS AND STILES TO LENGTH AND WIDTH. ALLOW EXTRA LENGTH ON STILES. THESE "HORNS" ARE CUT OFF AFTER ASSEMBLY.

2

USE DADO HEAD TO PLOW A 3/8" DEEP GROOVE ALONG INSIDE EDGES OF RAILS AND STILES. GROOVE WIDTH IS 1/3 STOCK THICKNESS.

3

LAY OUT AND CUT MORTISES THROUGH STILES. MORTISES ARE EXACTLY ALIGNED WITH GROOVES. DIMENSION X EQUALS STILE WIDTH LESS 3/4".

4

USE TENON JIG FOR SAFETY ON VERTICAL CUTS

LAY OUT TENONS WITH 45° SHOULDERS ON FACE SIDES OF RAILS. DIMENSION Y EQUALS 1/3 STOCK THICKNESS. ADJUST FENCE AND SET BLADE HEIGHT TO EQUAL DIMENSION Z. TO CUT SHORT CHEEK, RESET FENCE AND RAISE BLADE TO CUT LONG CHEEK.

5

USING MITER GAUGE TO PUSH WORKPIECE OVER BLADE, CUT TENON SHOULDERS ACROSS BOTH FACES OF RAILS.

6

INCLINE BLADE TO 45°, THEN ADJUST HEIGHT SO IT JUST GRAZES TENON CHEEK. ALIGN BLADE WITH 45° LAYOUT LINE AND REMOVE SMALL PIECE OF WASTE.

7

USE CHISEL TO CHOP OUT SMALL TRIANGLE OF WASTE AT CORNER OF SHOULDER

8

ADJUST BLADE AND FENCE TO CUT 45° BEVEL FULL LENGTH ON GROOVED FACE EDGES OF RAILS AND STILES

9

LAYOUT AND CUT AWAY A PORTION OF TENONS TO FORM HAUNCH. ASSEMBLE FRAME AND PANEL AND TRIM OFF HORNS.

and screwed to part B as shown. Also, small filler blocks (S) are used to plug the dado groove cutouts in the back edge of parts C, D, and E.

Final sand all parts, giving all edges a thorough rounding to simulate years of wear. Stain to suit. We would suggest a stain that provides an antique look, and one of our favorites (with pine) is a single coat of Minwax Special Walnut followed by two coats of their Antique Oil Finish.

While we can't provide a source for an exact reproduction of the knob, we can suggest a 1¼ inch diameter wooden knob available from Horton Brasses, Nooks Hill Rd., Cromwell, CT 06416. It's painted black with a brass face. Order part no. WCT-2. A small mortise is cut in the inside of part A to accept the knob's locking lever.

Early American Wall Cupboard

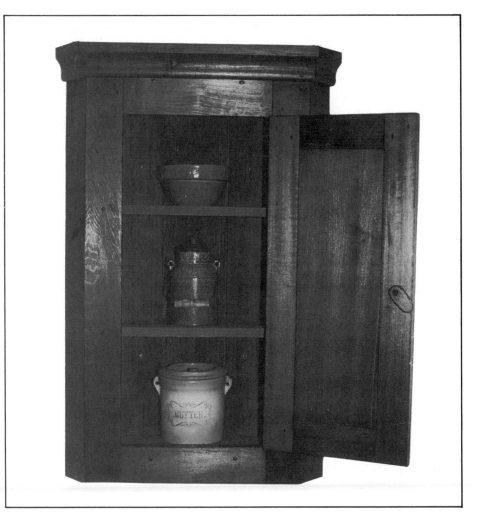

With space at a premium in the homes of most early Americans, wall cabinets enjoyed a great deal of popularity because they added some much needed storage area.

While not an original piece, the one shown offers many of the characteristics that make early American designs so appealing to many of us. To simplify construction, dowels are used for most joints, although experienced woodworkers will no doubt choose to incorporate the mortise and tenon. Pine is used throughout, except for the plywood back (part G and H).

Begin by making the bottom (A), top (C), and two shelves (B). As shown in the detail, all four parts are identical. An eight foot length of 1 x 12 stock (¾ inch by 11¼ inch actual) will provide enough material. It's important that the angles be cut accurately, so check your saw before starting. Also, make sure the dimensions are cut exactly as shown.

To make part D, rip 1 inch stock (¾ inch actual) to a width of about 3⅜ inches, then set the table or radial arm

saw blade to a 22½ degree angle and cut a bevel along one edge. Return the blade to the zero degree position and with the beveled edge against the fence, rip the piece to its finish width of 3 inches.

Cut part E to the dimensions shown in the Bill of Materials. Be sure both ends are square. Referring to the detail, drill parts E and D for ⅜ inch diameter by 2 inch long dowel pins. If you have one, a doweling jig will be helpful here. Drill the holes slightly more than 1 inch deep to allow room for any excess glue in the hole.

Parts D and E can now be joined to form the outer frame. Apply glue to the mating surfaces of both parts and also to the dowel pins. Keep in mind that the dowel pins must have a lengthwise groove to allow trapped air and glue to escape, otherwise you may not be able to close the joint. Assemble parts D and E and clamp securely with bar or pipe clamps. Apply only enough pressure to bring the mating surfaces in firm contact - too much pressure will squeeze most of the glue out of the joint. Use small scraps of wood as clamp pads to protect the frame. It's important that the frame be square, so check this before setting aside to dry. Make adjustments as necessary.

Make the two back pieces (parts G & H) next. We recommend that plywood be used here. Note that part H is wider than part G. Also, part H has a ¼ inch deep by ½ inch wide rabbet along one edge.

The cabinet can now be partially assembled. Sand thoroughly parts A, B, C, frame parts D and E, and back parts G and H. If there are deep scratches or dents, you may need to start with 80 grit aluminum oxide paper, otherwise start with 100 grit. For a proper sanding job you also need to remove all planer marks (the marks made at the mill by the cutter blades of a surface planer). Follow the first sanding with a second sanding using 120 grit. A third and fourth sanding with 150, then 220 grit will result in a smooth finish that will take a stain nicely.

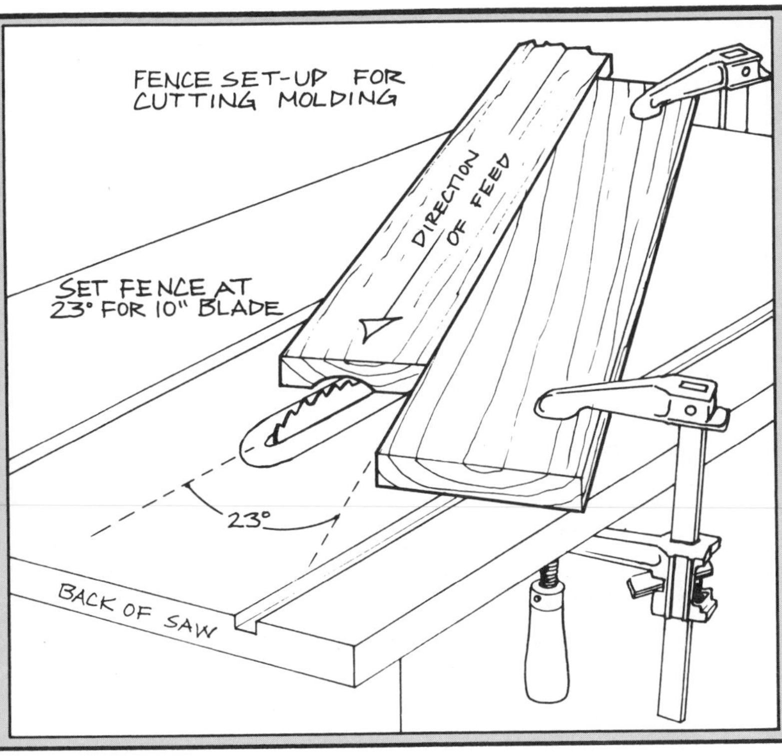
FENCE SET-UP FOR CUTTING MOLDING
DIRECTION OF FEED
SET FENCE AT 23° FOR 10" BLADE
23°
BACK OF SAW

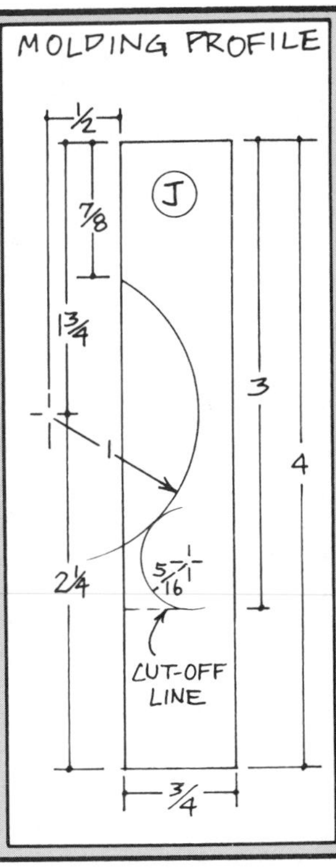
MOLDING PROFILE
½
⅞
J
1¾
3
1
4
2¼
5/16
CUT-OFF LINE
¾

If you plan to paint or stain the cabinet, now is the best time to do it - before the parts are assembled. These cabinets often had painted interiors (in this case, parts B, the top of A, the bottom of C, and inside of G & H) with all other parts stained. If you use paint, choose one of the early American colors available at many paint stores. If you can't get one locally, several attractive colors can be ordered from Cohasset Colonials, Cohasset, MA 02025.

After the stain and/or paint has dried, the back parts (G & H) can be assembled to parts A, B, and C. Lay out and mark the location of parts A, B, and C, then join to the back parts with 1¼ inch x #8 countersunk wood screws. The front frame (parts D and E) can also be added at this time. I used square nails to give the piece a more authentic look. Before driving the nails through, I first drilled pilot holes in order to prevent the wood from splitting. The general locations of the nails are shown in the photo. A good source for old-fashioned cut and decorative nails is the Tremont Nail Company, P.O. Box 111, Wareham, MA 02571.

The two sides (part F) can now be made. Rip the stock to about 2½ inches, then cut a 22½ degree bevel along one edge. Now measure the actual opening on the cabinet and rip the stock so that it has an exact fit. Drill pilot holes, then secure with cut nails.

To make the molding (J), the table saw is set up as shown above. A 23 degree angle is used for a 10 inch blade. Other size blades will require some experimentation to get the correct angle.

Lower the blade so that it is barely (about 1/32 inch) above the table. When properly set up, just the very top of the highest tooth should contact the board at a point 2¼ inch from the edge. Make the first cut with the blade set at a height of 1/32 inch. Use two push sticks, one to hold the workpiece against the fence, the other to feed the stock. After each pass raise the blade another 1/32 inch. It will take around a dozen passes to complete the cove cut.

Rip the stock to three inches (see above), then round off at the cut-off line using a sharp plane followed by a good sanding. The plate (I) is cut to shape and glued to the top as shown. The molding is mitered at 22½ degrees, then attached to the plate with glue and finishing nails, countersunk and filled.

With the cabinet completed, the frame and panel door can be made next (parts K, L, and M). Cut parts K and L to size as shown. At this point, it's best to use actual measurements from the cabinet to determine dimensions. The 5/16 inch deep by ¼ inch wide groove can best be cut with a router. Note that the groove must be stopped short of the ends on part K.

The center panel (M) is the visual highlight of this piece, so try to select stock that has a pleasing wood figure. The tapered edge can be cut on the table saw, radial arm saw, or with a panel raising cutter on the shaper.

Sand all parts thoroughly, then stain or paint as desired. Assemble the door as shown. Use glue to join parts K and L, but do not glue the panel (M) in place. It must be free to expand and contract in the frame.

Various kinds of commercial door latches are available but the one shown is most authentic. The door hangs on a pair of 1¼ inch brass butt hinges which are mortised into parts D and K.

Stained surfaces can be finished with two coats of Minwax Antique Oil Finish. Painted surfaces can be left as is.

Bill of Materials
(All Dimensions Actual)

Part	Description	Size	No. Req'd
A	Bottom	See Detail	1
B	Shelf	See Detail	2
C	Top	See Detail	1
D	Cabinet Stile	¾ x 3 x 32	2
E	Cabinet Rail	¾ x 3 x 12	2
F	Side	¾ x 2 x 32	2
G	Left Back	½ x 13¾ x 32	1
H	Right Back	½ x 14 x 32	1
I	Plate	¾ x 2 x 21	1
J	Molding	See Detail	
K	Door Stile	¾ x 2½ x 26	2
L	Door Rail	¾ x 2½ x 7	2
M	Panel	½ x 7½ x 21½	1

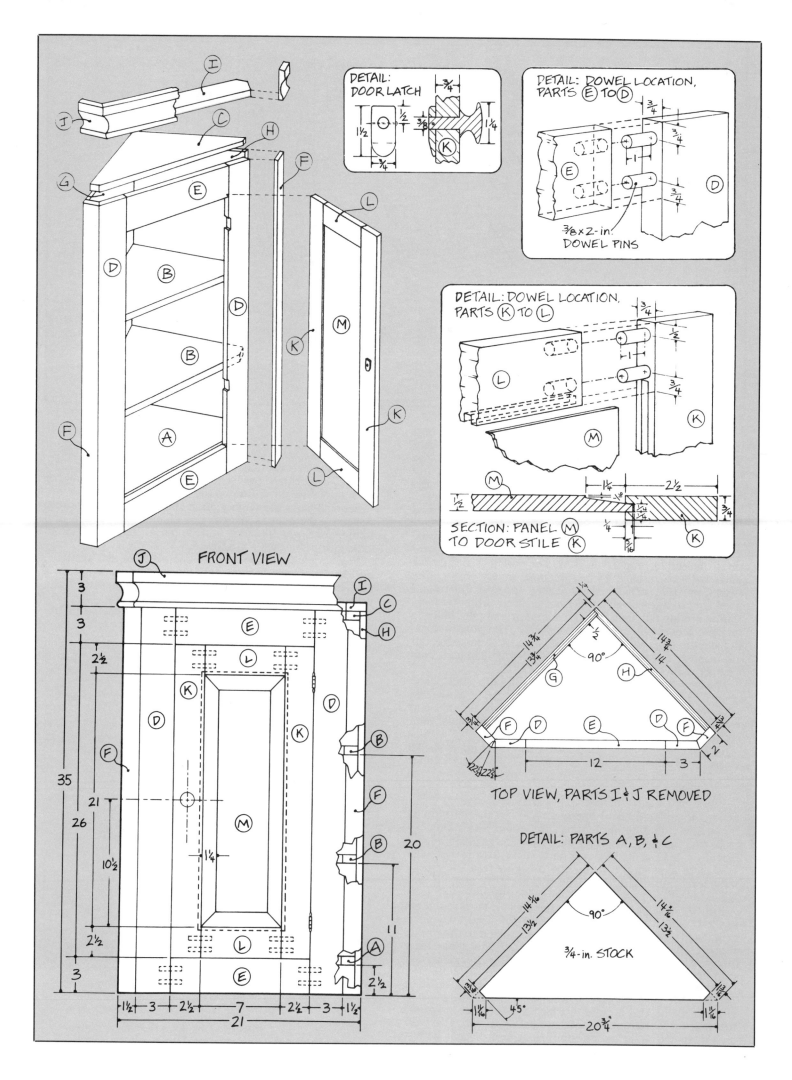

DETAIL: DOOR LATCH

DETAIL: DOWEL LOCATION, PARTS E TO D

⅜ × 2-in. DOWEL PINS

DETAIL: DOWEL LOCATION, PARTS K TO L

SECTION: PANEL M TO DOOR STILE K

FRONT VIEW

TOP VIEW, PARTS I & J REMOVED

DETAIL: PARTS A, B, & C

¾-in. STOCK

Candles will often make lovely additions to a festive occasion, especially if attractive holders are used. The one shown is made from walnut, although any hardwood that's suitable for turning can also be used. With a little practice this becomes a fairly easy turning job, making it a good item to consider for sale at craft fairs and gift shops.

Note that the project consists of three separate parts, a base, stem, and bowl. The stem is spindle turned and should present no special problems. The base is faceplate turned, and again no special problems should be encountered. For the bowl though, there are a few suggested procedures.

We used 2 inch nominal (1¾ inch actual) stock to make the bowl. Secure the stock to the faceplate, then turn the top half of the bowl, including the 5/16 inch deep by 3-3/16 inch candle well. This includes a ⅛ inch diameter pilot hole for the bottom of the spike. Sand thoroughly before removing from the faceplate. Carefully center a small faceplate in the candle well and fasten with short screws. The bottom half of the bowl can now be turned and sanded. After removing the faceplate, the screw holes in the well are filled with a mixture of sawdust and glue.

A center spike will add some stability to the candle and can be made using a 1 inch x #7 brass wood screw. Turn the screw into the pilot hole, then remove. Cut off the screw head and file this end to a point. Now, with a pair of pliers holding the pointed end, turn the screw into the bowl.

Apply glue to the spindle tenons and assemble the three parts. Several coats of Watco Danish Oil will provide an attractive final finish.

Candle Holder

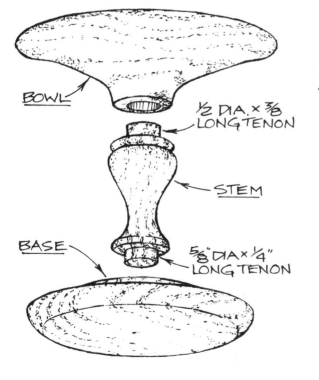

BOWL

½ DIA. x ⅜ LONG TENON

STEM

BASE

⅝" DIA x ¼" LONG TENON

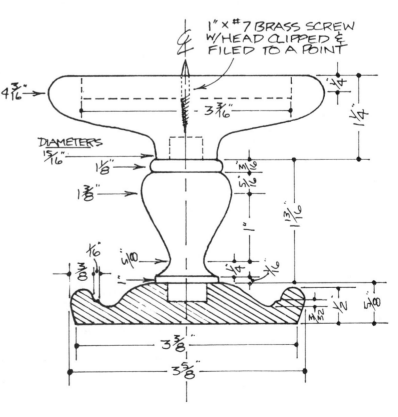

1" x #7 BRASS SCREW W/HEAD CLIPPED & FILED TO A POINT

4³⁄₁₆"

3³⁄₁₆"

¼"

¼"

DIAMETERS
15⁄₁₆"

1⅛"

³⁄₁₆"

5⁄₁₆"

1⅜"

1"

1³⁄₁₆"

7⁄₁₆"

3⁄₈"

1⁄₁₆"

¼"

1⁄₁₆"

1⁄₁₆"

3⁄₃₂"

½"

3⅜"

3⅝"

Chest of Drawers

This small chest of drawers, made from pine, is a fairly typical example of Danish country furniture from the early part of this century.

Begin by making the two front legs (part A). Cut each to 1⅝ inch square x 28¼ inch long, then lay out the locations of the four mortises for parts D and E. Use a sharp chisel to cut to the dimensions shown. The ¼ inch wide x ⅜ inch deep x 19 inch long groove is best cut with a router equipped with a ¼ inch straight bit. Note that it is stopped 9¼ inches from the bottom.

The two back legs (B) are cut to the same overall dimensions as the front legs. Two, ¼ inch wide by ⅜ inch deep by 19 inch long grooves are cut on each back leg, and again the grooves are stopped 9¼ inches from the bottom. Also, to accept the inside tenon on part G, part B has a short (¼ inch wide by ⅜ inch deep by ¾ inch long) groove cut at its top. A sharp chisel will make this groove in short order.

Refer to the step-by-step illustrations to make the curve shape on all four legs. Once the template is made, the profile can be quickly traced to the

stock, and all four legs can be cut in surprisingly little time.

The two sides (part C) are next. Since part C measures 13 inches wide (including the front and back tongue), it will be necessary to edge-glue two pieces of stock in order to get enough width. Two, 42 inch lengths of 1 x 8 stock (which actually measures ¾ inch x 7¼ inch) will provide enough material to make both sides and still allow for some final trimming. Locate and drill about three dowel pin holes along the mating edges of the 42 inch long boards. These dowel pins will primarily serve to align the boards as they are glued and clamped. Apply glue to both mating surfaces, then clamp securely with bar or pipe clamps. Allow to dry overnight. When dry, rip the board to a width of 13 inches. The ¼ inch wide by ⅜ inch long tongue can best be cut using a dado head cutter although repeated passes with a regular table or radial-arm saw will yield the same results. Check for a comfortable fit in the leg grooves. After the tongues have been made, the board can be crosscut into 19 inch lengths.

The three dividers (part D) and the

top divider (part E) are cut to the length and width shown in the Bill of Materials. The tenons are cut to the dimensions specified in the details. A tenon jig will be helpful here, but the joint can also be cut with a dado head cutter, or by hand with a back saw.

Next, the lower back frame (F), and the upper back frame (G) are cut to length and width. The tenons, shown in the details, are cut in the same manner as the dividers. Note that both parts have a ¼ inch wide by ⅜ inch deep groove along the entire length to accept the back (J).

After cutting the ¼ inch thick plywood back to length and width, the chest frame is ready for assembly. Sand all parts thoroughly, then assemble as shown using glue and bar or pipe clamps. Allow to dry thoroughly.

The drawer supports (H) are joined to the sides (C) with 1½ x #8 wood screws. Four screws are required for each support. The screw holes through part H should be slightly slotted so that part C will be free to expand and contract with changes in humidity. No glue should be used, except perhaps for a 2 inch long area at the middle. The drawer guide (I) can now be cut and glued to part H, but it should not be glued to part C.

The three drawers are made as shown on the drawing. Drawer pulls can be made as shown, although a number of ready-made commercial pulls would also look good.

The molding (L) is carved from ⅜ inch stock, then glued to the front legs. Drawer stops (K) are cut to size and glued in place.

Like the sides, the top (M) is made of edge-glued stock, and it is joined in the same manner. To add the molded edge, use a router equipped with a piloted 5/32 inch Roman ogee bit, then use sandpaper to round-off the lower edge. The top is joined to the rest of the cabinet with 1¼ x #10 round head wood screws (and washers) driven up through slotted holes in parts E and G, and also through a slotted block screwed and glued to the center of each side (C).

A stain like Minwax's Special Walnut looks good on a project like this. When dry, add several coats of their Antique Oil Finish for a soft, low luster final finish.

Bill of Materials (All Dimensions Actual)			
Part	Description	Size	No. Req'd
A	Front Leg	1⅝ x 1⅝ x 28¼	2
B	Back Leg	1⅝ x 1⅝ x 28¼	2
C	Side	¾ x 13 x 19	2
D	Divider	¾ x 1⅝ x 22½	3
E	Top Divider	¾ x 1⅝ x 22½	1
F	Lower Back Frame	¾ x 1½ x 21¾	1
G	Upper Back Frame	¾ x 1⅝ x 21¾	1
H	Drawer Support	¾ x 1½ x 10	6
I	Drawer Guide	¾ x ⅞ x 10	6
J	Back	¼ x 21-11/16 x 17-7/16	1
K	Drawer Stops	¼ x 1 x 2	6
L	Applied Molding	See Detail	2
M	Top	¾ x 16¾ x 26¾	1
N	Drawer	See Detail	3

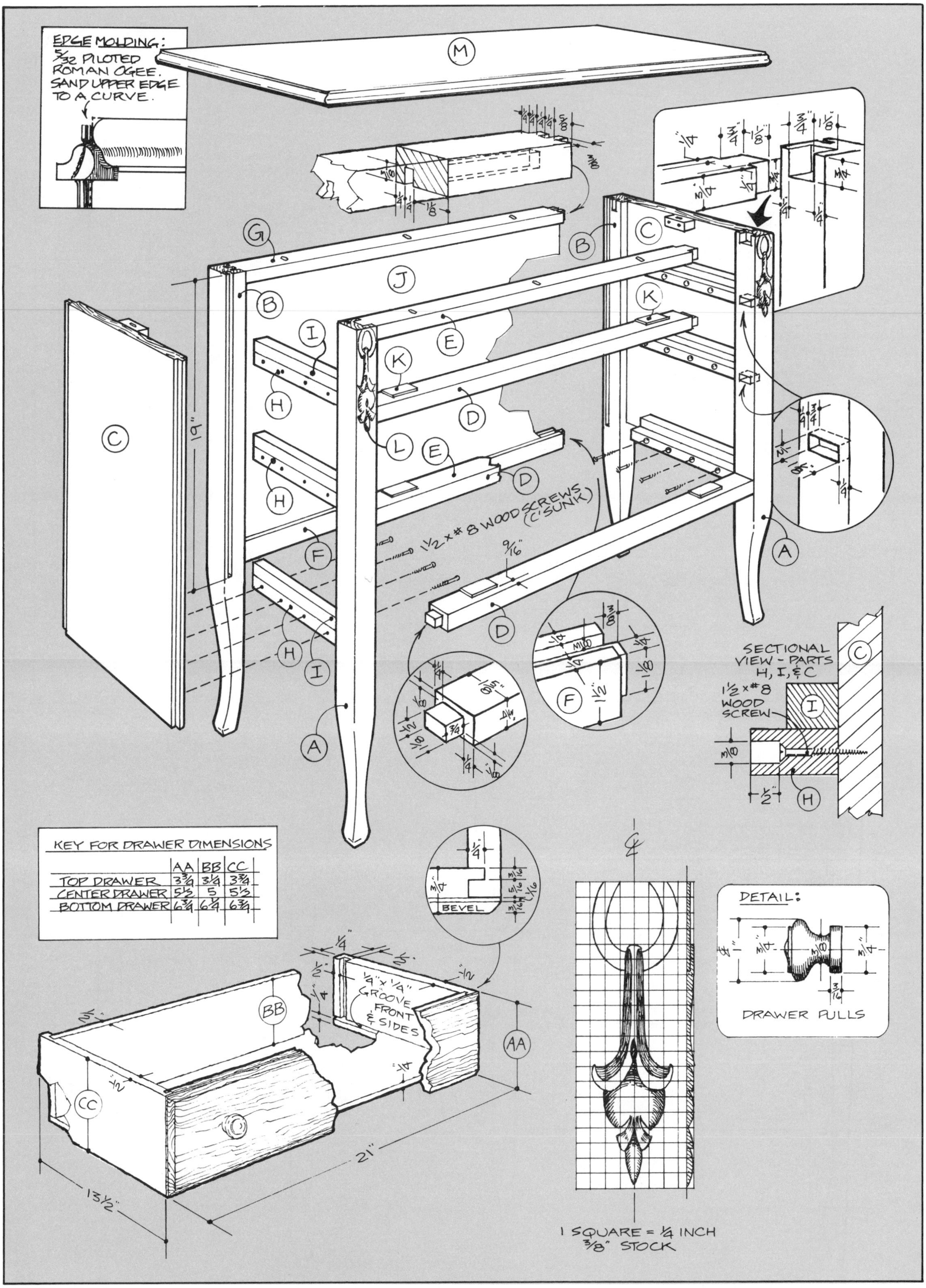
EDGE MOLDING:
5/32 PILOTED ROMAN OGEE. SAND UPPER EDGE TO A CURVE.
1 1/2 x #8 WOOD SCREWS (C'SUNK)
SECTIONAL VIEW - PARTS H, I, & C
1 1/2 x #8 WOOD SCREW
KEY FOR DRAWER DIMENSIONS
AA BB CC
TOP DRAWER 3 3/4 3 1/4 3 3/4
CENTER DRAWER 5 1/2 5 5 1/2
BOTTOM DRAWER 6 3/4 6 1/4 6 3/4
BEVEL
1/4" x 1/4" GROOVE FRONT & SIDES
21"
13 1/2"
DETAIL:
DRAWER PULLS
1 SQUARE = 1/4 INCH
3/8" STOCK

Cutting Leg Curves

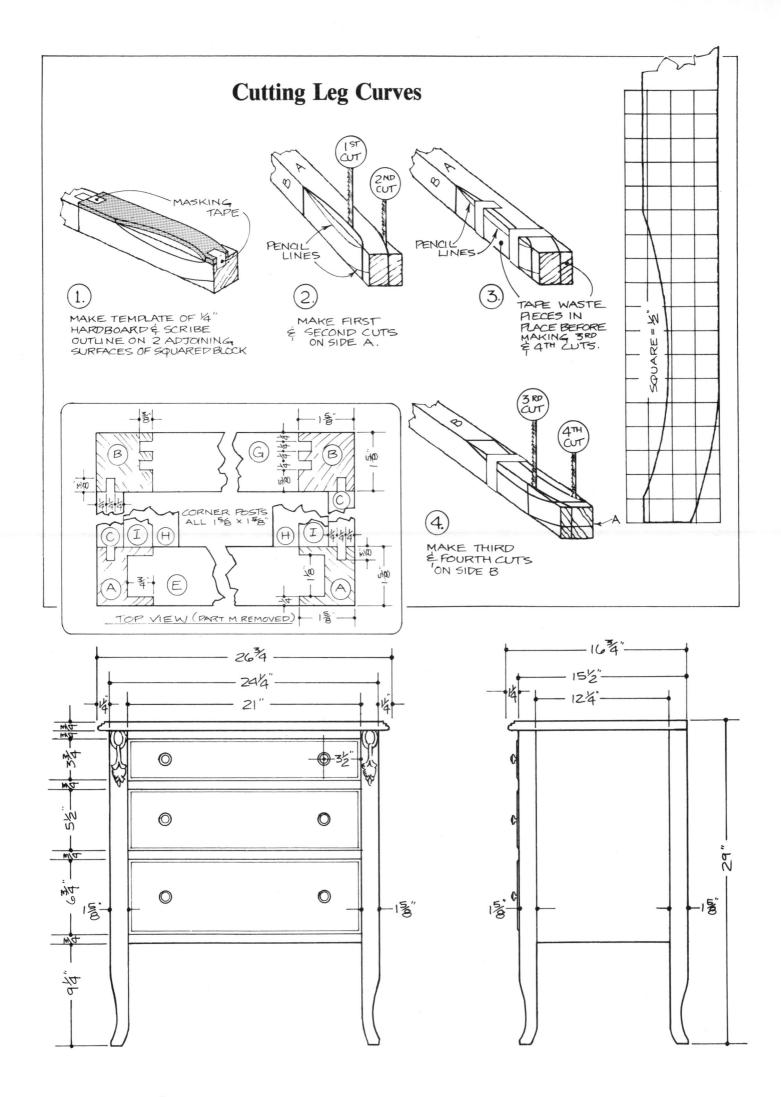

1. MAKE TEMPLATE OF ¼" HARDBOARD & SCRIBE OUTLINE ON 2 ADJOINING SURFACES OF SQUARED BLOCK

MASKING TAPE

2. MAKE FIRST & SECOND CUTS ON SIDE A.

PENCIL LINES

1ST CUT

2ND CUT

3. TAPE WASTE PIECES IN PLACE BEFORE MAKING 3RD & 4TH CUTS.

PENCIL LINES

SQUARE = ½"

4. MAKE THIRD & FOURTH CUTS ON SIDE B

3RD CUT

4TH CUT

CORNER POSTS ALL 1⅝" × 1⅝"

TOP VIEW (PART M REMOVED)

The dimensions of these lovely pine shelves are nearly identical to a Shaker original that hangs at the Hancock Shaker Village in Hancock, Massachusetts. The only significant difference is in the thickness of the stock - ours is ¾ inch while the Hancock piece was made from ⅝ inch lumber. The Shaker pegs (F) can be turned to the profile shown or purchased from Shaker Workshops, P.O. Box 1028, Concord, MA 01742.

Cut the two sides (A) from 1 x 8 nominal stock, then use an adjustable dado head cutter to make the ¼ inch deep by ¾ inch wide rabbet for part B. The ¼ inch deep by ¾ inch wide dadoes for parts C and D can be cut at the same time. Next, lay out the curved profile (see grid pattern), before cutting with a band or saber saw.

After cutting shelves B, C, and D, and pegboard E to dimensions shown, give all parts a thorough sanding. Assemble with glue and clamp securely. When dry, remove clamps, then add the ¼ inch diameter by one inch long dowel pins as shown. Use a sharp plane to bevel the front edge of the two upper shelves. Glue pegs (F) in place, then give the entire project a final sanding. Ours was stained with Minwax's Fruitwood stain, followed by a final finish of Minwax's Antique Oil.

Two counterbored holes permit the pegboard to be secured to the wall. A pair of leather laces, tied in a loop, allows the shelf to be hung from the two pegs - a common practice of the Shakers.

Shaker Shelves

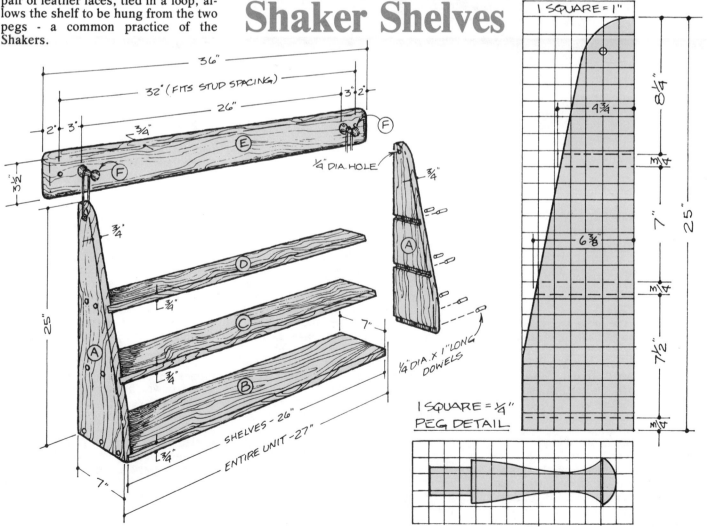

Cider Press Lamp

As we studied an antique cider press, it occurred to us that it could make a lovely lamp with just a few modifications. Basically, the modifications involved adding parts F and G (see Drawing) and some lamp hardware. However, if you'd rather have a working cider press, exclude parts F and G, but add plate (L) and cleat (M) as shown in the Detail.

Except for the press screw (K), all parts for the project can be obtained at most hardware stores. Part K can be ordered from Craftsman Wood Service Co., 1735 West Cortland Court, Addison, IL 60101. Order their part no. H0401.

The one shown is made from cherry, but most any other hardwood would be suitable. Softwoods should be avoided.

Begin by cutting the 1⅜ inch thick by 2¼ inch wide stock for the frame (parts A, B, and D), yoke (parts F and G), and feet (part C). You will need approximately nine linear feet. For the frame cut two pieces 12 inches long (for part A) and two pieces 13 inches long (for parts B and D). Apply a 9/16 inch wide by 7/16 inch deep lengthwise groove along the inside of parts A to accept the ⅜ inch threaded rod (I). Holding the uprights (A) in place on the bottom (B), mark where the inside of the groove falls. Drill a hole in the bottom to accept the rod. Also drill an angled hole for the lamp cord (see Front Elevation). Turn the uprights over onto the top (D) and repeat this.

Cut two 10 inch lengths of stock for the feet (C), chamfer as shown, then locate them under the bottom (B). Mark where the hole is to be drilled through the feet using the bottom as a template. First countersink the hole to a depth of ⅝ inch with a 1¼ inch spade bit, then drill a hole big enough to accept the threaded rod.

Cut two pieces of stock to 8⅞ inch (part F) and one piece 9½ inch (part G) for the yoke. Lay out and cut the dovetails (see Detail), and the tenons. Place the yoke assembly on the top frame piece (D) and mark for the mortises. Groove part G and the right side part F to hide the wiring, then mortise the top of the frame (D). At this time drill and counterbore part G for the lamp nipple and locknut. The counterbore is 1 inch diameter by ⅝ inch deep. The through hole is ⅜ inch diameter.

Also, part D can now be drilled for the threaded nut of the press screw (K). It's held in place with a pair of wood screws. The frame (A, B, & D), yoke (F & G), and feet (C), along with the threaded rods (I), can now be assembled with glue. Use the threaded rods to help clamp the frame and feet. Use additional clamps for the yoke.

Next make the support plate (E) for the barrel. Cut 1 inch stock to 9⅞ inch square, and cut off the corners at 45 degrees to make the 4-1/16 octagonal sides. Mark the center, and using a router and a trammel, groove the top of the plate. A ½ inch core-box bit was used to remove the remaining stock in between the grooves. The outside diameter of the groove should measure 8¾ inches. The completed groove measures ¼ inch deep by 1½ inches wide. Groove out for the spout in the same fashion without the trammel. After sanding, attach the plate in place with two #10 x 2 inch flat head wood screws.

To make the barrel, buy two lengths of ¾ inch wide x ⅛ inch thick iron strapping (J). If your hardware store has galvanized straps, lightly sand the coating. You will be amazed how thin the coating is. Mark for eighteen holes, 1½ inches apart, starting ½ inch from one end of a three foot strap. From one inch stock cut eighteen strips (H), 1⅛ inch thick by 8 inches long. Line them up on a surface and draw lines one inch from the top and bottom, across all pieces. Drill the straps and lay one over the wood strips, lining up the top edge of the strap with the top pencil line. Attach with ¾ inch round or flat head wood screws. The other strap is attached to the bottom in the same manner.

Bend the assembly into the barrel shape, then remove the screw from the first strip. Overlay the strap so that the holes line up and screw the first strip back in place through both straps. Cut off the excess metal. Chamfer the tops of the strips with a router or a plane, and place in the groove of the support plate.

Refer to the drawing for the arrangement of the lamp parts. The cord is fed down through the nipple and into the groove in parts G & F. It then runs down the inside of part A (use double pointed tacks), and through the angled hole in part B. When installed, the shade should just cover the socket.

Give all parts a final sanding. Apply a coat of Watco Danish Oil and while wet rub on a coat of Minwax Ebony stain. The result is an attractive antique look.

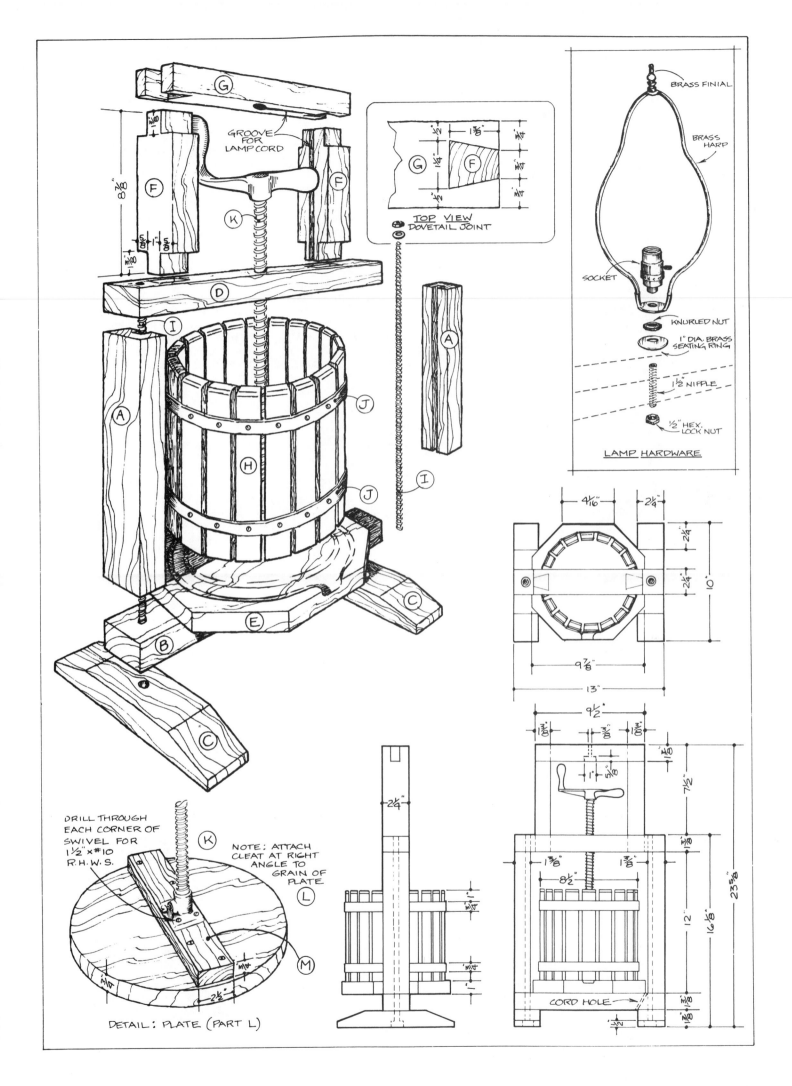

GROOVE FOR LAMP CORD

TOP VIEW
DOVETAIL JOINT

BRASS FINIAL

BRASS HARP

SOCKET

KNURLED NUT

1" DIA. BRASS
SEATING RING

1½ NIPPLE

½" HEX.
LOCK NUT

LAMP HARDWARE

DRILL THROUGH
EACH CORNER OF
SWIVEL FOR
1½" × #10
R.H.W.S.

NOTE: ATTACH
CLEAT AT RIGHT
ANGLE TO
GRAIN OF
PLATE

DETAIL: PLATE (PART L)

CORD HOLE

Firewood Rack

Readers in many parts of the country are no doubt starting to sample some of those uncomfortably chilly temperatures that come right along with the late fall season. It's a prelude to the long winter - one that many weather forecasters say will be unusually cold, not only here in New England, but also in most other areas of the country.

With those thoughts in mind, we decided a firewood rack was in order, so we designed one that could hold a pretty fair amount of wood, yet not take up the entire living room area. To save cost it's made using standard 2 by 4 construction lumber, although those who have access to oak or other hardwoods will want to consider putting them to use here. The lap joints and dowel pins make for very solid construction. Ours is sized for 18 inch logs. If you use shorter or longer logs, change dimensions to suit.

Select 2 by 4 stock that is well seasoned and free from any warp.

Avoid any with loose knots. Begin by cutting parts A, B, and C to the lengths shown. You'll need four pieces of each part. Set up a dado head cutter to make a ¾ inch deep cut, then proceed to cut the sixteen half-lap joints as shown in the exploded view. When cutting the joint in part A for the stretchers (C), make them slightly less than the width of the stretchers. Later when the stretchers are sanded, the slight reduction in width will make for a good snug fit.

Assemble the two frames (parts A & B) as shown. Use glue and clamp firmly with bar or pipe clamps to pull the edges in close contact. It's also a good idea to add a C-clamp at each corner to squeeze the lap joint faces together. Be sure to use clamp pads in conjunction with the clamps.

When dry, drill a 1 inch diameter hole through each joint to take a 1½ inch long dowel pin. Cut the pins so they protrude on each side about 1/32 of an inch. This allows them to be

sanded flush with the surface.

With a saber saw, apply the 1 inch radius to the corners, then use a router equipped with a ¼ inch piloted rounding over bit to round off all edges. Next, give all surfaces a complete sanding. Start with a grit that will remove planer marks with a minimum of effort. We started with 80 grit, then followed with 100, 150, and 220.

Use the router to round-over the outside edges of part C, but on the inside, stop the bit just short of the lap joint. Sand thoroughly, then joint to the frames with glue and clamps. Two ½ inch diameter dowel pins further secure the joint.

Final sand all parts, then stain to suit. Two coats of polyurethane varnish will provide a durable final finish. Four feet in the form of 1 inch diameter by ¾ inch long dowel pins, will help stabilize the rack on uneven floors. These feet are inserted in ⅜" deep holes so they will extend ⅜" from the bottom.

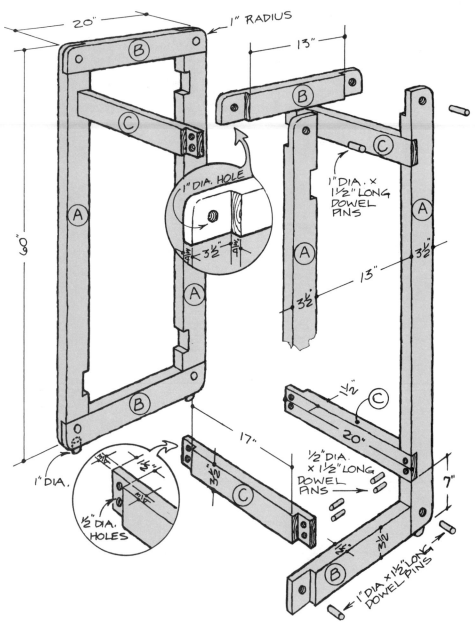

Woodpile Trivet

A firewood pile can often provide more than just BTU's on a bitter cold night. With a minimum of work, a short log can be transformed into an eye-catching trivet that's going to invite lots of compliments.

There's no hard and fast rule that dictates the size of the log, but we used one with a diameter of about 2¾ inches. Each disk was cut to a ½ inch thickness. You'll want the wood to have an interesting figure, so it may be necessary to slice a few logs to find one you like. However, be sure to use a log that's well seasoned or there will be splitting problems.

Locate the dowels 90 degrees apart, then drill 5/16 inch diameter by ⅜ inch deep holes for ¼ inch diameter dowel pins. The extra 1/16 inch hole diameter allows for any misalignment of the dowel pins. The pins are then secured in place with epoxy glue, which is fast setting and will fill any gaps in the hole. Sand both sides smooth, finishing with 220 grit, then final finish with an application of Watco Danish Oil.

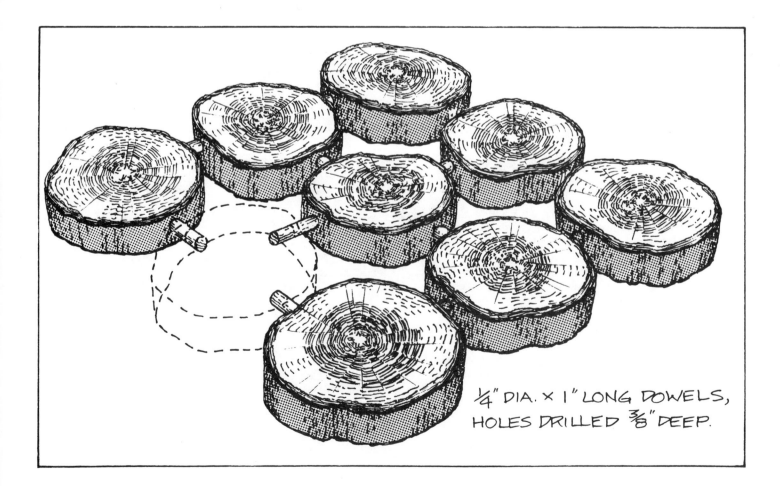

¼" DIA. × 1" LONG DOWELS, HOLES DRILLED ⅜" DEEP.

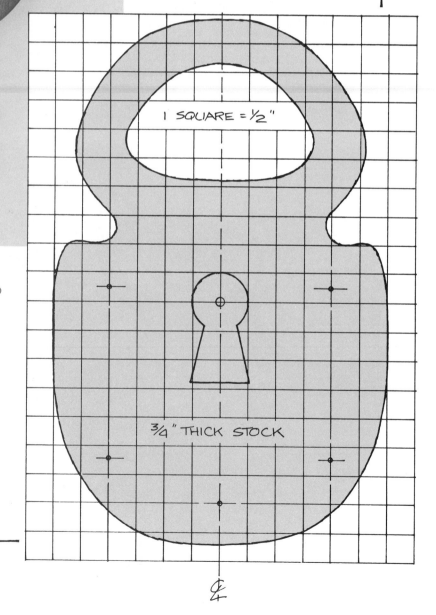

used to cut the ½ inch deep keyhole. The dovetail is cut to the same depth with a sharp chisel. We painted the bottom of the hole with a coat of flat black paint.

Give the part a complete sanding, taking care to make sure the edges are well smoothed. Two coats of polyurethane varnish will yield a durable clear final finish. Five ¾ inch brass cup hooks, available in hardware stores, will complete the project.

Secure to the wall with a wood screw through the keyhole. Paint the screw head with flat black paint.

Key Holder

This easy-to-make key rack will provide a handy place to hang the keys when you come into the house.

We used pine for ours, but just about any wood species will do. Since little stock is required, you may find your scrap box will provide plenty of material.

Cut to length and width, then transfer the pattern to the stock. Use a saber, band, or jigsaw to cut the profile. A one inch diameter spade bit is

1 SQUARE = ½"

¾" THICK STOCK

Wall Cabinet
With Reverse-Glass Stenciling

This very attractive pine cabinet owes much of its charm to the door panel which consists of a stenciled design on the back of a pane of glass. When covered with black enamel, the metallic powders used in the design catch the light and seem to glow from within.

The techniques for creating such panels are fairly simple and the materials needed are inexpensive. Once you've mastered the basics, you'll probably want to incorporate stenciled designs into many other woodworking projects.

Basically, the process of reverse-glass stenciling consists of cutting stencils and positioning them on a slightly tacky varnish surface. Using the fingertip wrapped in chamois, very fine metallic powders are rubbed on the varnish within the stencil units. The entire stenciled design is then covered with black enamel.

All of the design units used in the fruit and bowl design are shown full-size on page 91. To make stencils you only have to trace the designs on smooth paper or preferably architect's linen. The linen is semi-transparent so you can trace directly on it, dull side up, using a fine tip black felt-tip pen. Architect's linen is available at drafting supply stores. It's easy to cut and the stencils can be reused many times. When tracing, be sure to leave about 1 inch of space around each unit.

Cutting out the stencil units is best done with a pair of straight cuticle scissors sharpened right up to the tip. A small razor knife can also be used, working on a cardboard pad. After cutting the stencils, mark each unit with the color of metallic powder to be used, as shown in the key on page 91.

The metallic bronzing powders in this design are extra brilliant pale gold, extra brilliant copper and brilliant aluminum. The powders are sold in 1 oz. bottles and a bottle will last a long time since only small amounts are needed for one design.

Many stores that carry paints, wallpaper and decorating supplies also carry bronzing powders. If you cannot find them locally, or have the paint store order them for you,

they can be obtained from Wood Finishing Enterprises, 1729 North 68th St., Wauwatosa, WI 53213. They carry a full line of colors.

After the stencils have been cut, you're ready to varnish the pane of glass. Apply one coat of unthinned varnish to one side of the glass and make sure that all of the glass is covered. Finish off with the tip of the brush to pick up tiny bubbles on the surface, then set the glass aside in a dust-free place and wait for the varnish to become almost, but not quite dry. The proper stage has been reached when the surface is very slightly tacky but the fingertip leaves no mark.

On a piece of paper, pour small amounts of each of the three colored powders. The first unit to be stenciled is the bowl so place your stencil (shiny side down if architect's linen is used) on the varnished surface so that the bowl is centered as shown in the photo. It's a help to work over a black background.

Fold a piece of chamois (or velvet) around your index finger so that the tip is smoothly covered. Pick up a *very* small amount of gold powder with the fingertips and, with a *light circular* touch, apply the powder around the edges of the stencil. Take up more powder as needed and try to keep the brightest areas near the edges. After the brightest parts are done, go over them with more pressure to burnish the powder. Lift the stencil carefully, taking care to keep stray specks of powder off other areas of the glass.

The other units of the drawing are added in much the same way using the indicated colors. Note that the fruit and leaf units are not covered completely with powder but rather, the powder is applied around the edges of the stencil and allowed to fade. Separate stencils are used for the centers of flowers and the grapes and leaves are done by simply moving one or two single stencils around.

When the design has been completed, set it aside to dry for a few days; then cover the entire stenciled surface with flat black enamel from a spray can. If your first attempt is not quite right, you can clean the glass off with turpentine and try it again.

The cabinet sides (¾ x 6½ x 15¼) can be cut to size from standard 1 x 8 stock. Try to select good flat stock that has a pleasing figure. Referring to the drawing, lay out the locations of the holes for the shelf support pins, then bore holes to a depth of ⅜ inch. Next, cut the top (¾ x 6½ x 12¼) to length and width, then set up the dado head to cut the ¼ by ⅜ inch rabbet for the back panel as shown. Also, at this time cut the two rabbets in the side pieces.

The base is cut to size (¾ x 7 x 14), then a router equipped with a ⅜ inch rounding-over bit (piloted) is used to apply a bead to the front and sides.

After cutting the rail (¾ x 2 x 11½) to size, give all parts a complete sanding. The case can be assembled as shown. Use glue on all joints and clamp securely. Six counterbored wood screws secure the base. The ¼ inch plywood back can now be cut to fit.

The molding (see detail) can be purchased at most lumberyards. Miter the two corners and join to the case with glue and countersunk finishing nails.

All door rails and stiles are ¾ inch thick and 1¼ inches wide. A tenon jig used in conjunction with the table saw will simplify cutting the four slip joints. Take care when cutting the joints so they result in a good snug fit. Assemble with glue and clamps. When dry, use a ⅜ inch rabbet bit (piloted) to cut the door rabbet. The router bit will leave rounded corners which can be cleaned up with a sharp chisel.

Cut the adjustable shelf to size (¾ x 5½ x 11⅜) before giving the entire project a thorough sanding. Ours was stained with two coats of Minwax Golden Oak finish followed by an application of Watco Danish Oil. Four strips of ¼ inch quarter round molding, mitered at the corners are tacked in place to secure the glass.

(continued on next page)

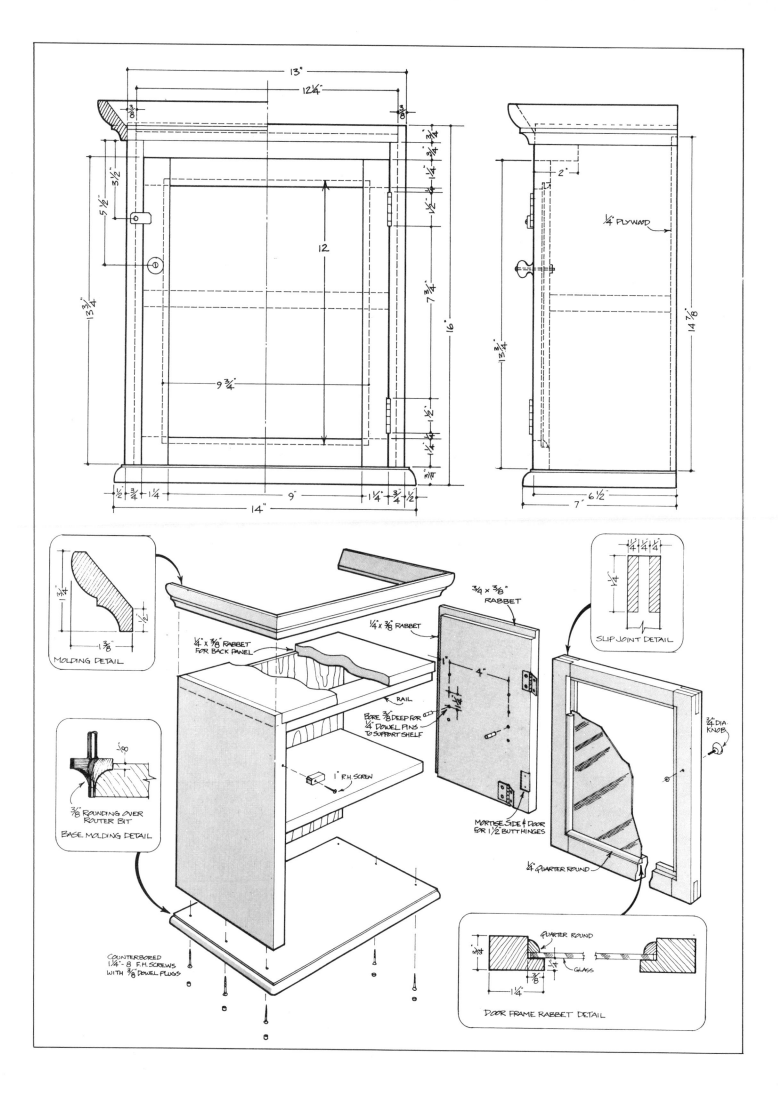

13"

12¼"

³⁄₈

³⁄₈

3½

5½

13¾"

13¾

9¾"

14"

½ ¾ 1¼

9"

1¼ ¾ ½

¾ ¾
¼
½

7¾

16"

¼ ½
¼
³⁄₈

¼ PLYWOOD

2"

13¾

14⅞

7" 6½"

MOLDING DETAIL

3¾

½

1³⁄₈

¹⁄₈

³⁄₈ ROUNDING OVER
ROUTER BIT

BASE MOLDING DETAIL

COUNTERBORED
1¼"-8 F.H. SCREWS
WITH ³⁄₈ DOWEL PLUGS

¼ × ³⁄₈ RABBET
FOR BACK PANEL

¼ × ³⁄₈ RABBET

RAIL

1" R.H. SCREW

¾ × ³⁄₈"
RABBET

4"

1¼

BORE ³⁄₈ DEEP FOR
¼ DOWEL PINS
TO SUPPORT SHELF

MORTISE SIDE & DOOR
FOR 1½ BUTT HINGES

¼ ¼ ¼

¼

SLIP JOINT DETAIL

¾" DIA.
KNOB

¼ QUARTER ROUND

QUARTER ROUND

¾

¼

³⁄₈

1¼

GLASS

DOOR FRAME RABBET DETAIL

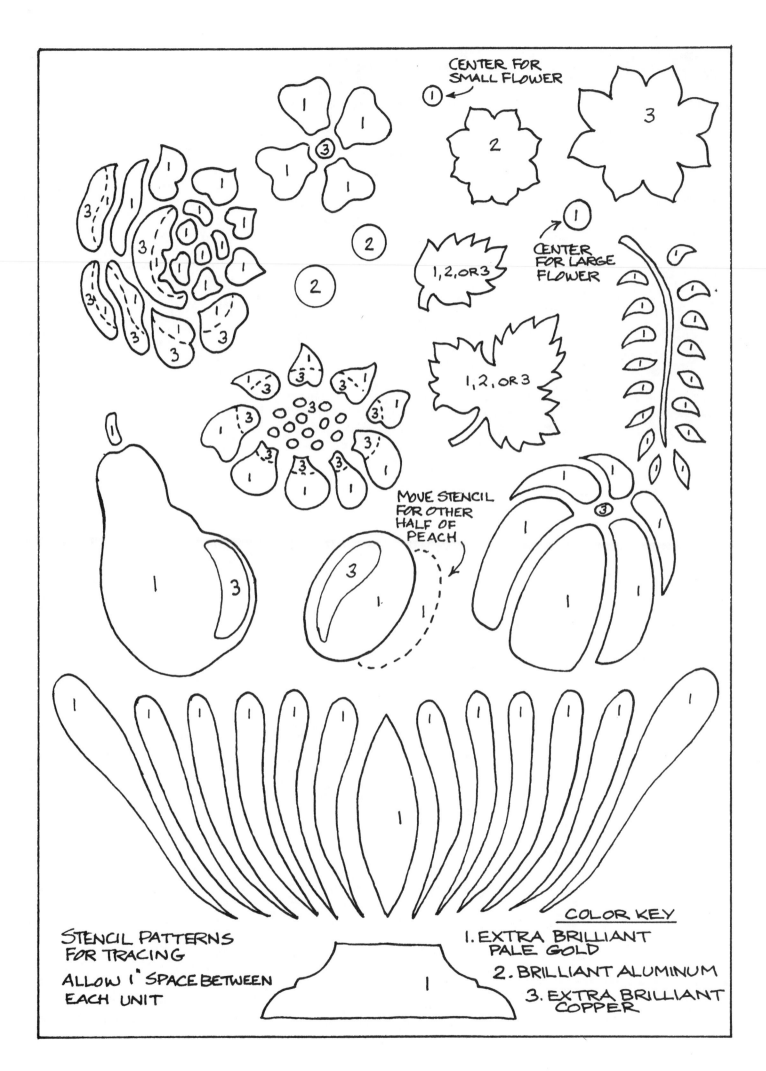

CENTER FOR
SMALL FLOWER

CENTER
FOR LARGE
FLOWER

MOVE STENCIL
FOR OTHER
HALF OF
PEACH

STENCIL PATTERNS
FOR TRACING

ALLOW 1" SPACE BETWEEN
EACH UNIT

COLOR KEY
1. EXTRA BRILLIANT
   PALE GOLD
2. BRILLIANT ALUMINUM
3. EXTRA BRILLIANT
   COPPER

Pine Cabinet

This small early American style cabinet can be put to use in just about any room in the house, especially if some extra storage space is needed. It's made from number two common pine, to keep costs to a minimum, although almost any kind of wood can also be used.

The two front pieces (parts A) can be made first. Cut to the length and width as shown in the Bill of Materials, checking to be sure all cuts are square. The ⅜ by ¾ inch rabbet can best be cut with a dado head cutter, but if you don't have one, repeated passes with a table or radial arm sawblade will produce satisfactory results. The 1½ inch bottom radius can be cut with a band or saber saw.

Next, the sides (parts B) can be cut to length and width. Referring to the drawing, lay out and mark the location of the ⅜ by ⅜ inch dadoes for the shelf (G) and the bottom (F). Cut out using the dado head cutter or use the repeated pass technique. Note that part B also has a ¼ by ⅜ inch rabbet along the inside back edge to take the back (part I).

The bottom (part F) and the shelf (part G) are identical parts. Cut to size, then apply the ⅜ by ⅜ inch rabbet on each end as shown. Try to cut the rabbet for a tight fit in the side (B) dado. Later, when parts F & G are sanded, a good snug fit should result.

The top (Part H) is made from ¾ inch thick stock cut to a width of 12¾ inches and a length of 31½ inches. If you can't get stock that's at least 12¾

inches wide, it will be necessary to edge-glue two or more narrower boards. Three or four ¼ inch diameter by 1½ inch long dowel pins in each edge-joint will make it easier to align the boards. Apply a thin coat of glue to each edge, then clamp firmly with bar or pipe clamps. Allow to dry thoroughly.

Note that the back edge of part H has a ¼ x ⅜ rabbet that's stopped at a point 1⅛ inch from the corner. Later, the back (part I) will fit into this rabbet. This cut can best be made using a router equipped with a ¼ inch piloted rabbet bit. The cut will be round where it is stopped, but this can quickly be squared-up with a sharp chisel.

Knotty pine plywood is a good choice for the back (part I), although fir plywood can also be used, especially if the cabinet is to be located where the back can't be seen.

The door components, parts C, D, and E, can be made next. Both the stiles (C) and rails (D) are made from ¾ inch stock ripped to a 2½ inch width. Note also that both parts require a ¼ inch wide by ⅜ inch deep groove along their inside edge. A dado head cutter can cut this groove, although two or three passes with the table or radial arm saw will also do the job.

The tenon on each end of parts D can be cut by using any of several methods, but perhaps the easiest one is to use a table saw tenon jig. With the saw blade set to a height of one inch, adjust the jig to cut the ¼ inch wide tenon.

A ¼ inch mortising chisel will make quick work of the mortise in part C. Make it slightly deeper than one inch to allow for any excess glue or wood chips.

The large center panel (E) is made of ¾ inch stock although ½ inch material can also be used if it's available. Like the top, the panel will probably require edge-gluing in order to get enough width. The gluing techniques are the same.

Cut the panel to length and width, then use the dado head to make the ¼ by ⅜ inch rabbet as shown. This step is not necessary if ½ inch stock is used. The bevel can be cut on the table saw with the blade tilted to about 8 degrees. Adjust the rip-fence to properly locate the bevel, then pass the stock, on edge, over the blade. When you approach the end of each cut, make sure the panel is firmly supported at the back of the table to avoid any tendency for the stock to dip into the blade.

Give all parts a thorough sanding, then assemble as shown using glue and clamps. Join parts A to B first. Allow glue to dry, then drill holes and add the dowel pins. Next, assemble parts G and F, again adding dowels after the glue has dried. The top (part H) can now be secured to the case with glue and dowel pins as shown. The back (I) is now added with glue and finishing nails.

The door components are assembled at one time. The mortise and tenon joints are glued, but the panel (E) is not. It must be free to expand and contract with changes in humidity.

The 1½ inch brass butt hinges are mortised into both the front (A) and the door stile (C). The knob can be turned to the shape shown, although a similar profile can be found in most hardware stores. The small turnbutton (J) will serve to keep the door closed.

Give all parts a final sanding, then stain and finish to suit. We applied two coats of Minwax's Golden Oak Wood Finish followed by an application of their Antique Oil Finish.

Bill of Materials (All Dimensions Actual)			
Part	Description	Size	No. Req'd
A	Front	¾ x 5 x 22¼	2
B	Side	¾ x 11⅜ x 22¼	2
C	Stile	¾ x 2½ x 20¾	2
D	Rail	¾ x 2½ x 17	2
E	Panel	¾ x 15½ x 16¼	1
F	Bottom	¾ x 11 x 29¼	1
G	Shelf	¾ x 11 x 29¼	1
H	Top	¾ x 12¾ x 31½	1
I	Back	¼ x 29¼ x 20⅞	1
J	Turnbutton	See Detail	1
K	Knob	See Detail	1

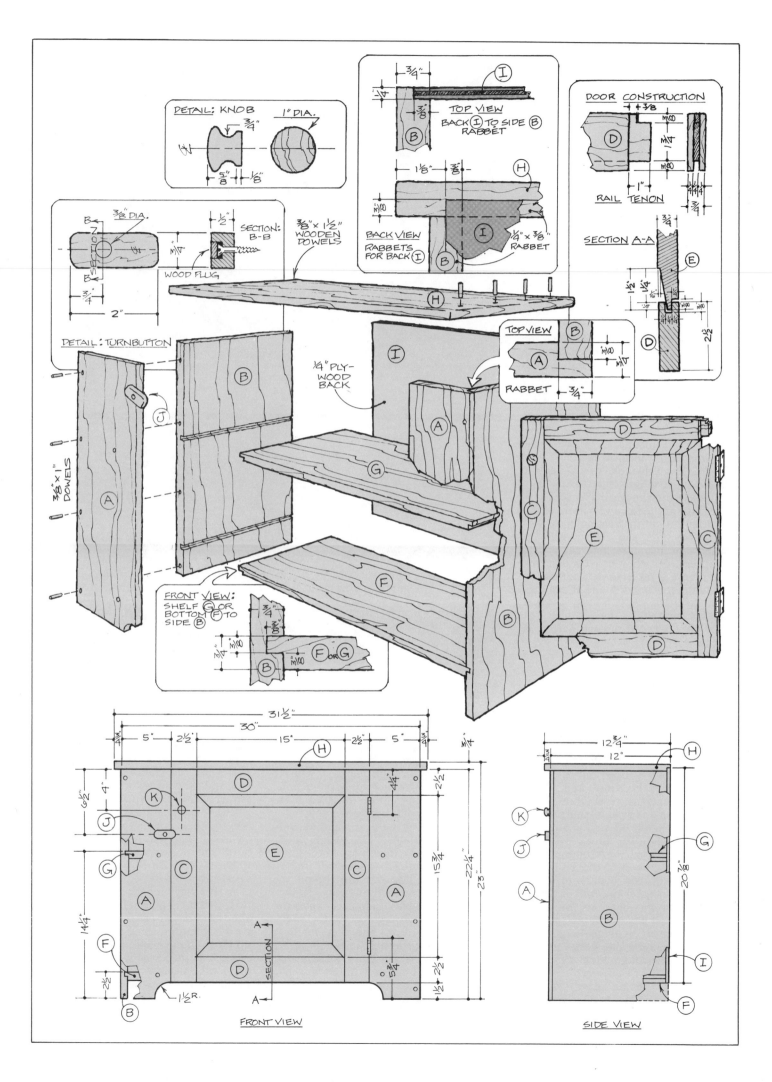

DETAIL: KNOB

1" DIA.

3/4"

5/8" 1/8"

SECTION: B-B

3/8" DIA.

B

1/2"

WOOD PLUG

3/4"

2"

DETAIL: TURNBUTTON

J

A

3/8" x 1" DOWELS

B

3/8" x 1 1/2" WOODEN DOWELS

H

1/4" PLY-WOOD BACK

I

G

A

F

FRONT VIEW: SHELF G OR BOTTOM F TO SIDE B

3/4"

3/8"

3/4"

B

F or G

TOP VIEW BACK I TO SIDE B RABBET

3/4"

3/8"

B

I

H

1 1/8" 3/8"

3/8"

BACK VIEW RABBETS FOR BACK I

B

1/4" x 3/8" RABBET

TOP VIEW

B

A

RABBET 3/4"

DOOR CONSTRUCTION

3/8

D

RAIL TENON

1"

3/4

SECTION A-A

3/4

E

1/2 1/4

D

2 1/2

D

C

E

B

C

D

FRONT VIEW

31 1/2"

30"

3/4" 5" 2 1/2" 15" 2 1/2" 5" 3/4"

H

D

K

J

G

C

A

F

E

C

A

D

A

B

1 1/2"R

4"

6 1/2"

14 1/4"

2 1/2"

4 1/4

2 1/2

15 3/4"

22 1/4"

25"

5 3/4

2 1/2

1 1/2

SECTION

SIDE VIEW

12 3/4"

12"

3/4

H

K

J

A

G

B

I

F

20 7/8"

Nautical Table Lamp

Resembling the heavy block and tackle rigs that were common to all old-time sailing ships, this handsome pine lamp has a look that is unquestionably nautical. It requires only standard 4/4 (¾ inch thick) and 5/4 (1⅛ inch thick) stock, and since construction is fairly basic, even the novice woodworker should be able to build it with little difficulty.

Begin by making the two outer shells (parts A) and the inner shell (part B). For each part cut 5/4 stock (which actually measures 1⅛ in. thick) to seven inches wide by nine inches long, then transfer the shape of the oval pattern from the grid pattern to the stock. On the two parts A, also mark the location of the one inch diameter center hole. On part B, mark the location of the ½ in. wide by five in. long slot and the ⅜ in. top and bottom hole. By the way, this slot simply serves as a means to shorten the length of the ⅜ in. drill hole. Without the slot, the drill hole would have to run the entire length of part B.

To make the slot, drill a ½ inch diameter hole at the top and bottom of the slot, then cut out the remaining material with the saber saw. The ⅜ inch top and bottom holes are best cut with a drill press, but they can be done by hand if care is taken to insure that the hole is square. Parts A and B can now be cut to shape using a band or saber saw. Following this, the one inch diameter hole is bored in each part A as shown.

Parts C and D are made from ¾ inch thick stock. Transfer the shape from the grid pattern, then cut out and give all edges a good sanding. Although it is possible to glue and clamp the entire block assembly at once, we found it easier to first assemble parts C and D to part A. At this point we also checked the rope for an easy sliding fit. When dry, these two sub-assemblies were joined to part B. Glue and clamp securely at each stage. Before gluing though, drive a couple of short brads, then clip the heads off so that about ⅛ inch is exposed. The brads will keep the mating parts from sliding when clamped. Just be sure the brads are not in line with the location of the ½ inch dowel pin holes that will be drilled later to join the base to the shell. When the shell has dried, cut one inch diameter dowel plugs to length and glue in place in the side holes. Cut the plugs slightly long, then sand the excess flush.

The base is made from 1⅛ inch stock cut to seven inches wide and nine inches long. A compass is used to scribe a 1¼ inch radius at each corner. This radius is then cut out with a band

or saber saw. A shallow cove is applied all around with a piloted ⅜ inch cove bit. Locate and mark the centerpoint on the underside of the base, then drill a one inch diameter by ¾ inch deep hole. At the centerpoint of this hole, finish boring through the base with a ½ inch diameter drill bit. Connecting the one inch hole to the back edge of the base is a ¼ inch diameter hole.

On the top of the base, lay out and mark the location of the two ½ inch diameter by 1¼ inch long dowel pins that secure the base to the shell. Drive a short brad into the centerpoint of each hole location, then clip off the heads so that about ⅛ inch is exposed. Sand a slight flat area across the shell bottom, then center the shell on the base. Be sure the hole in the base is aligned with the slot in the shell, then carefully press the shell to the base so that the brad points mark the shell bottom. Now separate the shell from the base and remove the brads with a pair of pliers. Using the brad holes as centers, drill 11/16 inch deep holes to

accept the ½ inch diameter dowel pins. Also at this time, locate and drill the four holes for the rope ends.

Give all parts a thorough sanding, particularly the edges of the shell, then assemble the shell to the base. Use glue and clamp firmly. Stain to suit and final finish with two coats of polyurethane varnish.

Cut ¾ inch diameter rope (hemp) to length, taking care to tape the ends tightly before cutting. Insert in the holes and glue in place. If necessary, a finishing nail can be added to further secure each rope end.

A five inch length of ⅛ inch I.P. threaded lamp pipe is inserted into the shell to a depth of ¾ inch. The lamp cord is then fed through the base and up through the shell and out the lamp pipe. A ⅝ inch spacer and 4 inch long brass tube slip over the lamp pipe. The harp is added and the cord is connected to the socket. The socket then threads to the top of the lamp pipe. The addition of a bulb and lamp shade completes the project.

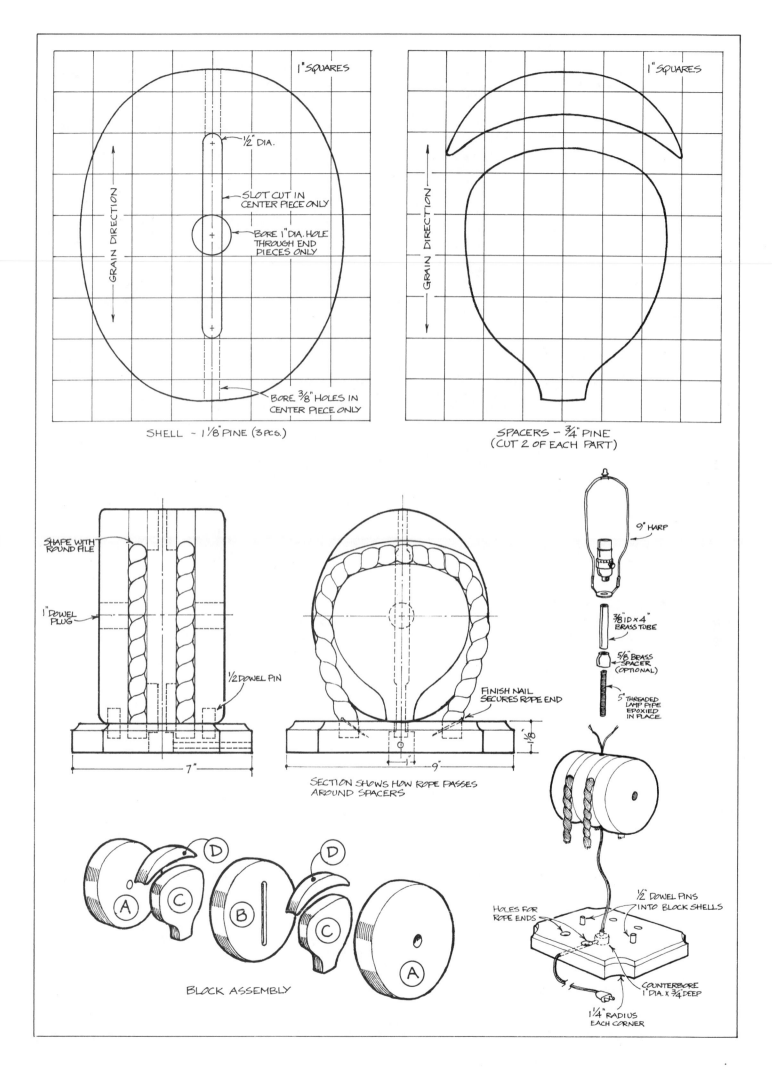

1" SQUARES

½" DIA.

SLOT CUT IN
CENTER PIECE ONLY

BORE 1" DIA. HOLE
THROUGH END
PIECES ONLY

GRAIN DIRECTION

BORE ⅜" HOLES IN
CENTER PIECE ONLY

SHELL – 1⅛" PINE (3 PCS.)

1" SQUARES

GRAIN DIRECTION

SPACERS – ¾" PINE
(CUT 2 OF EACH PART)

SHAPE WITH
ROUND FILE

1" DOWEL
PLUG

½" DOWEL PIN

7"

FINISH NAIL
SECURES ROPE END

SECTION SHOWS HOW ROPE PASSES
AROUND SPACERS

1"

9"

⅛"

9" HARP

⅜" ID x 4"
BRASS TUBE

⅝" BRASS
SPACER
(OPTIONAL)

5" THREADED
LAMP PIPE
EPOXIED
IN PLACE

D

A

C

B

D

C

A

BLOCK ASSEMBLY

HOLES FOR
ROPE ENDS

½" DOWEL PINS
INTO BLOCK SHELLS

COUNTERBORE
1" DIA. x ¾" DEEP

¼" RADIUS
EACH CORNER

Balance

Occasionally it's fun to make something that doesn't really have a function other than to be purely decorative. Undoubtedly, this project falls into that category. However, we've found one thing it can do, and that is generate quite a bit of conversation. More than likely you'll be asked if it actually works. If made carefully, the answer is yes - it's a reasonably accurate balance.

The base (B) and the scales (D) can best be made by faceplate turning the stock, although it's also possible to make both parts with a router. If a router is used, part B must be made from two pieces of stock, one piece 1 in. thick, the other ¾ in. thick. The two pieces are glued up after the routing is completed on each piece.

Because we lathe turned ours, we used maple stock in order to take advantage of its excellent turning qualities. Cherry would be another good choice.

Begin by making the base (part B). Cut 1¾ in. thick stock to seven inches square, then scribe corner to corner diagonal lines to locate the centerpoint. From this centerpoint use a compass to scribe three circles, the first to match the diameter of your faceplate (ours was 6 in. dia.), the second to 6½ in. diameter, and the third to 6¾ in. diameter. Next, use a band or saber saw to cut the stock to the 6¾ in. diameter circle.

With the scribed circle as a centering guide, the faceplate can now be screwed to the stock and then the entire unit attached to the lathe. Use the gouge to true up the stock, turning it down to the scribed 6½ in. diameter circle. With the lathe still turning, use a pencil to mark a line one inch from the faceplate. Keeping this one inch thickness, use the parting tool to make a ½ in. deep cut. Working left to right, continue making ½ in. deep cuts until a ¾ in. wide step is formed. Next, use a pencil to mark a line establishing the ¼ in. step for the ½ in. radius cove, then use a gouge or round-nose scraper to form the cove. The ½ in. outside radius can now be applied with the skew.

With the stock still in the lathe, give it a thorough sanding. Start with 100 grit aluminum oxide paper to remove any rough turning marks. Follow this with 150, then 220 grit. Remove the base from the faceplate and fill the screw holes with wood filler.

On the top surface of the base, lay out and mark the location of the ⅜ in. thick by 1½ in. wide by 1-5/16 in. deep mortise. Most of the mortise can be cut by drilling a series of holes with a ⅜ in. drill bit. The remaining waste stock can be removed with a sharp

chisel. Note that the mortise is cut slightly deeper than the tenon length to allow room for any excess glue.

To make the scales (part D), cut ¾ in. thick stock to 4½ in. square, then scribe corner to corner diagonal lines to locate the centerpoint. From this centerpoint use a compass to scribe two circles, one measuring 3¾ in. diameter, the other measuring 4 in. diameter. Use a band or saber saw to cut out to the 4 in. diameter.

Since the underside of the scales can be seen, the faceplate can't be screwed directly to the scale. If it is, the unsightly filled screw holes will show. Instead the faceplate is screwed to a backing block which is then glued (with paper in between to allow easy removal) to the scale. To make the backing block, cut ¾ in. thick stock (pine is suitable) to 3½ in. square. Scribe diagonal lines to locate the center then use the compass to scribe two circles, the first to match the diameter of your faceplate (ours was 3 in. diameter), the second to 3¼ in. diameter. Now use the band or saber saw to cut the backing block stock to the 3¼ in. diameter.

At this point, to aid when centering the backing block on the scale, it's a

good idea to add a 3¼ in. diameter circle to the scale stock. With a piece of heavy (brown grocery bag) paper in between, glue (with wood glue) the backing block to the scale stock, taking care to center it on the scribed circle. The two parts will have a tendency to slide over each other so before gluing drive two small brads into the scale stock, then clip off the heads so about ⅛ in. is exposed. Just make sure the brads are located a safe distance from where the turning tools will cut. When dry the faceplate can be screwed to the backing block and then the entire unit attached to the lathe.

To insure that the stock rotates smoothly it's a good idea to first true up the backing block using the parting tool. Use the gouge to true up the scale stock, turning it down to the scribed 3¾ in. diameter. A ½ in. gouge will do a good job of rounding the outside edge to the profile shown on the drawing. In order to shape the entire curve, though, it will be necessary to partially cut into the backing block.

Next, arrange the tool rest so that it faces the face surface of the stock. To dish out the scale, begin by using a pencil to mark a 3⅜ in. diameter on the turned stock. This establishes the diameter of the dished-out area. With this line as a guide, use a parting tool to make a ¼ in. deep cut. Working toward the center from this groove, use a ½ in. gouge to remove the remaining material. Sand completely using the same procedure as was used for the base. Remove the stock from the lathe. Now remove the faceplate, then use a chisel and mallet to knock off the backing block. Sand off the remaining paper before drilling three ⅛ in. chain holes located 120 degrees apart.

The post (part C) is cut to 1⅛ in. wide by 12½ in. long. The tenon can be cut in a variety of ways, but we chose to use the dado head in conjunction with the table saw. No matter what method you choose though, make sure the tenon fits snugly in the base mortise. The ¼ in. wide notch for the beam (A) can also be cut in a variety of ways. We used a tenon jig. With the table saw blade set for a height of 2⅛ in., the notch was cut with three or four passes over the blade. Next, use a ruler to scribe the top to bottom taper, then a smooth or jack plane to cut to shape. Add the ¼ in. chamfer with a file or drawknife.

The beam (A) is made next. If you don't have ¼ in. thick stock it can be resawn from thicker stock on the band or table saw. Transfer the grid pattern shown, then cut to shape. A ⅛ in. ring hole is added at each end.

Sand part A so that it pivots freely in the post notch. A ¼ in. dowel pin is glued in place and sanded flush with the surface. Several coats of Deftco Danish Oil produces a nice finish.

We used brass cafe curtain rings and light brass chain available at most hardware stores. The links were opened to fit in the scale holes, then closed over. A piece of felt, glued to the bottom, completes the project.

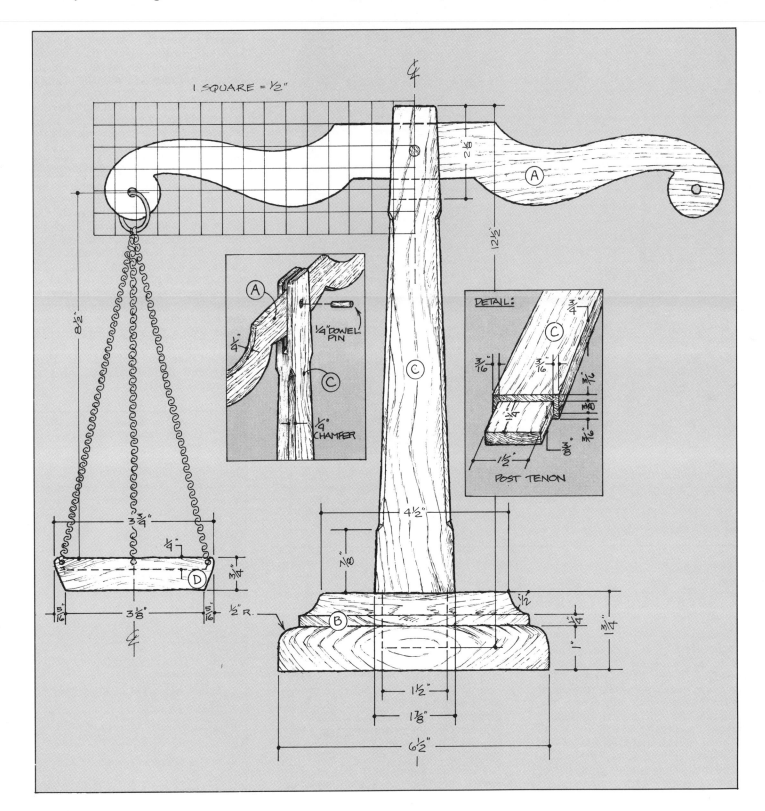

Punched Tin Spice Cabinet

Made from pine, this small piece makes a handsome and versatile cabinet for home or apartment. The pierced tin panels provide a nice detail and can be made with little effort. The project requires only a small amount of lumber so you may find your scrap box will yield enough material. And if you don't have enough scraps around, it can be made from the judicious use of a six foot length of 1 x 8 stock.

The two sides (A) are cut to length and width, and a ½ inch wide by ¼ inch deep dado is cut into each to accept the bottom (D) as shown. Next, referring to the drawing, drill five pairs of ¼ inch diameter by ¼ inch deep holes in each side for the shelf adjusting pegs. The bottom (D) and shelf (E) can now be cut to size.

The base (B) and top (C) are cut from ¾ inch thick stock and a molding applied to the front and sides. To make the molding, use a ⅜ inch rounding-over bit with pilot to apply the ⅜ inch radius and ⅛ inch step. The ¼ inch radius is applied with a file or Surform tool.

Now assemble the top, base, sides, and bottom, checking to be certain that the cabinet is square. Note that counterbored 1 x #6 flat head wood screws secure the top and base to each side. Make sure that the bottom is flush with the sides at the front. Plug your screw holes, and sand the plugs off flush after the glue has dried.

Next, use a ¼ inch bearing guided rabbeting bit, set for a ¼ inch depth, to rout the ¼ in. x ¼ in. rabbet all around the back of the cabinet to accept the back (F). Note that where the bottom sets into the sides, you'll need to stop and then restart the rabbet, since the bottom will interfere with the bearing. However, as the dado for the bottom is also ¼ in. deep, you shouldn't have to do much cleaning up to keep the rabbet consistent. A little hand work with the chisel will square the corners to accept the square back, or as an alternate you could round the corners of the back to match the radius of your rabbeting bit.

Select good flat stock for the door rails (H), stiles (G) and divider (I). Cut to size and check their fit to the cabinet opening. Next, cut a ¼ inch deep by 1 inch wide lap joint on the ends of all pieces and a ¼ inch deep by 1 inch wide dado centered halfway up the back of the stiles to accept the divider as shown. Glue and clamp the frame and check for squareness. When dry, use a router with a ¼ inch piloted rabbet bit to cut $^5/_{16}$ inch deep recesses for the tin panels (J) in the inside of the door frame and divider. Use a chisel to square the corners.

Bill of Materials
(All Dimensions Actual)

Part	Description	Size	No. Req'd
A	Side	½ x 6 x 16½	2
B	Base	¾ x 6⅞ x 10¾	1
C	Top	¾ x 6⅞ x 10¾	1
D	Bottom	½ x 5¾ x 9	1
E	Shelf	½ x 5¼ x 8½	1
F	Back	¼ x 9 x 17	1
G	Door Stiles	½ x 1 x 13	2
H	Door Rails	½ x 1 x 8½	2
I	Door Divider	½ x 1 x 8½	1
J	Tin Panel	.010 x 5½ x 7	2
K	Door Knob	⅝ in. ceramic	1
L	Turnbutton	(see detail)	1
M	Drawer Front	⅝ x 3 x 8½	1
N	Drawer Sides	½ x 3 x 5¼	2
O	Drawer Back	½ x 2½ x 7⅞	1
P	Drawer Bottom	¼ x 5$^5/_{16}$ x 7¾	1
Q	Drawer Knob	¾ in. ceramic	1
R	Molding	¼ in. quarter round	As Req'd
S	Drawer Stop	¼ x ¾ x 1½	1

Cut the drawer (parts M, N, O and P) to dimensions shown then cut a ⅜ inch deep by ⁹⁄₁₆ inch wide rabbet on each side of the front to accept the sides as shown. Cut a ¼ inch deep by ½ inch wide dado ¼ inch from the back end of each side to fit back (O). With a ¼ inch straight router bit or with the dado head, cut a slot ¼ inch deep by ¼ inch wide on the inside of the front and sides to accept the bottom. Note that the back fits flush with the sides at the top and rests on the bottom (P).

Assemble the drawer parts as shown. Nail the sides to the front with small finishing nails. Clamp securely and check for squareness. Next, cut the turnbutton, drawer stop, molding for tin panels and ¼ inch diameter by ¾ inch long shelf pegs. Glue the drawer stop in position on the base as shown.

Mount the door to the cabinet with two 1 inch by 1 inch loose pin brass hinges. Remove the hinges, sand, and stain the door and all other parts with one coat of Minwax Golden Oak Stain (No. 210B) and finish with Watco Danish Oil. Add the shelf, then secure the back with small finishing nails. Apply the turnbutton with a 1 x #6 brass flat head wood screw. The tin panels are held into place with ¼ inch quarter round molding tacked into place. Finally, mount the door and affix the ceramic knobs to the door and drawer.

Tin for the panels (J) can be purchased via mail-order from Country Accents, P.O. Box 437, Montoursville, PA 17754. Write to them for price and ordering information.

If desired, the tin can be made to have an antique finish, much like the look of pewter. Working in one direction only use very fine (220 grit) garnet or aluminum oxide paper and give the sheet a thorough sanding. Use even pressure and continue sanding until the bright shine is dulled. You'll find it easier to hold the tin if you place it on a rubber sink mat.

Next, wash the tin and dry it thoroughly, then place it in a shallow non-metallic container — a glass baking disk or plastic dish pan will do fine. Add vinegar to the dish until the tin is covered with about ¼ inch of vinegar. The longer the tin soaks in the vinegar, the darker it will get, but we found that 6-8 hours gives good results. If you have a small piece of scrap tin, it's not a bad idea to use it for a test. When you are satisfied with the results, remove the tin, then wash thoroughly and dry.

Now transfer the full-size pattern to the tin and place the panel on a scrap board for piercing. A variety of tools can be used for piercing — awls, nailsets, screwdrivers, even square flooring nails. Each tool imparts its own distinctive mark when struck with a hammer. For this project we used a ¹⁄₃₂ inch nailset to punch the holes to about ¹⁄₁₆ in. diameter. The holes were spaced about ⅛ in. apart.

PATTERN
PIERCED TIN DESIGN: FULL SIZE

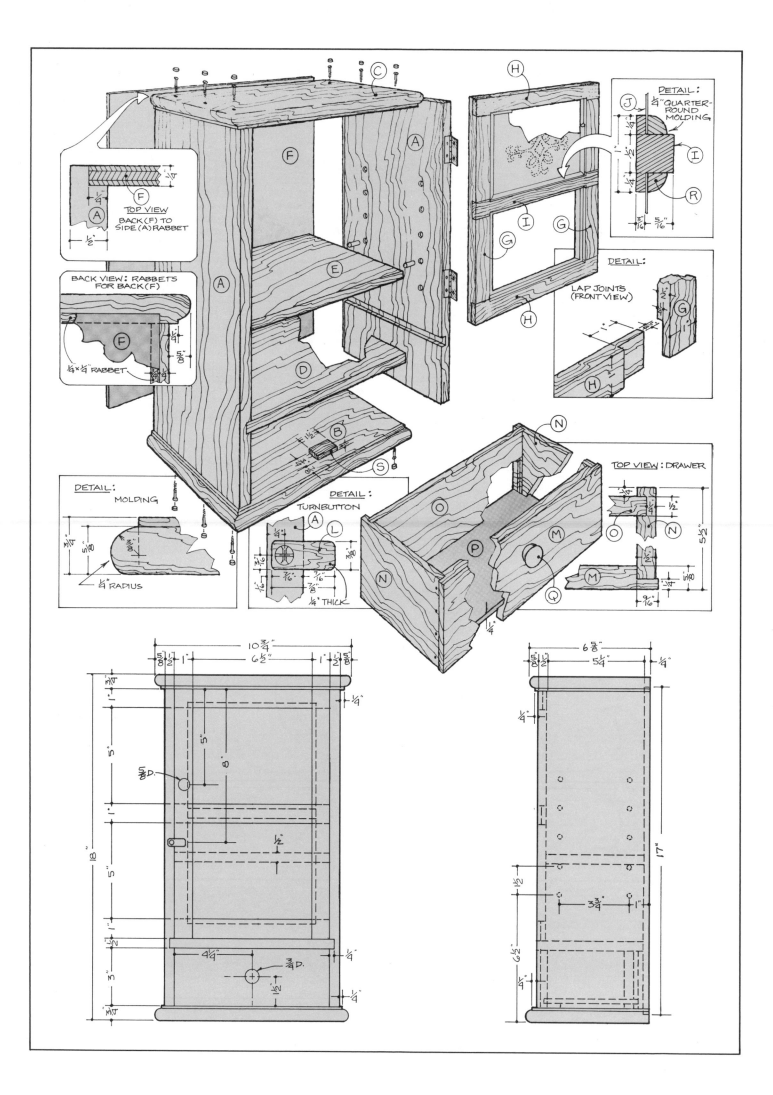

DETAIL: ¼" QUARTER-ROUND MOLDING

TOP VIEW BACK (F) TO SIDE (A) RABBET

BACK VIEW: RABBETS FOR BACK (F)

¼ × ⅜ RABBET

DETAIL: LAP JOINTS (FRONT VIEW)

DETAIL: MOLDING

¼" RADIUS

DETAIL: TURNBUTTON

¼" THICK

TOP VIEW: DRAWER

Mailbox

A minimum of stock and a few evenings in the workshop are all that's needed to construct this sturdy mailbox. Ours is made from pine, but cedar is also a good choice, especially if it will be exposed to the weather. To help keep rain from getting inside we've added a cove along the cleat (F) and inset the back (C) and cleat so that rain traveling down the outside of a building will run behind the mailbox. For further weather-proofing, it's important to use brass hinges, galvanized nails and a water-resistant glue such as the plastic resin type.

Begin by cutting the two sides (A) to size (¾ x 7 x 12½). The tapered top edge is cut at an angle of 16 degrees on the table or radial-arm saw. Transfer the pattern of the curve to the stock before cutting out with a band or saber saw.

Next, cut the front, part B, to ¾ x 6¼ x 14, the bottom, part D, to ¾ x 5¼ x 14, and the back, part C, to ¾ x 8 x 14. Two or more narrower boards will probably have to be edge-glued in order to get enough width for part C. Note that a 16 degree bevel is applied to the top edge of parts B and C.

To cut the cove in part F, it's best to start with a wide piece of stock. Clamp a guidestrip to the stock, then rout the cove using a ½ inch core box bit. Now, with the table or radial-arm saw blade set at 16 degrees, rip part F to the width shown.

After cutting the top (E) to size, give all the parts a thorough sanding. Assemble with plastic resin glue and finishing nails, countersunk and filled. Stain to suit, then finish with three coats of spar varnish.

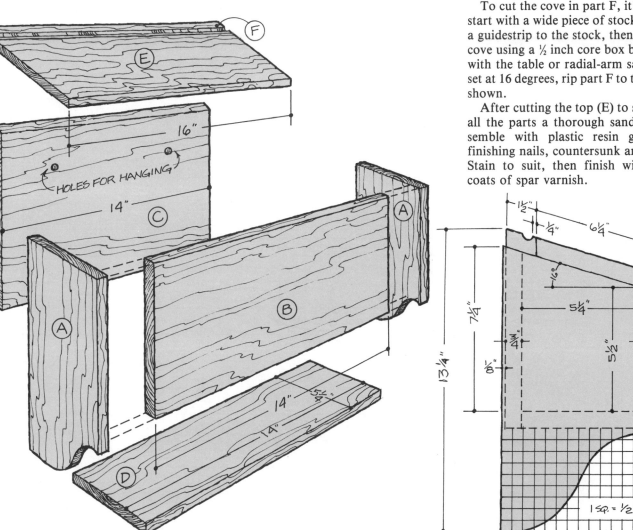

With its nicely shaped scroll pattern, this easy-to-build pine wall shelf will make an attractive addition to just about any room in the house.

The back can be made first. Since a 9 in. wide piece of stock is required, it will be necessary to edge-glue two or more narrower boards. To prevent the edges from sliding when clamped, it's a good idea to include two or three ¼ in. diameter dowel pins in the joint. Apply glue to the edges, then clamp firmly and allow to dry overnight.

Transfer the scroll pattern from the drawing to the stock, then cut out with a band or saber saw. Give the edges a thorough sanding. If you have one, a drum sander will be helpfull here. After smoothing the edge, use a router equipped with a ⅜ in. piloted cove bit to apply a cove all around the outside edge.

The shelf can be made next. If necessary glue up narrower boards, then transfer the grid pattern to the stock. Again, sand the edges and apply the cove detail.

Next, cut the bracket to the shape shown, then lay out and mark the location of the ⅜ in. dowel pins. Give all parts a thorough sanding before staining to suit. When dry, assemble with glue and clamp firmly. Use just a thin coat of glue in order to keep glue squeeze-out to a minimum. Allow to dry overnight. Final finish with two coats of polyurethane varnish, sanding lightly between each coat. Two angled holes drilled through the back and into the shelf provide a convenient means to hang the shelf.

Pine Wall Shelf

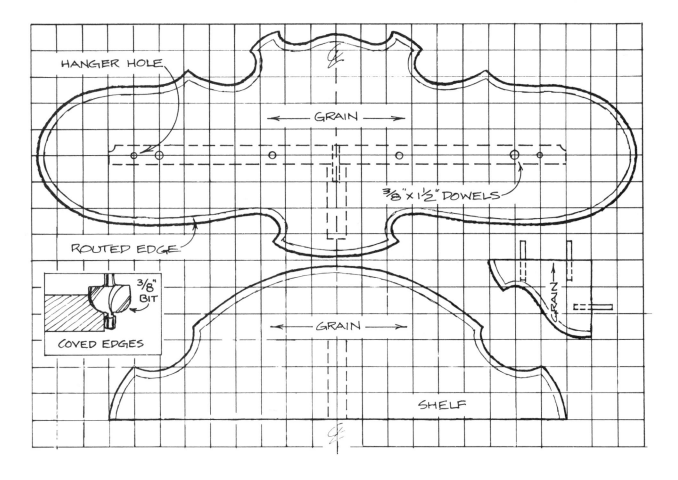

Mirror with Shelf

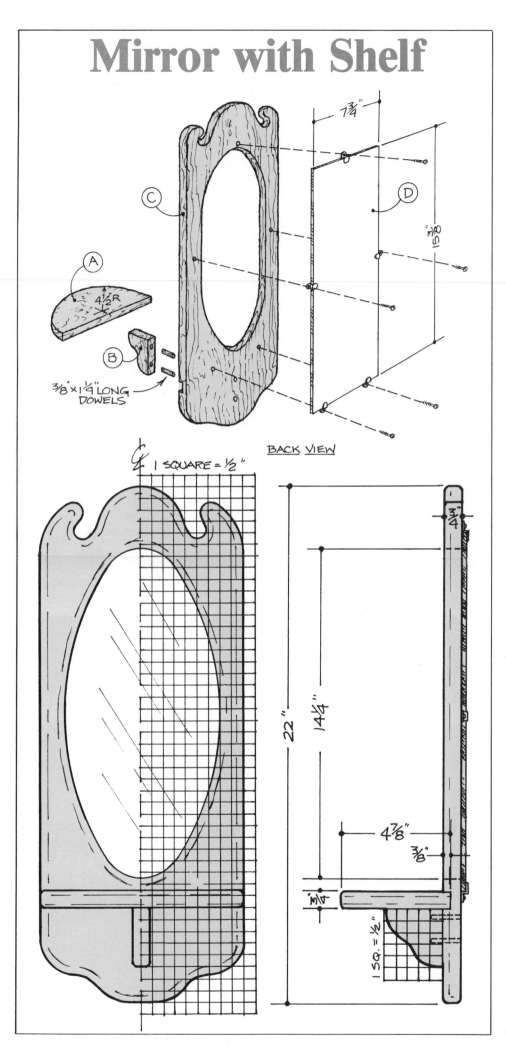

A — $4\frac{1}{2}R$

$\frac{3}{8}" \times 1\frac{1}{4}"$ LONG DOWELS

$7\frac{3}{4}"$

$15\frac{5}{8}"$

BACK VIEW

1 SQUARE = $\frac{1}{2}"$

22"

$14\frac{1}{4}"$

$4\frac{7}{8}"$

$\frac{3}{8}"$

$\frac{3}{4}"$

$\frac{3}{4}"$

1 SQ. = $\frac{1}{2}"$

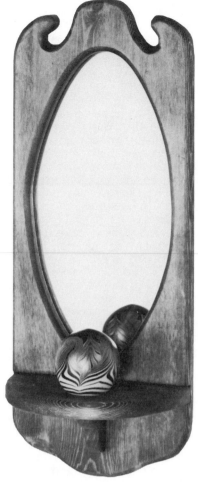

A few hours in the workshop are all that's needed to build this eye-catching oval mirror. Ours is made from pine, much in keeping with its Early American style.

The frame (part C) can be made first. Cut ¾ in. thick stock to a width of 9 in. and a length of 22 in., then mark the location of the ⅜ in. deep by ¾ in. wide dado for the shelf (part A). The dado can be cut with the dado head cutter or by making repeated passes over the sawblade.

Next, referring to the drawing, transfer the profile from the grid pattern to the stock. To cut out the oval, first drill a ⅜ in. hole in the waste stock, then with this as a starting point, use a saber saw to cut out the opening. The outer profile can be cut out with a band or saber saw.

The shelf (part A) is made from a piece of ¾ in. thick stock measuring 4⅞ in. wide by 9 in. long. Use a compass to lay out a 4½ in. radius, noting that the radius is centered at a point ⅜ in. from the back edge of part A.

After making part B, all parts can be thoroughly sanded. Part A can now be glued in place and secured with finishing nails. Part B can now be glued and clamped in place. When dry, drill through from the back for ⅜ in. dowels as shown. The mirror is held in place with five mirror clips as shown.

Stain to suit and finish with two coats of polyurethane.

Early American Wall Unit

A wall unit can be put to good use in any room in the house, perhaps explaining why they are always so popular. This one, made of pine, has a distinctive Early American look, a style that continues to appeal to a great many people. The three small drawers come in handy for storing a variety of odds and ends.

Except for the drawer fronts (H), the drawer bottoms (K), and the drawer stops (L), all parts are made from ½ in. thick stock. If you don't have a planer, most millwork shops, for a small charge, will plane down ¾ in. thick stock to ½ in. Three six-foot lengths of 1 x 6 stock will provide enough material for the entire project.

Begin by cutting the two sides (parts A) to overall length and width and laying out the location of the three ¼ in. by ¼ in. dadoes for parts C, E, and F. Using the table or radial-arm saw, the dadoes can be cut using the dado head cutter or by making repeated passes with a regular sawblade. Next, transfer the curved profile from the grid pattern, then cut out with the band or saber saw.

The top shelf (C), the lower shelf (E), and the bottom (F) can now be cut to length and width. The ends must be square, so before cutting to length, check your saw set-up. The ¼ in. by ¼ in. rabbet on each end can be cut using either the dado head cutter or by making repeated passes over the sawblade. Make each cut with care and check for a snug fit in the side dado. Keep in mind that the stock will be reduced in thickness after sanding. In fact, if a lot of sanding is required, it's a good idea to do the heavy sanding before cutting the rabbets. Note that in addition to the end rabbets, part C has a ½ in. wide by ¼ in. deep rabbet along the back edge as shown in the side view of the drawing. Also note that the top of part F and the bottom of part E have ⅛ in. deep by ½ in. wide dadoes to accept the dividers (G). If you use the dado head cutter, a good fit can best be insured by first making a test cut in scrap stock, then checking the cut with the divider stock. Again keep in mind that the divider stock will be reduced in thickness after sanding.

Parts A, C, E, F and G can now be assembled. Give all parts a thorough sanding, taking particular care to smooth the curved edges of the sides (A). We assembled ours by first gluing the dividers to the lower shelf (E) and the bottom (F), using four handscrews to hold everything together. It's important not to use too much glue or else there will be problems with glue squeezing out of the joint. Before these glue joints set up, we immediately glued the two sides (parts A) and the top shelf (part C) using bar clamps to secure them in place. Clamp pads were used to protect the stock. At this point it's important to check for squareness and make any necessary adjustments.

Next, the back (B) can be cut to fit snugly between the two sides. Once satisfied with the fit, the curved profile can be transferred to the stock and cut out with a band or saber saw. The apron (D) can also be cut to fit at this time. With the stock held face side against the table saw miter gauge and the sawblade set for a height of 1½ in., the notch on each end can be cut with two or three passes over the blade. A good fit here is important so make the cuts carefully. Following this, use the dimensions shown to lay out the apron pattern. Use a ⅜ in. drill bit to cut the seven holes, then cut the curves with the saber saw. Parts B and D can now be sanded and glued in place.

The drawers are made as shown and assembled with glue and finishing nails. Check for a good sliding fit before gluing the drawer stops (L) in place.

Give the entire project a complete final sanding with 220 grit aluminum oxide sandpaper. Any areas of glue squeeze-out should be cleaned up with a sharp chisel. Give all edges and corners a generous rounding-over.

As always, the type of finish is a matter of personal preference. Ours was stained with two coats of Minwax's Golden Oak stain. An inexpensive foam brush makes it easy to apply — and it can be tossed out when the job is over. Allow the stain to dry thoroughly. For a clear final finish we applied two coats of polyurethane varnish. Three wooden knobs, stained and varnished, are added to complete the project.

Bill of Materials
(All Dimensions Actual)

Part	Description	Size	No. Req'd
A	Side	½ x 5½ x 16¾	2
B	Back	½ x 4⅜ x 19	1
C	Top Shelf	½ x 5 x 19½	1
D	Apron	½ x 1¾ x 19½	1
E	Lower Shelf	½ x 5½ x 19½	1
F	Bottom	½ x 5½ x 19½	1
G	Divider	½ x 5½ x 2¾	2
H	Drawer Front	¾ x 2½ x 6	3
I	Drawer Side	½ x 2½ x 4⅝	6
J	Drawer Back	½ x 2 x 5⅜	3
K	Drawer Bottom	¼ x 5¼ x 4³⁄₁₆	3
L	Drawer Stop	¼ x 1 x 1	6

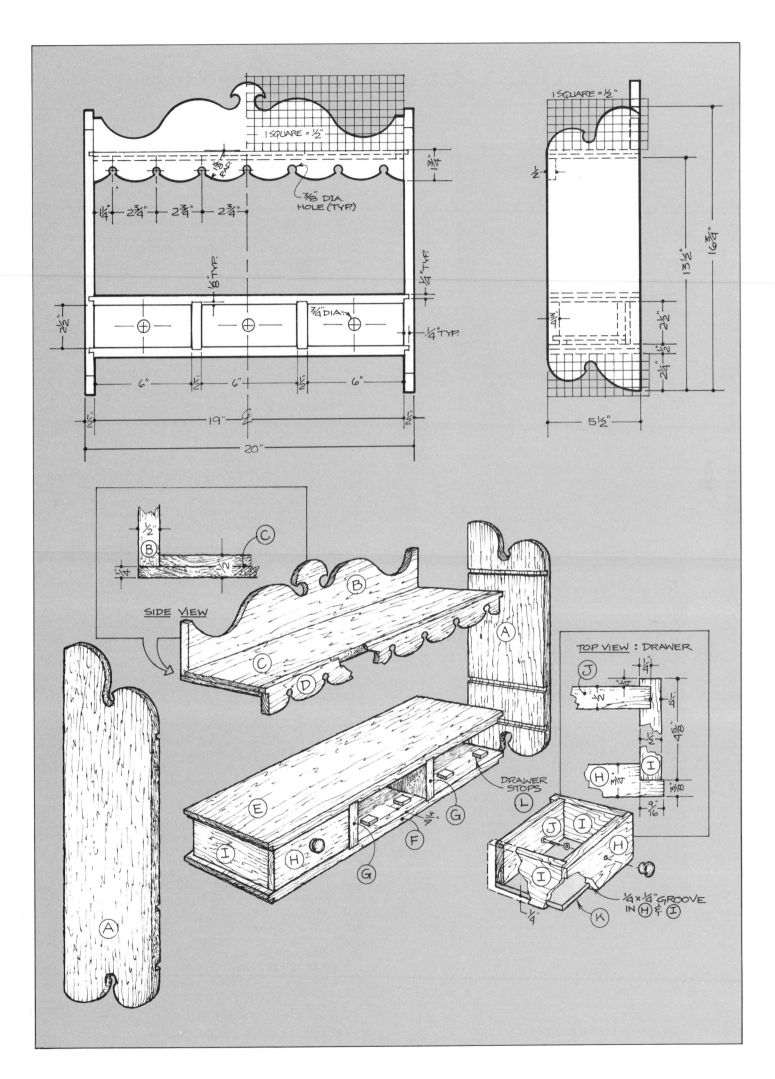

1 SQUARE = ½"

3/8 R.

3/8 DIA. HOLE (TYP.)

¼" 2¾" 2¾" 2¾"

¾"

⅛" TYP.

¼" TYP.

2½"

¾" DIA.

¼" TYP.

6" ½" 6" ½" 6"

½" 19" ½"

20"

1 SQUARE = ½"

½

¾"

16¾"

13½"

2½"

2¼" ½"

5½"

½"
¼"
B
C
½"

SIDE VIEW

B

C

D

A

TOP VIEW : DRAWER

J

¼"
¼"
1"
¼"

½"

45"

I

H

3/8"

9/16"

A

E

I

H

F

G

G

DRAWER STOPS

L

J

I

H

K

¼"

¼ x ⅛" GROOVE IN H & I

Pine Corner Cupboard

The left back (part A) and right back (part B) can be made first. Most lumberyard and building supply centers now carry ¾ in. pine in wide glued up panels, usually in widths of 18 in. and 24 in. Considering the time they save, it's probably the way to go.

Of course, if you prefer, the back parts can be made by edge-gluing two or more narrow boards. Cut the stock to allow a little extra on both length and width. To make it easier to keep the board edges in line when clamping, it's a good idea to include 4 or 5 dowel pins in each joint. Since the pins only serve to align the boards it is not necessary to glue them in place. Apply glue to each mating edge, then clamp securely with bar or pipe clamps. When dry, cut to overall length and width, keeping in mind that the right back (B) is ⅜ in. narrower than the left back (A).

Continuing work on parts A and B, lay out the location of the five ¾ in. wide by ¼ in. deep dadoes. A radial-arm saw equipped with a dado head cutter is probably the best way to cut them. If you don't have a dado head cutter, the same cut can be made by making repeated passes with a regular sawblade. A router can also do the job. Use a guide strip clamped to the stock. The router can also be used to cut the ¾ in. wide by ⅜ in. deep rabbet along the back edge of part A. To complete work on the back parts, use the table saw (with the blade at 45 degrees) in conjunction with the rip fence to cut the bevel on each front edge.

The top (part C) and the five shelves (parts D) are made next. As shown in the cutting diagram, the shelves can be cut from a six foot length of 1 x 12 stock. Take care to cut the 45 degree angles with accuracy. The plate groove can be cut with a router equipped with a ⅜ in. core-box bit. Clamp guidestrips to the stock to guide the router.

The side (part F) can now be cut to overall width and length. The two ¼ in. wide by ⅛ in. deep grooves (see cross-sectional detail) can be cut on the table saw. Set the sawblade to a height of ⅛ in., then adjust the rip-fence to properly locate the blade. Run the stock, face down, along the rip-fence to make each cut.

Next, part E, the rail, and part G, the base, are cut to size. Transfer the grid pattern from the drawing to the stock, then cut out with a band or saber saw.

Cut the two doors (part I) and the four battens (part J) to size. The routed groove in the door is a nice detail and can be made with little difficulty with a router. Using ¼ in. plywood, make a template to the dimensions shown on the drawing. Center this on the door front and tack in place with four small brads. Be sure to locate the brads so that they will not interfere with the travel of the router. Equip the router with a ¼ in. diameter straight bit and a 7/16 in. guide bushing. Start the router, then lower bit into the stock keeping the guide bushing against the template. Now, rout the groove by moving the router in a clockwise direction around the template. To get the feel of this step, it's a good idea to make one or two practice cuts on scrap stock.

Now all parts can be given a thorough sanding, taking particular care to remove any deep scratches. Assemble the back parts (A and B) with glue and finishing nails. Before nailing though, it's best to drill pilot holes to minimize any chance of splitting. The five shelves (D) and the top (C) can now be added, again using glue and finishing nails. Parts E, F and G are also glued, but look best if cut nails, which have an antique look, are used. The bed molding can be purchased at most lumberyards. Miter both ends, then glue and clamp in place.

Final sand before staining. We used two coats of Minwax's Early American stain. Following this we applied two coats of their antique oil finish.

Screw the two battens (J) to the back of each door. Attach the doors to parts F with 3 in. "H" hinges. Two 1 in. porcelain knobs complete the project.

Country furniture seems to be especially popular these days, perhaps because the style is characterized by clean lines and sturdy construction. This piece, made of pine, will make a charming addition to a kitchen or dining room. The joinery is basic throughout, so even a beginner should be able to tackle this one with confidence.

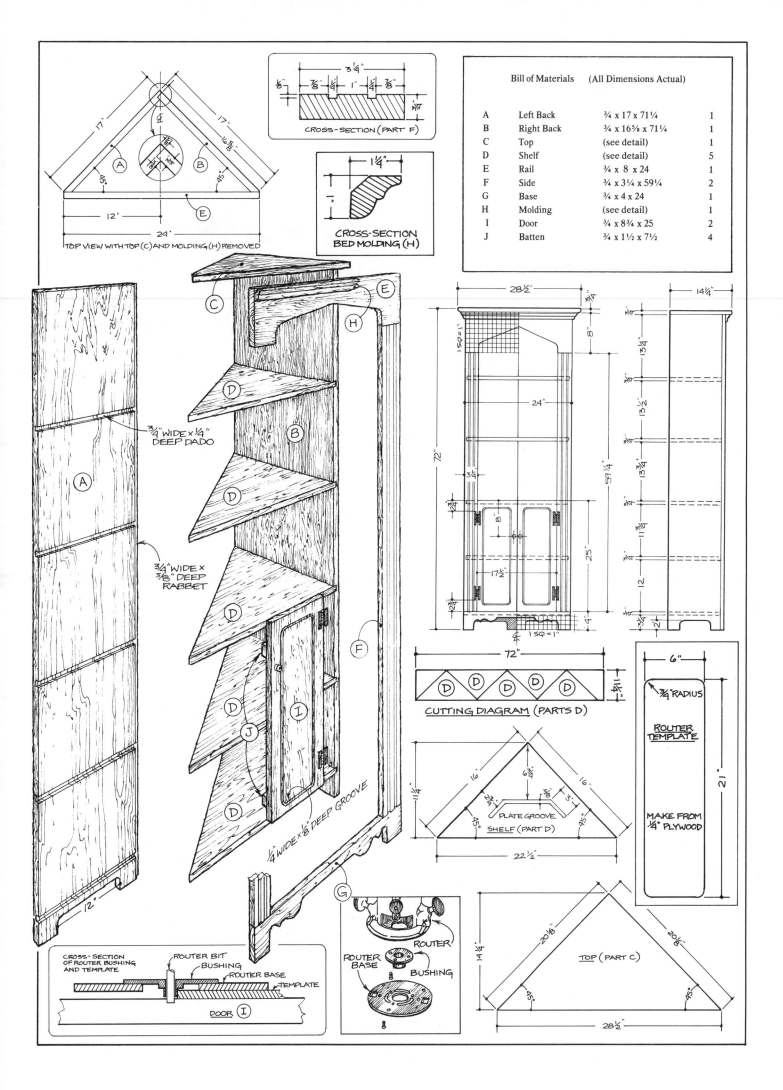

Early American Portable Bookcase

This appealing reproduction of an Early American portable bookcase provides a lovely setting for several small plants. It can also be used as a desk top organizer, or a display stand for curios. No matter how you use it, it's a nice accent piece and is fun to build.

All parts are of ½ in. number 2 white pine with the exception of the drawer bottoms which are ⅛ in. hardboard. If you don't have a planer, for a small charge most millwork shops will plane down ¾ in. stock to ½ in.

Begin by edge-gluing narrower stock for the two sides (A) the bottom (B), the shelf (C), the divider (D), and the back (E). Apply glue to both mating surfaces, then clamp securely with bar or pipe clamps. Allow to dry thoroughly.

Cut the two sides (A) to overall size (8½ in. wide by 11 in. long), then lay out the location of the ⅛ in. deep by ½ in. wide shelf dadoes. Cut the dadoes with a dado head cutter or by making repeated passes over a regular sawblade. The ¼ in. deep by ½ in. wide rabbet along the inside back edge can be cut using the same method. To complete work on part A, transfer the profiles from the grid pattern to the stock, then cut out with a saber saw. To make the handle first drill two ¾ in. diameter holes to establish the ends, then cut out.

The back can now be cut to size (12 in. wide by 17 in. long). Transfer the curved profile to the stock and cut to shape. Note that the bottom edge has a ¾ in. deep cut-out stopped 1¼ in. from each end.

Next, cut the bottom (B) and shelf (C) to size, noting that both measure 8½ in. wide by 16¾ in. long. Also, cut the divider to 8 in. wide by 2¼ in. long. Following this give all parts a complete sanding, paying particular attention to the curved edges of the sides and back. Assemble the divider in place with glue and finishing nails, taking care to make sure that it is square to the front. The sides and back can now be added, again using glue and finishing nails.

After the two drawers are made and assembled, give the entire project a thorough final sanding. Be sure to round all corners to simulate years of wear. Some judicious distressing will also add to the authentic look. Add the two ⅛ in. thick drawer stops as shown.

Stain to suit, then final finish with two coats of polyurethane varnish.

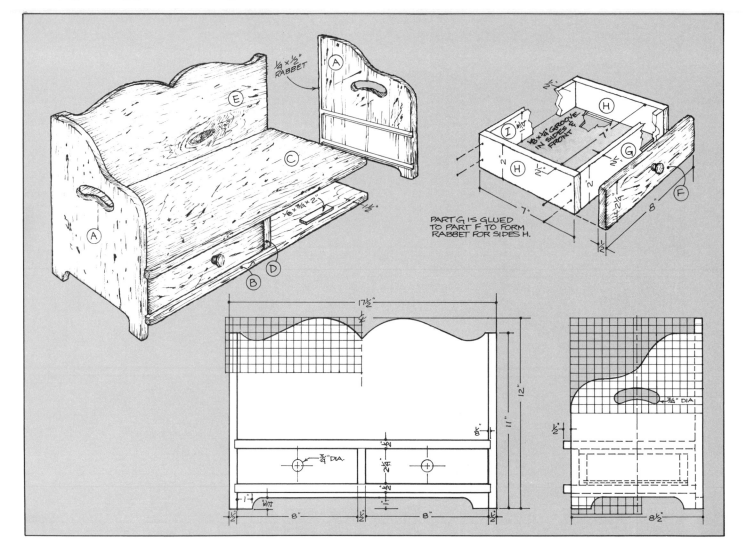

Salt Box Planter

Resembling the wall boxes that were so common during our Colonial period, this well-proportioned planter will provide an eye catching setting for a favorite houseplant. Cut the back to length and width, then transfer the grid pattern to the stock. Lay out the location of the ½ in. notch, then cut out both grid pattern and notch with a band saw. After cutting the bottom to size, a router equipped with a piloted beading bit is used to make the molding. The front is rabbeted as shown in the detail. Sand all parts, then assemble with glue and countersunk wood screws.

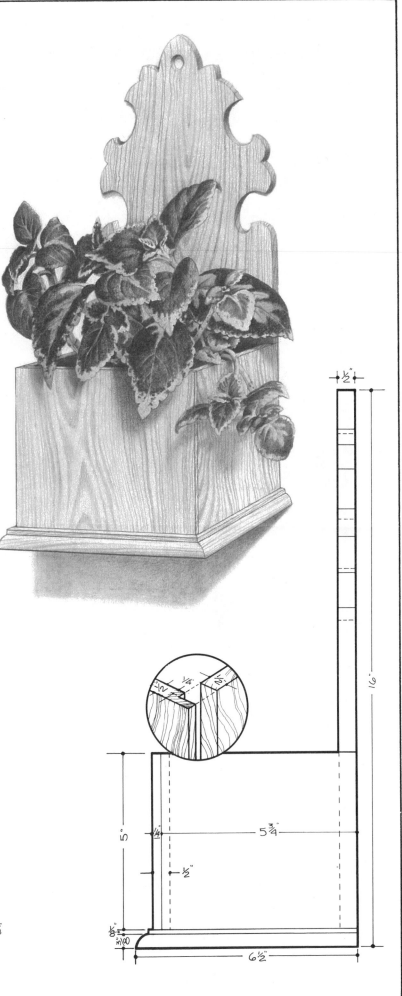

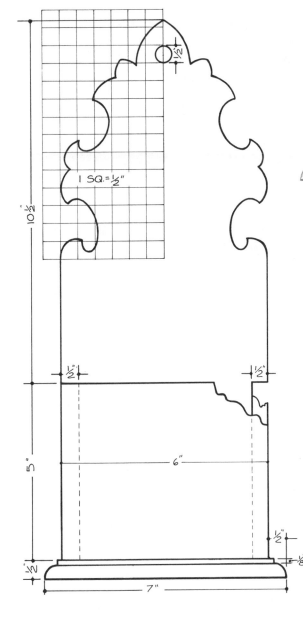

1 SQ. = ½"

Shaker Desk

We discovered this lovely example of a Shaker writing desk at a local cabinetmaker's shop. While not an exact reproduction, the overall design is very nearly the same as the Shaker original.

Cherry was used for this piece, a wood commonly chosen by the Shakers. The drawer sides, back, and bottom are made of pine, although maple could also be used here.

The four legs (A) can be made first. From 2 in. stock (which actually measures 1¾ in.), rip each leg to a width of 1¾ in. Although the overall length of the legs is 27⅛ in., it's best to initially cut them slightly oversized, then trim them to final length later on.

Lay out and mark the location of the apron mortises on each leg. To cut each mortise, use a drill press equipped with a ⅜ in. diameter bit and drill a series of holes. This will remove most of the material and what remains can be cleaned up with a sharp chisel. Be sure to cut the mortise about 1/16 in. deeper than the tenon length. This extra depth will allow room for any excess glue that may be in the joint when it is later assembled. If the joint does not have

room for excess glue, it becomes just about impossible to make it close.

At this time, also cut the small mortises for the drawer frame (parts D and E) tenons. These can best be cut with a chisel.

Referring to the drawing, note that each leg is tapered down to 1 in. on two sides. The taper starts at a point just below the apron (B), 5¼ in. from the top of the leg. If you have a tapering jig for your table or radial-arm saw, this is a good time to use it, although a good sharp hand plane will also do the job in little time.

The two side aprons (B) and the back apron (C) can be made next. Cut to the length and width shown in the bill of materials, making sure to include the tenon length. Although the tenons can be cut by hand using a back saw, we generally prefer to use a table saw equipped with a dado head cutter. Set the dado head to a height (about 3/16 in.) that will provide a snug fitting tenon when both cheeks are cut, then use the miter gauge to pass the stock over the cutter. Make some test cuts on scrap stock before starting.

Cut the inner and outer dividers (parts F and G) to overall length from ¾ in. square stock. Use a sharp hard pencil to lay out the dovetail profile, then use a dovetail or fine-toothed back saw to cut out. For best results, cut just on the outside of the line, then use a sharp chisel to pare the material exactly to the line.

Next, make the upper and lower drawer frame (parts D and E). Cut to overall length from ¾ in. square stock, then lay out the location of the dovetail pins. To insure accuracy, use the divider dovetails as templates. And to avoid confusion later on, label each divider dovetail and its corresponding pin on the drawer frames. Once marked, use a dovetail saw and chisel to remove the pin material. Cut just inside the line and use the chisel to pare to an exact fit.

Before assembly, give the legs, aprons, drawer frame members and dividers a thorough sanding. Be sure to remove any unsightly planer marks that tend to give a washboard effect to the stock.

Assemble each side apron (B) to a pair of legs as shown. Apply glue to the apron tenon, then assemble the leg and clamp with a bar or pipe clamp. Use scrap stock as clamp pads to prevent marring the legs. Check for squareness before setting aside to dry.

The inner and outer dividers (F and G) can now be glued to the upper and lower drawer frames (D and E). Use glue and clamp lightly. When dry, this frame unit and the back apron (C) can then be joined to the two previously glued sub-assemblies consisting of the side apron and legs. Again, use bar or pipe clamps and check for squareness before setting aside to dry.

Now the side apron and long apron cleats (H and I) can be cut to length from ¾ in. square stock. Properly cut, they should fit snugly inside the legs. To permit the cleats to be screwed and glued to the aprons, drill and countersink each one for ¾ in. x #8 flat headed wood screws.

The lower cleats serve as a means for the bottom (L) to be attached. They can now be secured in place, keeping in mind that they are located ¾ in. from the bottom edge of the apron (see drawing).

The upper cleats provide a means for attaching the top (M) and need to be predrilled and countersunk before assembly. To permit expansion and contraction of the top, these holes should be slotted.

The bottom (L) can now be cut to size from ¾ in. thick birch plywood. Note that it will have to be notched at the corners in order to fit around the legs. With the desk base unit upside down, drop the bottom in place, then drill and countersink holes for 1¼ in. x #8 flat head wood screws.

Next, cut the inner and outer drawer guides (parts J and K) to length so they fit snugly between the dividers and the back apron cleat. Secure to the bottom (L) with round headed wood screws and washers. It's best to make the drawer guide holes slightly slotted so they can be adjusted later on when the drawers are added.

Part M, the top, is made from ½ in. thick stock. If you can't get ½ in. stock, most millwork shops will plane down ¾ in. material. Or, if you have a band saw, you can resaw narrow stock to ½ in. thickness.

Cut the top boards a bit on the long side (about 40 in.) before edge joining. Since the edges have a tendency to slip over each other when clamp pressure is applied, it's a good idea to add two or three ¼ in. diameter dowel pins to each edge joint. Apply glue to all mating surfaces (the dowel pins don't need any) then clamp firmly with bar or pipe clamps. Following this, the back (O) can be made in the same manner.

The battens (part N) serve to stiffen the top and prevent warping. They are cut to fit just inside of parts I, but are attached only to the top. Four slotted holes (to allow expansion and contraction of the top) are drilled in each batten to take ⅞ in. x #8 round head wood screws and washers.

The dovetailed drawer boxes (parts P and Q) are made from ⅜ in. thick stock as shown. Once the dovetails are cut, the boxes are assembled as shown. Again, use glue and clamp firmly. Check for squareness before setting aside to dry.

Both the top (M) and the back (O) can now be thoroughly sanded. Work through 220 grit to insure a smooth surface.

The base can now be attached to the top. Place the top upside down on a blanket or other protective surface, then locate the base in its proper position. With the bottom (L) removed, mark the location of the holes in cleats. Remove the base and drill pilot holes for 1 in. x #8 flat head wood screws. Attach the base, then add the bottom (L).

The drawer boxes (parts P and Q) are not glued to the top. Instead, angled screws are driven through the bottom of the box and into the top. Two are driven at the front of the box and two at the back. The back (O) is also screwed in place.

After the drawers are made, the entire project can be final sanded. Note that the bottom edge of drawer backs (T) and (X) must be notched to fit over the drawer stops (AA). Lightly round all corners. Check drawers for a good sliding fit and adjust as necessary. Three coats of Watco Danish Oil complete the project.

Bill of Materials
(All Dimensions Actual)

Part	Description	Size	No. Req'd
A	Leg	1¾ x 1¾ x 27⅛	4
B	Side Apron	¾ x 5 x 15¼ (incl. tenon)	2
C	Back Apron	¾ x 5 x 36¼ (incl. tenon)	1
D	Lower Drawer Frame	¾ x ¾ x 36¼ (incl. tenon)	1
E	Upper Drawer Frame	¾ x ¾ x 36¼ (incl. tenon)	1
F	Inner Divider	¾ x ¾ x 4¼ (incl. dove)	2
G	Outer Divider	¾ x ¾ x 4¼ (incl. dove)	2
H	Side Apron Cleat	¾ x ¾ x 13½	4
I	Long Apron Cleat	¾ x ¾ x 34½	3
J	Inner Drawer Guide	¾ x ¾ x 14¾	2
K	Outer Drawer Guide	¾ x ¾ x 14¾	2
L	Bottom	¾ x 15½ x 36½	1
M	Top	½ x 17½ x 39	1
N	Batten	½ x 2 x 14	4
O	Back	½ x 8⅝ x 39	1
P	Box Top & Bottom	⅜ x 9¾ x 9¾	4
Q	Box Side	⅜ x 9¾ x 5	4
R	Base Drawer Front	¾ x 3½ x 10½	3
S	Base Drawer Side	½ x 3½ x 14⅝	6
T	Base Drawer Back	½ x 3½ x 10½	3
U	Base Drawer Bottom	½ x 9⅞ x 14⅛	3
V	Box Drawer Front	¾ x 4¼ x 9	2
W	Box Drawer Side	½ x 4¼ x 9⅛	4
X	Box Drawer Back	½ x 4¼ x 9	2
Y	Box Drawer Bottom	½ x 8⅜ x 8⅝	2
Z	Drawer Knob	See Detail	5
AA	Drawer Stop	¼ x 1 x 1½	10

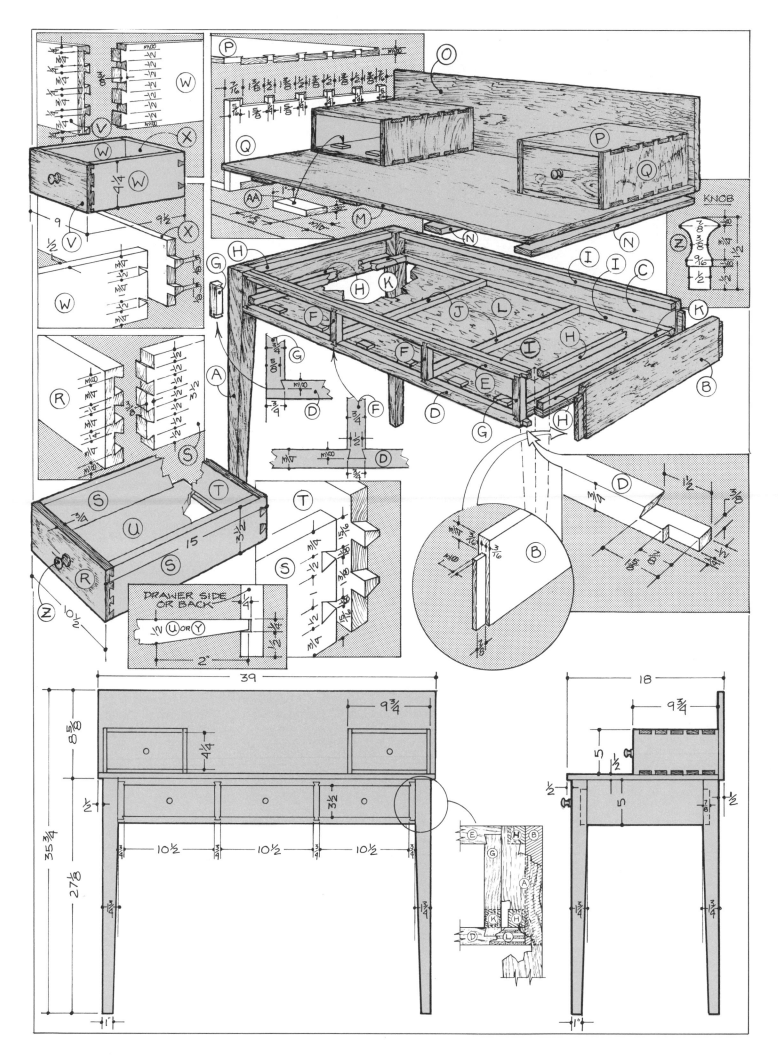

DRAWER SIDE
OR BACK

KNOB

Early American Spoon Rack

This rack will provide a lovely setting for your favorite spoon collection. Ours, with its Early American styling, is made from pine, although cherry would also be a good choice.

If you don't have ½ in. thick stock, most millwork shops will plane down ¾ in. material. Also, you can re-saw narrow stock on the table saw, then edge-glue it to get enough width for the front (A) and the back (B). Or you can get it the way our forefathers did by going to work on thicker stock with a well sharpened hand plane.

The front (A) can be made first. Cut to a width of about 4¾ and a length of about 18½ in. These dimensions will be trimmed later on. Transfer the profile of the top edge to the stock, then cut out with a band or saber saw.

The back (B) measures 18 in. wide, so it will be necessary to edge-glue two or more narrower boards. Apply glue to all mating edges, then clamp firmly with bar or pipe clamps. To keep the edges from sliding out of alignment, it's helpful to clamp two pairs of cleats (made from scrap stock) across the width of the board. To prevent sticking, use wax paper between the cleats and the stock. Once dry, remove the clamps, then transfer the curved profile of the top. Cut out with a band or saber saw.

Once the sides (C) have been made, the spoon holders (Parts E and F) can be cut to length and width. Mark the location of each spoon, then bore a ½ in. diameter hole as shown. The hole should be centered along the 1 in. width. The notches can then be cut out with a dovetail or back saw. Readers should keep in mind though, that some spoon designs may require slightly different cutouts.

Give all parts a thorough sanding, taking particular care to smooth the curved edges. Assemble as shown. Use glue and finishing nails, countersunk and filled. Final sand before staining to suit. Several coats of a good penetrating oil, such as Deftco, will provide an attractive final finish.

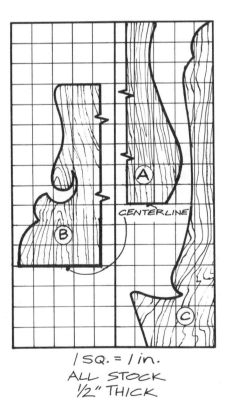

1 SQ. = 1 in.
ALL STOCK
½" THICK

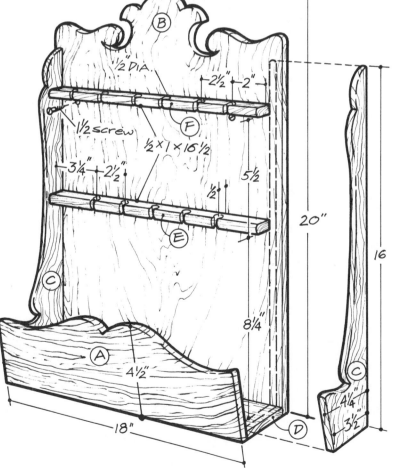

Canning Jar Storage Shelves

If you're one who enjoys putting garden products up in jars, as we do, we think you'll find this project to your liking. It's a solidly constructed storage rack with room for plenty of canning jars. The one shown is made from solid oak stock, with oak plywood for the shelves (parts F). However, for a project like this, just about any wood can be used, even pine.

The two front legs (parts A) and the two back legs (parts B) can be made first. Cut each leg to overall width and length, then lay out and mark the location of the mortises for the rails (parts C).

To cut each mortise, use a ¼ in. diameter drill bit to bore a series of holes. This removes most of the waste material. What remains can be cleaned out with a sharp chisel. Be sure to cut the mortise about 1/16 in. deeper than the tenon length in order to allow room for excess glue. If you neglect to add this extra depth, and there is excess glue, the joint won't close.

A well made mortise should be square to both the edge and face surfaces of the leg. A drill press, if you have one, will make this step fairly easy. However, if done with care, a hand brace or portable electric drill will do as good a job.

The stretchers (parts D) and back (part E) are joined to the legs with single half-lap through dovetails. This joint is not as difficult to make as you might think, and it adds considerably to both the strength and visual interest of the piece. Cut parts D and E to overall length and width, then lay out the location of the ⅜ in. deep by ¾ in. wide dado that's cut to accept the shelves (parts F). This cut is best made with a dado head cutter, although you can get the same result by making repeated passes with a regular saw blade.

Next, using the same procedure, cut a ⅜ in. deep by ¾ in. wide rabbet on the end of each part D and E. This step forms the half-lap portion of the joint.

Now, referring to Details A and B, lay out the dovetails as shown. For maximum accuracy, it's best to use a sharp knife or pencil to scribe the lines. Use a dovetail saw or a fine tooth backsaw to remove the waste.

The dovetail pins on the front and back legs (parts A and B) can best be laid out and scribed by using the finished dovetails as a template. Use a square to carry the scribed lines to the face of the board. The next step is to make the two saw cuts establishing the angled sides. Again, use a dovetail saw or fine tooth backsaw to make these cuts. For an accurate cut, lay the saw blade on the waste side of the scribed line, just grazing it.

The waste between the cuts is removed with a chisel and mallet. With a sharp knife, score the original line at the base of the waste. Next, with the bevel of the blade down, use a chisel to make a V-cut into the line. This prevents the grain from splintering behind the line. Now, lay the flat of the chisel against the back of the V-cut and proceed to chop away the waste material. When halfway through, flip the stock over and start from the other side.

A well fitted joint should go together with only light tapping from a mallet. If necessary, trim further with the chisel.

The shelves (parts F) can now be cut to overall length and width. The edging (parts G) is glued to both ends as shown. Use pipe clamps to secure until dry. It's best to cut the edging a bit wider than necessary. After clamping it can be planed flush.

The rails (parts C) can now be cut to overall length and width. The tenon can best be cut using the dado head cutter.

Sand all parts thoroughly, then assemble parts A, B, and C as shown. Use glue and pipe clamps. When dry, assemble part E and the three back stretchers (parts D), again with glue and clamps. Finally, complete assembly by adding the shelves (parts F) and the four front stretchers.

Final sand, then finish with two coats of polyurethane varnish.

Bill of Materials (All Dimensions Actual)			
Part	Description	Size	No. Req'd
A	Front Leg	¾ x 2 x 38½	2
B	Back Leg	¾ x 2 x 40½	2
C	Rail	¾ x 2 x 6¾	4
D	Stretchers	¾ x 2 x 30	7
E	Back	¾ x 5 x 30	1
F	Shelf	¾ x 8¼ x 28	4
G	Edging	¼ x ¾ x 8¼	8

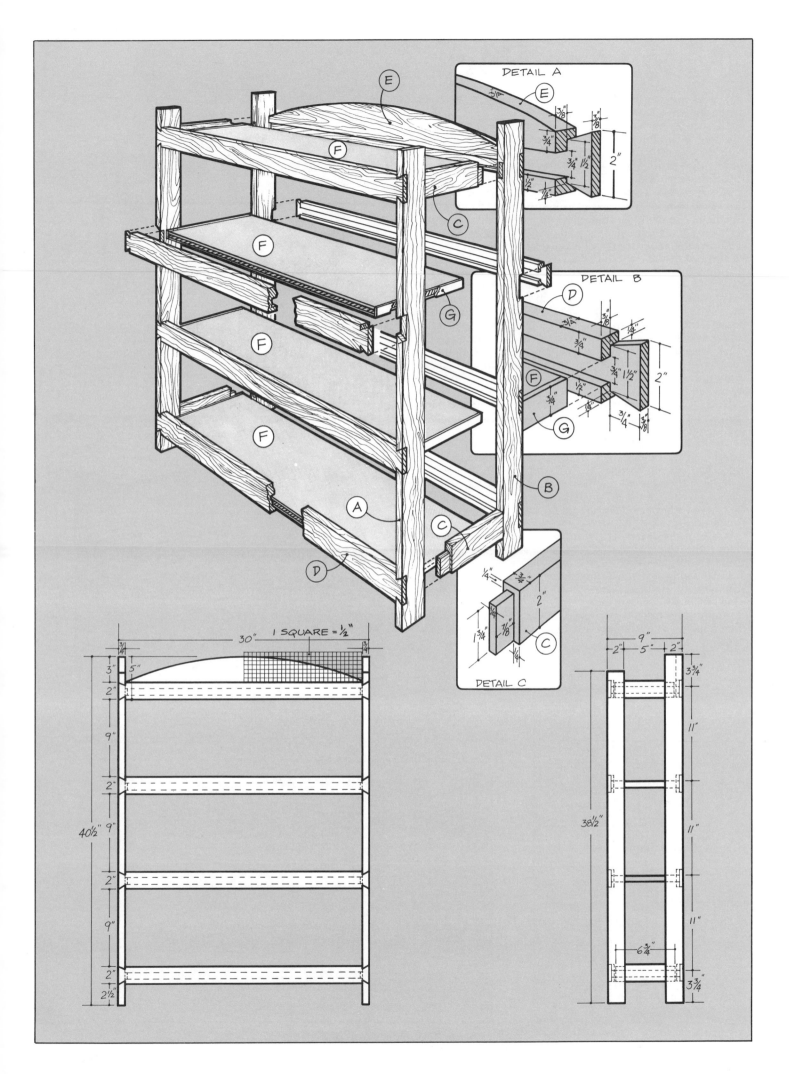

DETAIL A

DETAIL B

DETAIL C

E

F

C

G

D

A

B

F

1 SQUARE = ½"

30"

40½"

3"
5"
2"
9"
2"
9"
2"
9"
2"
2½"

9"
2" 5" 2"

3¾"

11"

11"

38½"

11"

6¾"

3¾"

115

Magazine Rack

A weekend in the workshop is all that's needed to complete this project. With its Early American styling, pine is a good choice, particularly since it's relatively inexpensive. We used ¾ in. thick stock throughout.

Begin by cutting the two sides (D) to overall length and width from ¾ in. thick stock. If necessary, edge-join stock to get the 6 in. width.

Referring to the drawing, lay out and mark the location of the ¾ in. wide by ⅜ in. deep dado for the bottom (E). To cut the dado, use the table saw equipped with a dado-head cutter or use a regular saw blade and make repeated passes.

Since the dadoes for the dividers (Parts A, B and C) must be stopped at the bottom dado, it's best to use a router for this operation. Equip the router with a straight bit. If you have a ¾ in. diameter bit, each cut can be made with one fence setting, although you'll need at least three depth adjustments to get the ⅜ in. depth. Smaller bits will take more passes and the edge-guide will need to be relocated after each pass. To cut the dadoes, clamp the edge guide to the stock, then hold the router against the guide as you make the cut. A piece of scrap stock that has a straight edge will make a good edge guide. Be sure to stop the cut at the point it meets the bottom dado.

Next, transfer the profile from the drawing to the sides, then cut out with a band or saber saw. This completes preliminary work on the sides.

The dividers (Parts A, B and C) can now be cut to overall length and width as shown. Transfer the grid pattern to the stock and cut out with a band or saber saw.

After cutting the bottom to size (¾ x 6 x 24 in.), all parts can be given a complete sanding. Give special attention to the curved edges, as these should be well smoothed with no rough areas.

Assemble as shown. Use glue and wood screws to join the sides (D) to the dividers (A, B and C) and the bottom (E). Countersink the wood screws, then plug with wood plugs.

Final sand all parts. Give the corners and edges a good rounding to simulate years of wear, and sand the wood plugs flush with the surface.

Apply stain to suit (we used Minwax's Early American), then apply two coats of polyurethane varnish as a final clear finish.

¾" WIDE + ⅜" DEEP
DADO
FOR DIVIDERS

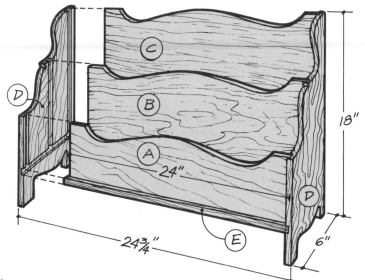

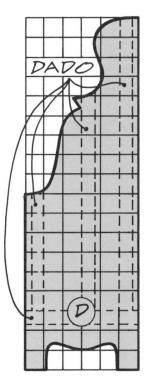

DADO

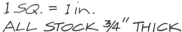

1 SQ. = 1 in.
ALL STOCK ¾" THICK

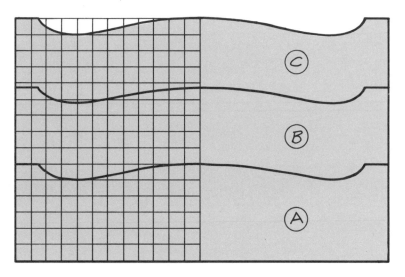

Bootjack

Boots seem to be as popular as ever today, in spite of the fact that getting one off almost always results in an annoying struggle. We suspect that, in one form or another, this simple tool has been around nearly as long as the boot itself. Our version, made of ash, can be built in just a few hours in the workshop — time well spent if you own a pair of troublesome boots.

To make the base you'll need a piece of ¾ in. thick stock measuring 5 in. wide by 15 in. long. Transfer the grid pattern, then cut out with a band or saber saw. The stand is made as shown, then glued to the base using a pair of ⅜ in. by ¾ in. long dowel pins. Sand thoroughly, rounding all edges, then apply two coats of polyurethane varnish to complete the project.

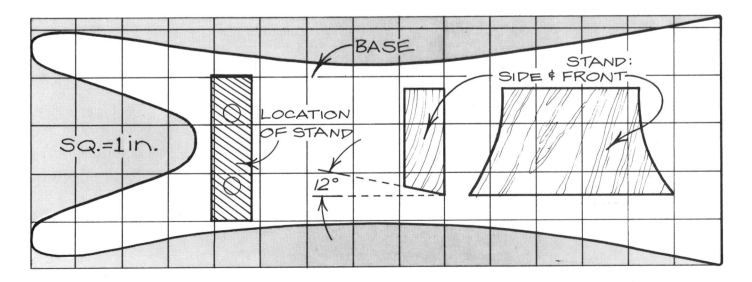

Mitten Box

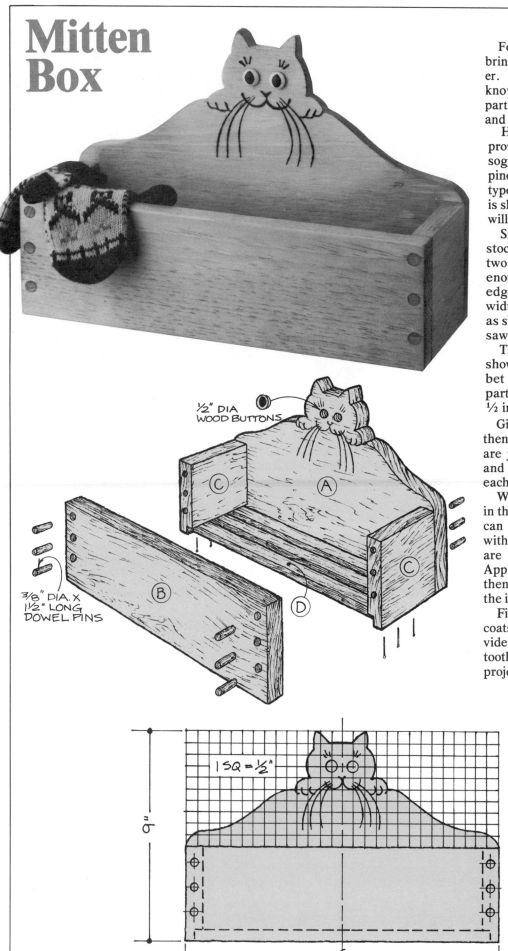

For many of us, a long winter season brings plenty of cold and snowy weather. If you've got kids, you probably know that wet mittens are as much a part of the winter scene as rosy cheeks and cold toes.

Here's a weekend project that will provide a handy place to store those soggy mittens. We used ¾ in. thick pine for ours, although just about any type of wood can be used. The bottom is slatted to allow for ventilation which will help dry things out.

Since the back (A) requires wide stock, it will be necessary to edge-glue two or three narrower boards to get enough width. Once stock has been edge-glued, cut to overall length and width, then transfer the kitten profile as shown. Cut out with a band or saber saw.

The remaining parts are cut as shown. Note that a ½ in. by ½ in. rabbet is cut along the bottom edge of parts C. The slats (parts D) are cut to ½ in. thick by ¾ in wide.

Give all parts a thorough sanding, then assemble as shown. The slats (D) are joined to the sides (C) with glue and a single finishing nail through each end.

We used a woodburning tool to burn in the kitten's face and whiskers. They can also be carved, or simply added with a felt marking pen. The "eyes" are a pair of ½ in. dowel buttons. Apply a coat of enamel to the button, then use a black felt marker to darken the inside.

Final sand, then stain to suit. Two coats of polyurethane varnish will provide a good final finish. A pair of sawtooth picture hangers completes the project.

½" DIA WOOD BUTTONS

⅜" DIA. X 1½" LONG DOWEL PINS

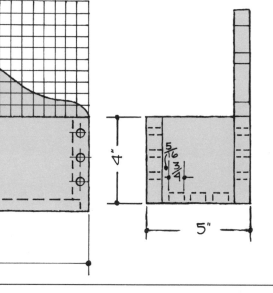

1 SQ = ½"

9"

14"

4"

5"

5/16

3/4

Coal Scuttle

Not too many years ago, the coal scuttle was an important piece of equipment in many homes. We used pine to make this charming adaptation of one, and found that it can be put to a number of uses around the home. We use it to hold magazines, but it also serves well as a planter or wastebasket. Kindling wood stacks nicely in it too.

The sides (parts A) can be made first. Since each side is 14½ in. wide, you'll need to edge-glue two pieces of 1 by 8 stock (which actually measures ¾ in. thick by 7¼ in. wide). Apply glue to both mating surfaces, then use bar or pipe clamps to clamp the stock together. Once dry, remove the clamps, then transfer the curved profile from the drawing. Cut to shape with a band or saber saw.

Note that the front (part B), the back (part C), and the bottom (part D), all require wide stock, so it will be necessary to edge-join material for all these parts.

Assemble with glue and finishing nails. To prevent splitting, be sure to first drill pilot holes.

Give all parts a thorough sanding, taking care to round over all edges. To give ours an "antique" look we did some judicious distressing with a hammer.

For a final finish we applied two coats of Minwax's Golden Oak stain followed by an application of their Antique Oil finish.

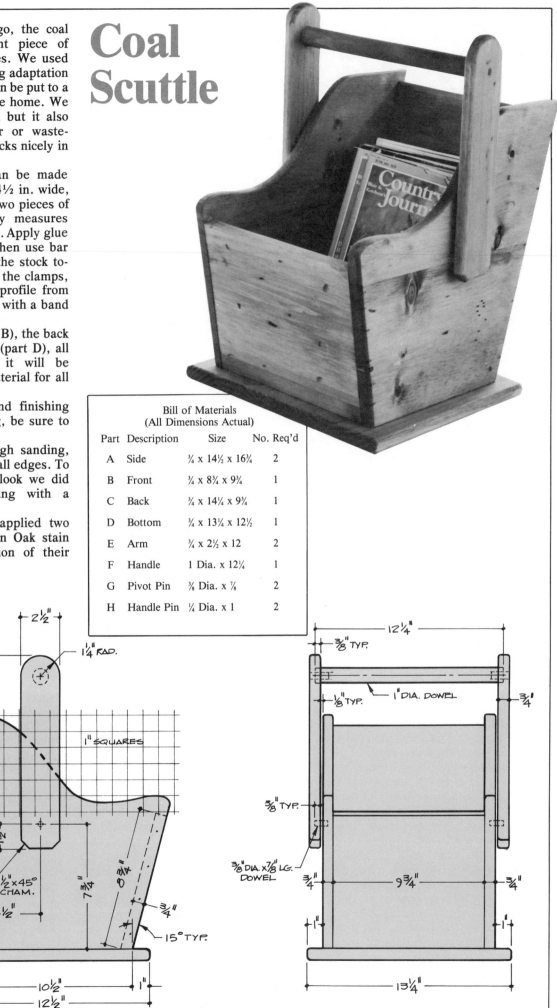

Bill of Materials
(All Dimensions Actual)

Part	Description	Size	No. Req'd
A	Side	¾ x 14½ x 16¾	2
B	Front	¾ x 8¾ x 9¾	1
C	Back	¾ x 14¼ x 9¾	1
D	Bottom	¾ x 13¼ x 12½	1
E	Arm	¾ x 2½ x 12	2
F	Handle	1 Dia. x 12¼	1
G	Pivot Pin	⅜ Dia. x ⅞	2
H	Handle Pin	¼ Dia. x 1	2

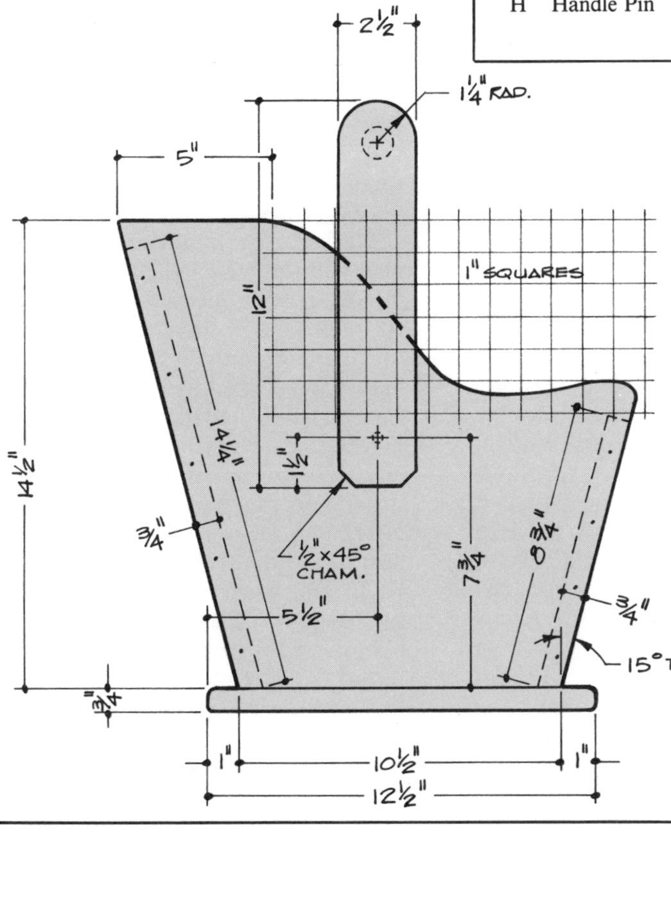

Shaker Chest of Drawers

The clean lines that typify Shaker style are very much evident in this handsome piece. Solid cherry, a wood commonly chosen by Shaker craftsmen, was used for all parts, except the drawer sides, backs, and bottoms.

The two sides (parts A) and the top (part B) can be made first. Since these parts are rather wide, it will be necessary to edge-glue two or more narrow boards in order to get enough width. It's best to cut the boards so that the glued up stock will be slightly wider and longer than necessary.

Perhaps most important to the success of an edge-joint is a clean, smooth surface on both mating parts. This permits close contact between both surfaces and results in maximum glue strength. When a board is ripped on a table or radial-arm saw, it usually results in a fairly rough edge, so it's best to clean it up using the jointer.

When edge-joining boards of this length, it's a good idea to use three or four dowel pins. Although the pins don't add strength to this joint, they make it easier to keep the edges aligned when the boards are clamped.

Apply a thin coat of glue to both mating surfaces, then clamp the stock together with bar or pipe clamps.

There's no need to add glue to the dowel pins. Avoid overtightening the clamps which can cause too much glue to squeeze out, resulting in a weakened joint.

Once dry, remove the clamps and cut part B to overall length and width. Cut parts A to length, but don't trim them to final width yet. It's best to do that after the drawer frame dovetail grooves are cut.

The top, part B, can now be temporarily put aside while the two sides, parts A, are worked.

The dovetail grooves for the six drawer frames are made next. Carefully lay out the centerline location of each groove, extending the line across the entire width of part A. Next, at a point ⅜ in. on each side of the centerlines, scribe another line across the width. This pair of lines establishes the ¾ in. thickness of the dovetail groove.

Equip the router with a ½ in. dovetail bit (we used a Sears bit, p/n 9-25531) and adjust it for a ⅜ in. deep cut. Cut a guidestrip of suitable length from *straight* stock and clamp it to the side. The distance between the guidestrip and the bit (dimension "A" in figure 1-A) should be such that the cut establishes one leg of the dovetail. The guidestrip must be parallel to the guidelines. Make the cut with the router held firmly against the guidestrip.

Now, transfer the guidestrip to the other side of the slot and again clamp it in place. The distance between the guidestrip and the bit (Dimension "A" in figure 1-B) should be such that it establishes the ¾ in. dovetail width. With the guidestrip parallel to the guidelines, make another cut, again holding the router firmly against this guidestrip. Repeat this process for each of the drawer frames.

The two sides can now be trimmed to final width. Then, using the dado head cutter, add a ½ in. by ¾ in. rabbet along the back edge as shown. This rabbet can also be cut by making repeated passes with a regular saw blade.

The dovetails that join parts A to part B can now be cut. Lay out the dovetails very carefully using a hard, sharp pencil. Once the tails have been laid out on the top (B), mark the waste material between the tails with an "X" to avoid confusion. In addition to scribing the tail layout on the face of the board, carry the lines across the end grain. Now clamp the top in a vise and use a fine-tooth dovetail saw to make the angled cuts that will establish the tails. Cut just on the waste side of the line, grazing but not removing it. Bring the cuts almost — but not quite — to the scribed bottom line. A coping saw is now used to cut across the grain and remove the waste. Take the top from the vise, clamp it flat on the workbench over a scrap board, and use a sharp chisel to dress the sides and bottoms of the cutouts.

The pins on the sides (A) should be laid out and marked using the finished dovetails as a template. To do this, clamp the side vertically in a vise, lay the dovetailed top in position on the side and trace the dovetails with a sharp pencil or X-acto knife. Use a small square to carry the scribed lines onto the face of the board.

Mark the waste portion between the pins with an "X", then cut out using the same technique as for the dovetails. A well-fitted dovetail should fit together with only light tapping from a mallet and scrap block. If needed, trim further with a sharp chisel.

Next, cut part D, establish the dovetail on the ends, and notch the sides to fit the dovetail.

The six drawer frames are made next. The top frame consists of parts K, L, and M, the bottom frame consists of parts K, L, M, and N, and the remaining four frames consist of parts K and L. Note that a ¼ in. wide by 1¼ in. deep groove is cut along the inside edge of each part K. This groove serves as a mortise for the tenon on each end of parts L.

Parts L for the top frame and the

bottom frame require a ¼ in. wide by 1¼ in. deep groove along the inside edge to accept the tenon for parts M. Parts L for the remaining four frames do not require any grooves.

Parts L and M have ¼ in. thick by 1¼ in. long tenons on each end. These are cut to fit in the mortises in parts K and L. Parts M also have a ¼ in. by ⅜ in. groove along each edge.

The dust panels, parts N, are made from ½ in. thick solid stock. Each edge is tapered to 3/16 in. (see cross-sectional view of drawer bottom for typical taper) to fit into grooves in parts L and M.

Once parts K, L, M, and N have been cut they can be assembled as shown. Use glue and clamp each frame securely. It's most important that the frames be square so check carefully and make adjustments as necessary. The dust panels (N) should not be glued in place. They should be free to "float" in the frame.

Part G and the five parts F can now be cut to size and glued in place. Use care here to make sure the top and bottom edges of parts F are flush with the top and bottom edges of the drawer frames. Only the top edge of part G should be flush.

The dovetails on each end of the drawer frames can best be cut using a router table. Using the same bit that

cut the dovetail grooves, run the drawer frames on edge through the cutter. In order to better support the frames, it's best to clamp a temporary tall fence to the router table fence. Be sure to measure carefully when setting up, and make several practice cuts to check for accuracy. Properly cut, the dovetails should be snug yet slide into the grooves with a minimum of effort. Remember, when the glue is applied later on, the wood swells slightly, so try to allow for this when cutting. Since the dovetails only show at the front edge, it's most important that the fit be accurate at that point.

We used a molding-head cutter (Sear's p/n 93212) to cut the molding (part P). To increase safety, it's best to cut the molding on the edge of a wide piece of stock, then rip it to its 1 in. width. Use push sticks to keep hands away from the cutter.

The dovetails on each end of part E

(continued on next page)

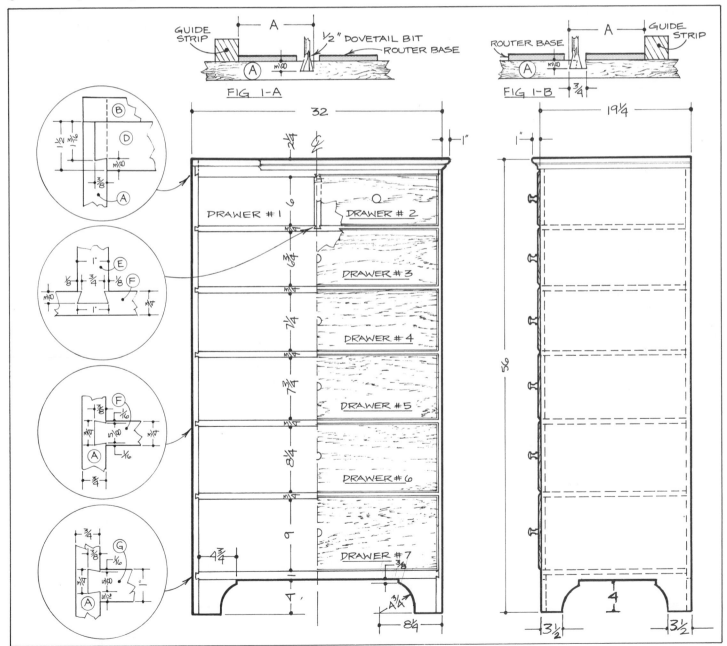

Bill of Materials (All Dimensions Actual)			
Part	Description	Size	No. Req'd
A	Side	¾ x 19¼ x 56	2
B	Top	¾ x 19¼ x 32	1
C	Back	¾ x 10⅜ x 55¾	3
D	Stretcher	¾ x 1½ x 31¼	1
E	Divider	¾ x 1 x 6¾	1
F	Edging	¾ x ¾ x 31¼	5
G	Edging	¾ x 1 x 31¼	1
H	Foot	¾ x 4¾ x 4	2
I	Glue Block	1¼ x 1¼ x 3¾	4
J	Guide	1 x 1½ x 17¾	2
K	Frame End	¾ x 3½ x 17¾	12
L	Frame Front & Back	¾ x 3½ x 26¾	12
M	Frame Divider	¾ x 3½ x 13¼	2
N	Dust Panel	½ x 10¾ x 11⅛	2
O	Runner	¾ x 1 x 17¾	1
P	Molding	See Details	As Req'd
Q	Drawers	See Details	7

are best cut with a dovetail saw. Once cut, transfer the profile to parts D and F, then use a sharp chisel to chop out the waste material.

After the remaining parts are cut to size, all can be given a thorough sanding. Begin assembly by joining the two sides (A), to the top (B). While gluing, use a pair of temporary stretchers to provide proper spacing across the bottom.

Once dry, the bottom drawer frame can be installed. Apply a coat of glue to the front half of the drawer support end (part K) and the back half of the dovetail groove in part A. When the drawer frames are slid in from the front, this gluing technique serves to spread the glue evenly. Once the frame has been slid in place, check for squareness and allow to dry. Once dry, follow the same procedure for all remaining drawer frames.

Although in theory we know that the cross-grain orientation of the drawer frames to the sides should create a serious wood movement problem, in practice, with a piece such as this, which is made of hardwood and has the sides essentially locked in by the series of dovetail frames, the problem never manifests itself. In case you wondered about the function of part J, it serves to prevent the two top drawers from tipping as they are opened.

The seven drawer knobs can be lathe-turned to the dimensions shown or a similar style can be purchased from Shaker Workshops, P.O. Box 1028, Concord, MA 01742.

All remaining parts can now be assembled. Each back piece (part C) is joined to the back of the drawer frames by a single screw through the center of each board. A single screw allows each board to expand and contract with changes in humidity.

The drawers are assembled as shown. Note that the dovetail spacing varies from drawer to drawer.

Give the chest a thorough final sanding, using 220-grit for the final effort. Check all drawers for a good sliding fit. Two coats of a good penetrating oil completes the project.

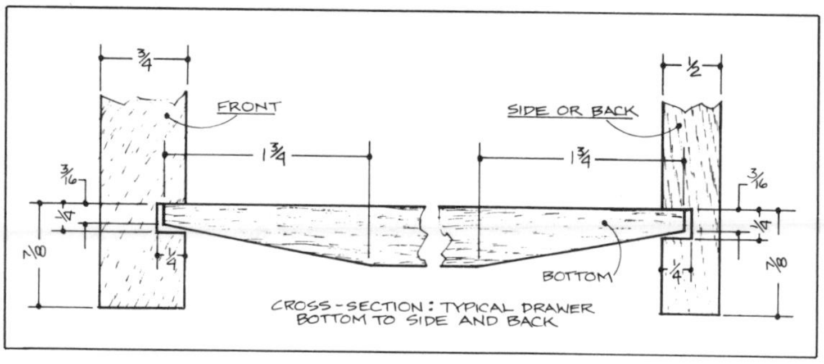

CROSS-SECTION: TYPICAL DRAWER BOTTOM TO SIDE AND BACK

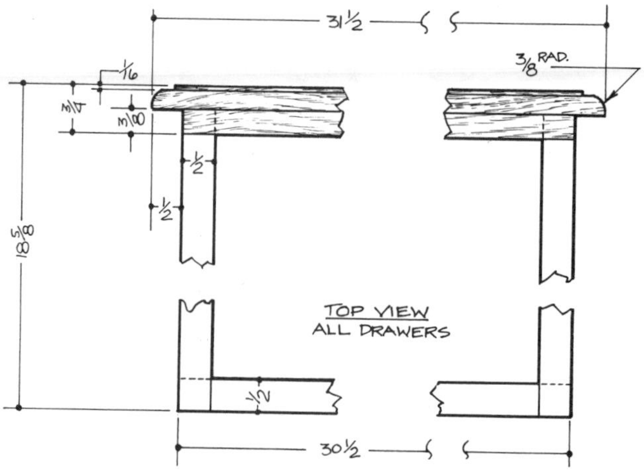

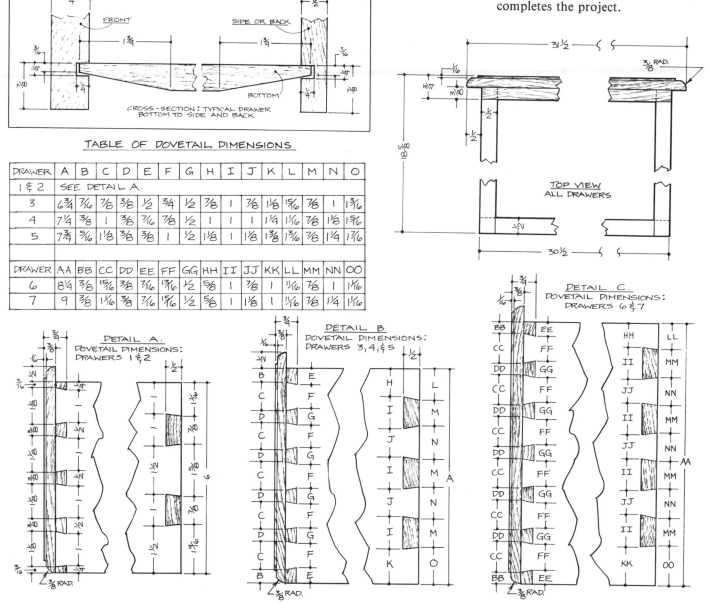

TABLE OF DOVETAIL DIMENSIONS

DRAWER	A	B	C	D	E	F	G	H	I	J	K	L	M	N	O
1 & 2	SEE DETAIL A.														
3	6¾	7/16	⅞	⅜	½	¾	½	⅞	1	⅞	1⅛	15/16	⅞	1	1 3/16
4	7¼	⅜	1	⅜	7/16	⅞	½	1	1	1	1¼	1 1/16	⅞	1⅛	1 5/16
5	7¾	5/16	1⅛	⅜	⅜	1	½	1⅛	1	1⅛	1⅜	1 3/16	⅞	1¼	1 7/16
DRAWER	AA	BB	CC	DD	EE	FF	GG	HH	II	JJ	KK	LL	MM	NN	OO
6	8¼	⅜	15/16	⅜	7/16	13/16	½	⅝	1	⅞	1	11/16	⅞	1	1 1/16
7	9	⅜	1 1/16	⅜	7/16	15/16	½	⅝	1	1⅛	1	11/16	⅞	1¼	1 1/16

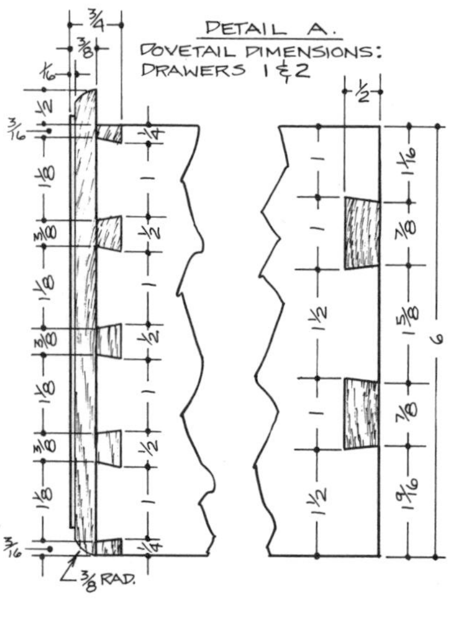

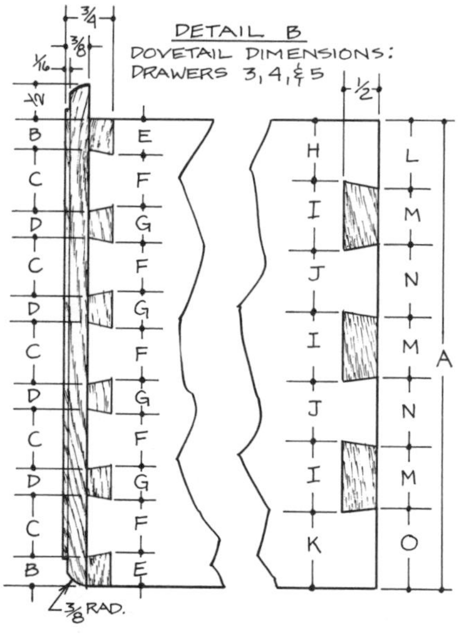

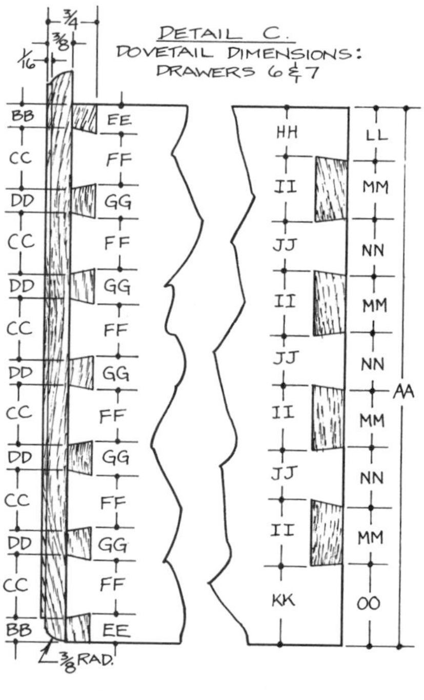

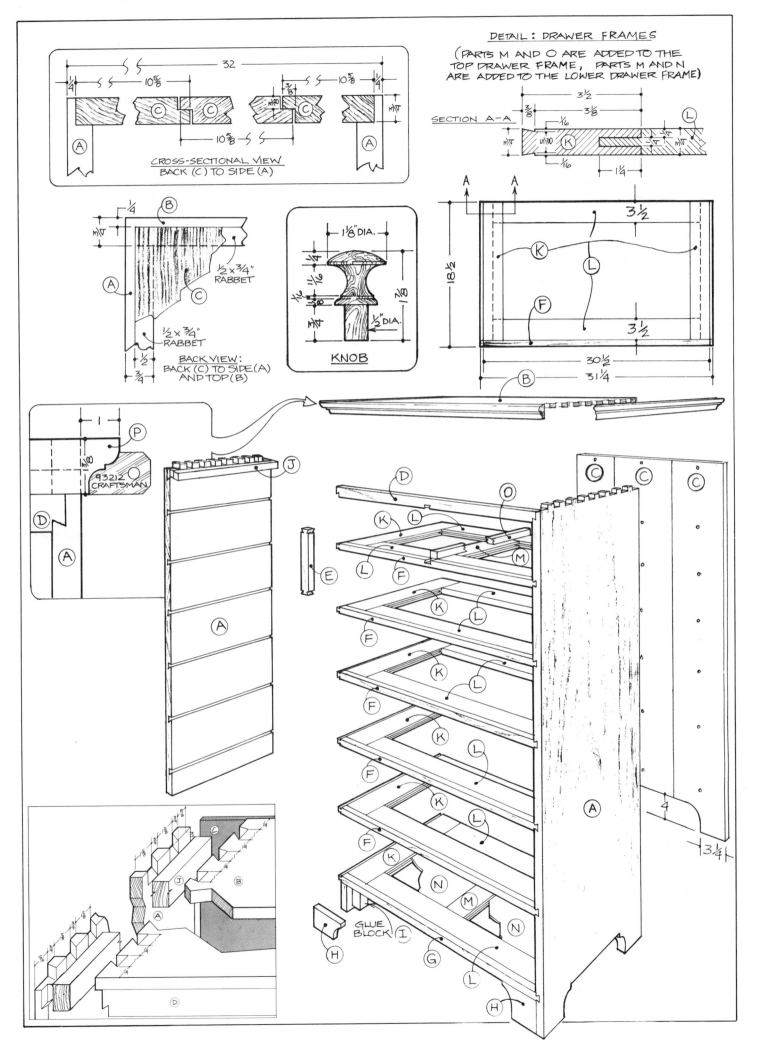

DETAIL: DRAWER FRAMES

(PARTS M AND O ARE ADDED TO THE
TOP DRAWER FRAME, PARTS M AND N
ARE ADDED TO THE LOWER DRAWER FRAME)

SECTION A-A

CROSS-SECTIONAL VIEW
BACK (C) TO SIDE (A)

BACK VIEW:
BACK (C) TO SIDE (A)
AND TOP (B)

KNOB

93212
CRAFTSMAN

GLUE
BLOCK

Hooded Doll Cradle

This scaled down version of an Early American cradle is made from ½ in. thick pine, although a hardwood such as cherry, oak or walnut can also be used.

With its compound angles this piece may at first glance seem challenging, but once the sides (A), front (B), back (C) and bottom (G) have been made and assembled, the remaining hood parts (D, E, F) are simply cut to fit. Since the hood parts are cut to fit after assembly, the dimensions in the bill of materials for parts D, E, and F are approximate.

Once you've prepared stock for the sides, front, and back, use the table saw to cut these parts to final size. Since the sides, front, and back of the cradle tilt out at 10 degrees, the butt joint where these parts meet will be a compound angle. The compound angle tables tell us that for a four-sided butt miter (with sides tilted at 10 degrees), the table saw miter gauge should be angled 9¾ degrees, while the blade is tilted 1½ degrees. However, if you are unable to achieve such accuracy on your table saw, we discovered that a 10-degree miter gauge setting and a 2-degree blade tilt will yield a good tight joint. The cuts on the ends of parts A, B, and C should establish the finish length of these pieces. Next, tilt the table saw blade to 10 degrees, and use the rip fence to establish the bevel on the bottom edge of parts A, B, and C.

Now set the miter gauge at 90 degrees, tilt the sawblade 22 degrees, and with the back edge of part A against the miter gauge, establish the bevel along the top. Next, lay out the curved profiles on the sides and front, using the grid patterns as a guide, and cut these profiles out with a scroll saw, jigsaw, or band saw. Also, on the table saw, establish the 32-degree angle on the top edge of the back, which will support the hood. These angles are accomplished on the table saw with the miter gauge tilted 22 degrees, and the ends of part C backed up to the miter gauge. Just make sure that the angle on the back will fall on a plane with the 22-degree cut you made earlier on the top edge of the sides.

After cutting the bottom to size, assemble the sides, front, back and bottom, using both glue and finishing nails. All the remaining parts, except the rockers (H), will be cut to fit the cradle case. Start with part D, which has the same compound angle cut on its ends as you cut on the ends of parts A and B. Although we show a finish length of 10³⁄₁₆, part D may have to be cut a little longer or shorter in order to fit the actual dimension across your cradle. Establish the 32-degree angles on the top of part D, and trim the ends until you have a perfect fit to the cradle. Then transfer the profile, and cut the curved shape along the lower edge of part D. After part D has been glued and finish nailed in place, you can cut parts E and F to fit. Note that one end of each part E and both ends of part F are cut at 16-degree angles. Let the other end of parts E run long so it overhangs the sides, then hold it in position, scribe a line along the underside where it overhangs, and trim flush. This cut to trim parts E flush with the sides must be made with the blade tilted 22 degrees.

Cut the rockers to size, lay out and cut their profile, and assemble them to the cradle. Final sand, stain if desired, and finish.

Bill of Materials			
Part	Description	Size	No. Req'd.
A	Side	(see detail)	2
B	Front	½ x 5¼ x 8¾	1
C	Back	½ x 10¼ x 9⅞	1
D	Hood Front	½ x 2½ x 10³⁄₁₆	1
E	Hood Top	½ x 4¾ x 4¼	2
F	Hood Center	½ x 4¾ x 4¼	1
G	Bottom	½ x 8½ x 16	1
H	Rocker	½ x 2 x 13	2

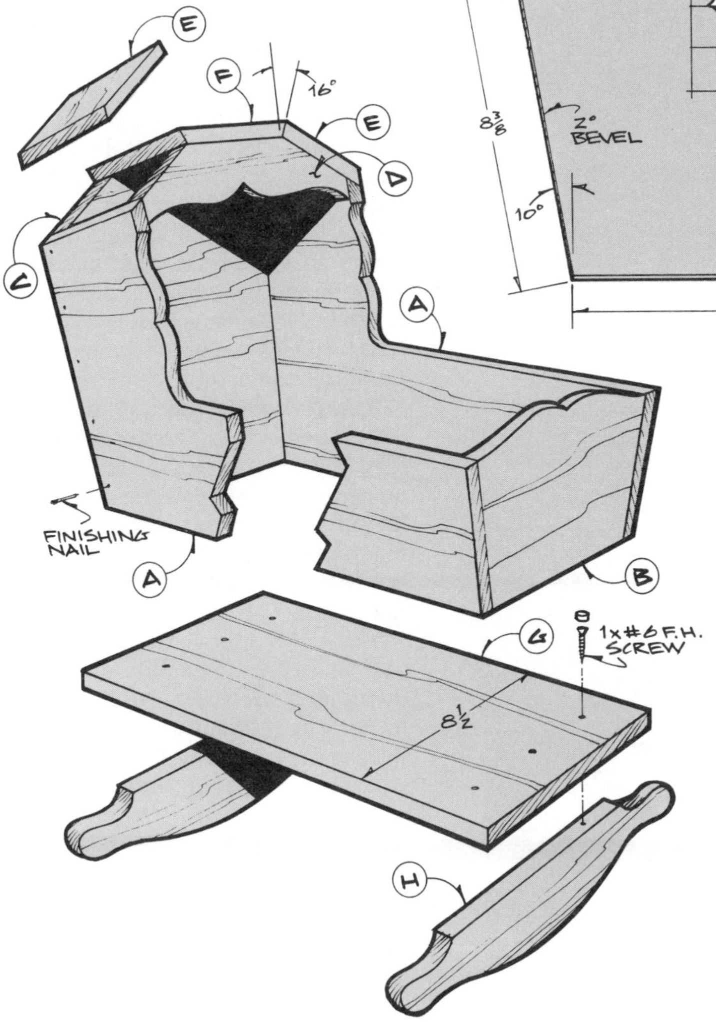
E
F
16°
E
D
C
A
FINISHING NAIL
A
B
G
1x#6 F.H. SCREW
8½
H

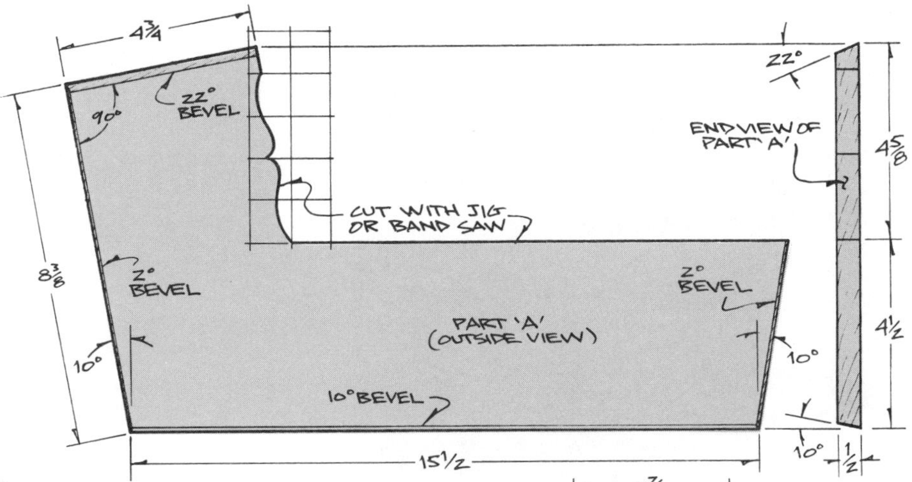
4¾
22° BEVEL
90°
CUT WITH JIG OR BAND SAW
8⅜
2° BEVEL
PART 'A' (OUTSIDE VIEW)
10°
10° BEVEL
2° BEVEL
10°
15½
22°
END VIEW OF PART 'A'
4⅝
4½
10°
½

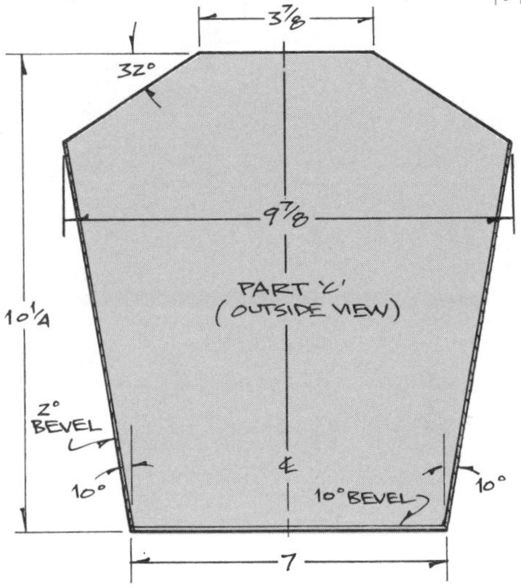
3⅞
32°
9⅞
PART 'C' (OUTSIDE VIEW)
10¼
2° BEVEL
10°
10° BEVEL
10°
7

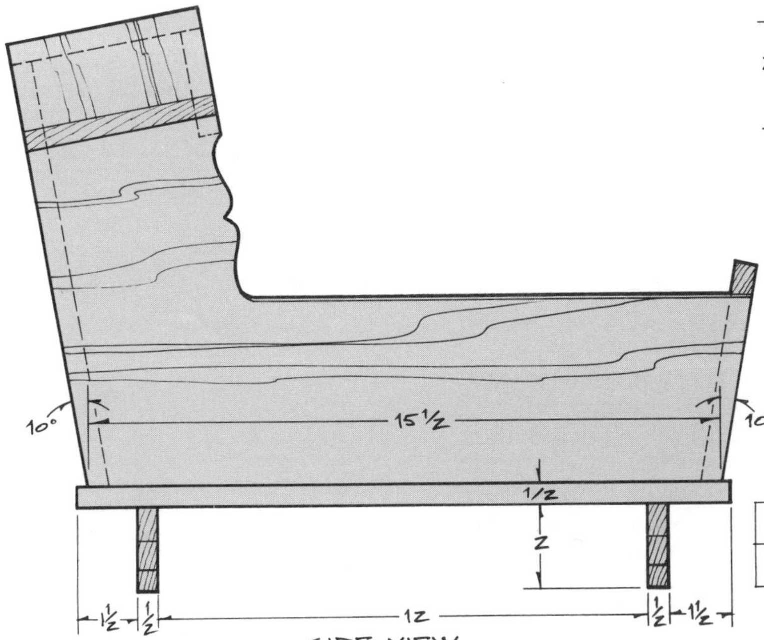
10°
15½
10°
½
2
1½
½
12
½
1½

SIDE VIEW

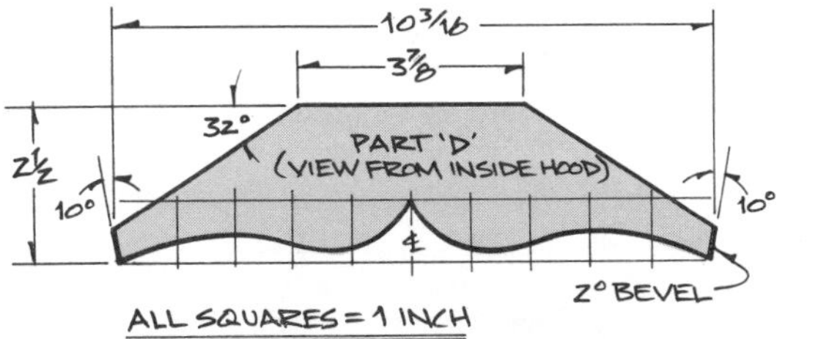
10³⁄₁₆
3⅞
32°
PART 'D' (VIEW FROM INSIDE HOOD)
2½
10°
10°
2° BEVEL

ALL SQUARES = 1 INCH

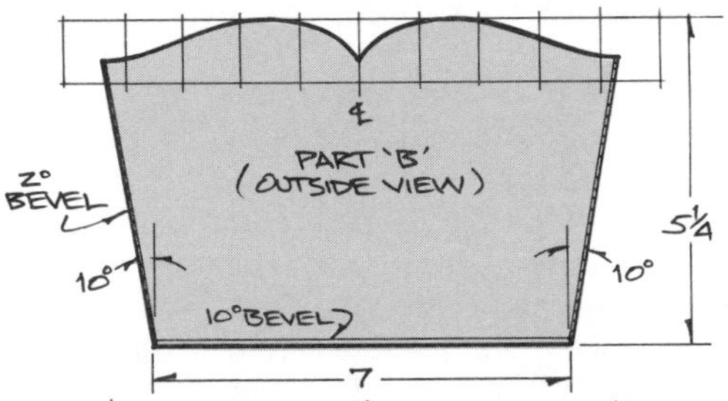
PART 'B' (OUTSIDE VIEW)
2° BEVEL
10°
10° BEVEL
10°
5¼
7

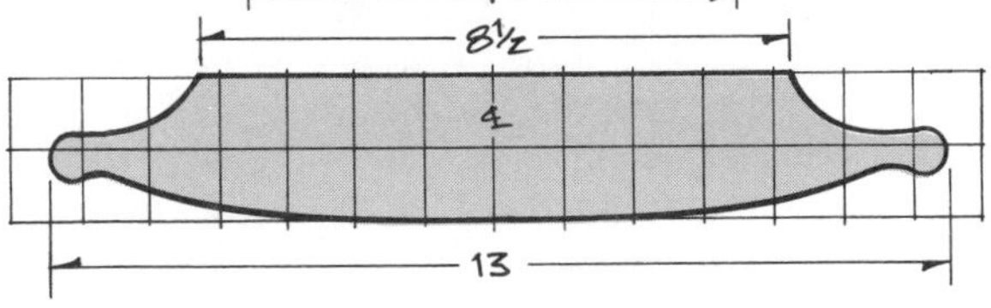
8½
13

Early American Wall Secretary

Early American furniture continues to enjoy a great deal of popularity in this country. This piece, made from pine, certainly has all the flavor, and the charm, of that style.

It's a piece that can be put to use almost anywhere in the house, but we think it can be particularly handy near a telephone since the front folds down to form a writing surface.

The two sides (parts A) can be made first. If you can't get 9¼ in. wide stock you'll have to edge-glue a couple of narrower boards in order to get the needed width. Apply glue to both mating surfaces, then use bar or pipe clamps to clamp together. Allow to dry overnight.

Cut both sides to overall length and width, then lay out and mark the location of the dadoes for the top (part B), upper shelf (part C), middle shelf (part D), and the bottom (part E). The dadoes for parts B and C are ⅜ in. deep by ¾ in. wide and go completely across the board. The dado for part E is also ⅜ in. deep by ¾ in. wide, but it is stopped at a point 1¾ in. from the front edge. The dado for part D is ⅜ in. deep by ¼ in. wide and is stopped at a point 1½ in. from the front edge.

The dadoes are best cut using the dado-head cutter in conjunction with the table saw, although a router can also do the job. It's a good idea to cut

the dadoes slightly less than the thickness of the mating board. Then, when the mating board is later sanded, the fit should be just right.

Next, use a router equipped with a ¼ in. piloted rabbet bit to cut the ⅜ in. by ¼ in. rabbet along the inside back edge. Note that the rabbet stops at the dadoes for parts C and E.

Now, the grid pattern for the side panels can be transferred from the drawing. A band or saber saw will cut it to shape in short order.

Parts B, C, D and E can now be cut to overall length and width. All are ¾ in. thick stock except for the ½ in. thick part D. A router with a ¼ in. straight bit will cut the ¼ in. by ¼ in. stopped dadoes (for parts H) in the bottom of part C and the top of part D. The tenons on each end of parts D and H and the dadoes in parts H for the horizontal divider (I) are best cut with the dado-head. Note that the front edge of part E is cut at a 45-degree bevel.

After part F is made, all parts can be given a thorough sanding, working up to 220-grit. Assemble as shown using glue and wood screws, countersunk and plugged with screw buttons, to secure parts A, B, C, and E. Check for squareness.

Apply glue to the back half of the tenon on each end of part D, then apply glue to the front half of its mating dado in part A. When part D is slid in from the back, this gluing technique serves to spread the glue out evenly. Parts H and I can be added in the same manner. Following this, the plywood back (G) is secured in place with finishing nails.

The door panel (part M) will require edge-glued stock. The bevel is best cut on the table saw with the blade tilted at an angle of about 9 degrees. It's a good idea to clamp a tall (about 6 in.) auxiliary fence to your rip fence in order to support the panel as it's passed over the blade.

The panel groove in parts J and K can be cut on the table saw with the dado-head. However, the panel groove in parts L is stopped, so a router will have to be used here.

After sanding all parts, the door is assembled as shown. Don't glue the panel in place, it must be free to float. Note that you'll need to add a door stop (N) and a bullet catch to hold the door closed.

The project can now be stained to suit. We used two coats of Minwax Golden Oak Wood Finish followed by several coats of their antique oil finish.

If not available locally, the door hinge (called a combination hinge support) is available from The Woodworkers' Store, 21801 Industrial Blvd., Rogers, MN 55374. Order part number D4750.

Bill of Materials			
Part	Description	Size	No. Req'd.
A	Side Panel	¾ x 9¼ x 41¾	2
B	Top	¾ x 6 x 29¼	1
C	Upper Shelf	¾ x 9¼ x 29¼	1
D	Middle Shelf	½ x 8 x 29¼	1
E	Bottom	¾ x 8½ x 29¼	1
F	Front Panel	¾ x 9 x 28½	1
G	Back	¼ x 17¼ x 29¼	1
H	Vertical Divider	½ x 5½ x 8½	2
I	Horizontal Divider	½ x 5½ x 13	1
J	Top Rail	¾ x 3 x 25	1
K	Bottom Rail	¾ x 3 x 25	1
L	Door Stile	¾ x 3 x 17¼	2
M	Door Panel	¾ x 11⅞ x 23⅛	1
N	Door Stop	¾ x 1 x 2	1

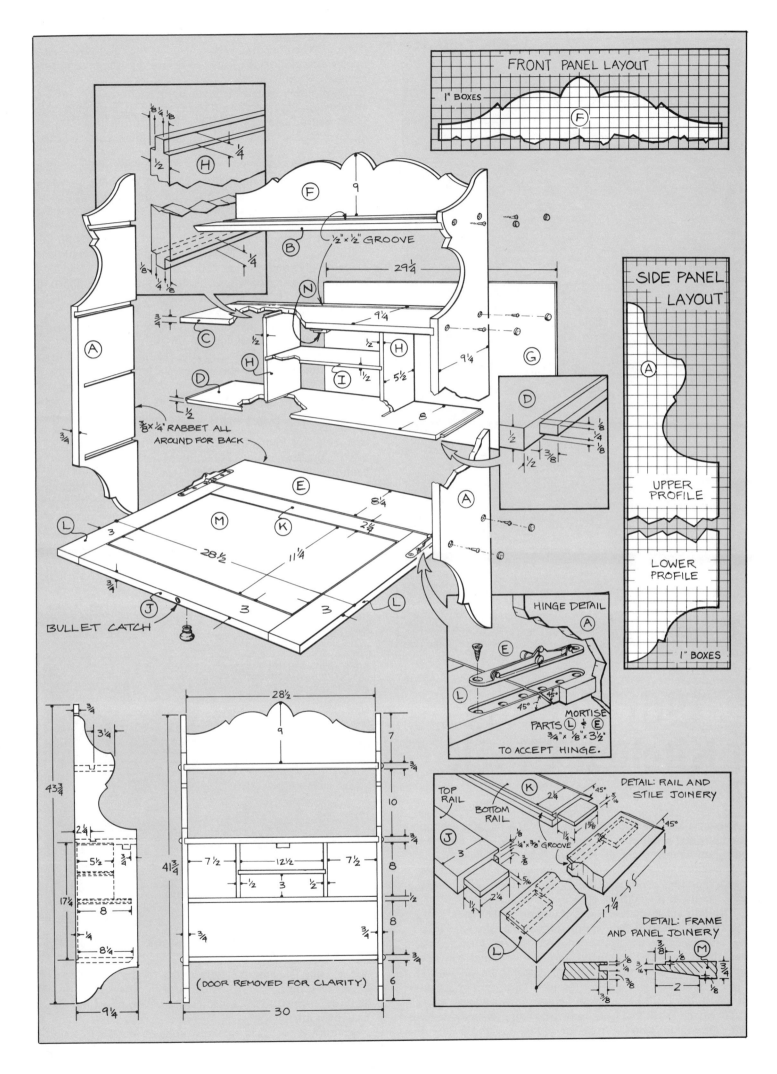

FRONT PANEL LAYOUT

1" BOXES

F

H

1/4
1/2
1/4
1/8
1/4
1/8

F

9

1/2" x 1/2" GROOVE

B

29 1/4

N

C

3/4

A

3/4

3/4

1/2

9 1/4

H

H

1/2

D

I

1/2

H

1/2

5 1/2

9 1/4

G

8

SIDE PANEL LAYOUT

A

UPPER PROFILE

LOWER PROFILE

1" BOXES

D

1/2

3/8

1/8
1/4
1/8

3/8 x 1/4" RABBET ALL AROUND FOR BACK

E

M

K

8 1/4

2 1/4

A

28 1/2

11 1/4

L

3

J

3

3

L

BULLET CATCH

3/4

HINGE DETAIL

A

E

L

45°

45°

MORTISE PARTS L & E 3/4" x 1/8" x 3 1/2" TO ACCEPT HINGE.

3/4

3 1/4

43 3/4

2 1/4

5 1/2

3/4

17 1/4

1/4

8

8 1/4

9 1/4

28 1/2

9

7

3/4

10

3/4

41 3/4

7 1/2

12 1/2

7 1/2

1/2

3

1/2

8

3/4

8

3/4

3/4

6

(DOOR REMOVED FOR CLARITY)

30

DETAIL: RAIL AND STILE JOINERY

TOP RAIL

BOTTOM RAIL

K

2 1/4

45°

5/16

1/8

1 5/8

J

3

1/4" x 3/8" GROOVE

3/8

45°

1 1/4

1/4

2 1/4

5/16

17 1/4

L

DETAIL: FRAME AND PANEL JOINERY

3/8

1/8

1/8
1/4
3/16

3/8

M

3/4

1/8

2

127

necessary. Allow to dry thoroughly before removing the clamps. When dry, sand the outside of the case, giving particular attention to the joints to insure that the mating surfaces are flush.

The molding (part L) is made up of sections X, Y, and Z as shown in Figure 1. You'll need a molding-head (available from Sears-Roebuck), a three bead cutter (Sears' part number 9-2352) and ¼-½ in. quarter-round cutter (Sears' 9-2351).

To make this type of molding, the rip fence must overlap the cutter, so it's mandatory that an auxiliary plywood fence, at least ¾ in. thick, be added to the regular rip fence. Since clamps tend to get in the way, it's best to attach the auxiliary fence with countersunk screws.

Also, the regular table saw insert can't be used with the dado-head, so it must be removed and replaced with one made of plywood. Perhaps the easiest way to do this is to simply cut a piece of ¼-⅜ in. thick by 3-4 in. wide plywood to approximately the length of the rip fence. Then, with the molding-head cutters below the level of the table top, securely clamp the plywood to the saw table after the rip fence has been properly located for the cut.

As shown in figure 1, step 1, the beading cut is made first. For maximum safety when using the molding head, it's a good idea to cut the molding on stock that's wider and longer than necessary and then trim to final dimension with a regular sawblade. Be sure to use a push stick and keep hands away from the cutter. A piece of 1⅜ in. thick stock that measures 3 in. wide by 36 in. long is a good choice.

To make the beading cut, equip the molding head with the beading cutters, then lower the cutters below the level of the table top. Locate and secure the rip fence (with auxiliary fence added). With the plywood insert against the rip fence, clamp the insert to the saw table. Start the saw and slowly raise the cutters to cut through the insert. Raise the cutters to slightly higher than the needed depth of cut, then lower them to the exact cutting height.

Check the set-up on a piece of scrap stock. If all looks satisfactory, run the stock through the cutter.

Replace the dado-head with a regular saw blade, remove the insert, then cut the stock to a width of 1½ in. Following this, locate the rip fence to cut section "Y" to a thickness of

19th Century Kitchen Clock

Called a Kitchen Clock, this clock was a popular item in the late 1800's. Millions were made and sold. We used red oak, but walnut or cherry would also be good choices.

If possible, select quartersawn material for the scrollwork (parts F and H) as it is less likely to cup later on. Also, make sure the stock is well dried.

The two sides (parts A) can be made first. From ½ in. thick stock, cut to overall length and width as shown. The ½ in. wide by ⅜ in. deep rabbet along the top, bottom, and back edges can best be cut on the table or radial-arm saw with a dado-head cutter, although repeated passes with a regular sawblade will also do the job. The ⅜ in. by 3½ in. notch on the front parts A can be cut in the same manner.

Give parts A, B, and C a complete sanding, then assemble with glue and clamps. Check for squareness and adjust if

¹¹⁄₁₆ in. (step 2). Another adjustment of the rip fence will allow the section "X" to be cut to a thickness of ⁷⁄₁₆ in. A final rip fence adjustment will cut part "X" to a 1 in. width (as shown in step 4).

Section "Z" is cut in basically the same manner as was used to cut sections "X" and "Y". Again it's best to use a piece of stock that's about 3 in. wide and about 36 in. long. Note that the cutter will cut into the auxiliary fence as it is raised to it's proper height. Once the molding cut has been made, use a regular saw blade to rip the stock to a width of 1¼ in. (as shown in figure 1, step 4).

Sections X, Y, and Z can now be glued and clamped (see figure 1, step 4). Once dry, sand any rough areas, then cut to length with mitered corners. Apply a coat of glue to the miters and clamp. An easy-to-make jig as shown in figure 2 will prove helpful here.

The base (part D) is made from ¼ in. thick stock. If you don't have a thickness planer, use the band or table saw to resaw thicker stock to ¼ in. Once resawn, cut to final length and width before sanding thoroughly. Part D can now be joined to the molding with glue and clamps.

Now that the base is assembled to the molding, the case (parts A, B, and C) can be joined to the base with glue and ⅝ x #6 flat head wood screws. Note that the back of the case is flush with the back of the base.

The scrollwork (parts F and H) is made from ⅜ in. thick stock. Transfer the profile to the stock, then cut out with a jig saw. Before using the jig saw though, use a ⅝ in. diameter drill bit to form the nine ⅝ in. diameter curves along the top of part F. Once cut out, sand all surfaces, taking special care to smooth the edges.

Lay out and mark the location of the incised lines, then use a "V" groove carving tool to form the cuts. Final sand, then glue the side scrolls (parts H) to the case. The upper scroll (part F) is not glued to the case but rather it is secured with cleats (parts J and K). The cleats are glued and screwed to the case as shown. The rosette (part G) is then face-plate turned and glued in place.

After final sanding all surfaces, we applied a coat of Minwax Golden Oak stain. The many curved surfaces make it difficult to brush on a final finish, so we chose to apply two coats of Deft spray finish.

The movement (part Q), gong (part R), dial plate (part S), and paper dial (part T), can be ordered from S. LaRose, Inc., 234 Commerce Place, Greensboro, NC 27420. Part numbers are shown in the bill of materials, and the gong is included with the movement.

Cut the back (part E) to size and secure to the case with four ¾ by #4 brass round head screws. Note that the width of the back is ⅛ in. less than the actual groove-to-groove dimension. The paper dial (part T) is glued to the dial plate (part S) with disc adhesive, the glue used to bond sanding discs to metal plates. Next, join the dial plate to the back side of the upper scroll (part F) with a pair of small sheet metal screws.

Bill of Materials
(All Dimensions Actual)

Part	Description	Size	No. Req'd.
A	Side	½ x 3½ x 14½	2
B	Top	½ x 3⅛ x 7¼	1
C	Bottom	½ x 3 x 7¼	1
D	Base	¼ x 4⅜ x 13¼	1
E	Back	½ x 7⅛ x 14⅜	1
F	Upper Scroll	⅜ x 9 x 13½	1
G	Rosette	(See Detail)	1
H	Side Scroll	⅜ x 2¼ x 7¾	2
I	Bracket	(See Detail)	1
J	Top Cleat	½ x ½ x 5½	1
K	Side Cleat	½ x ½ x 2	2
L	Molding	(See Detail)	as req'd
M	Door Side	½ x ⅞ x 12¾	2
N	Door Bottom	½ x ⅞ x 7½	1
O	Door Top	½ x ⅞ x 3⅛	3
P	Glass	⅛ x 6⅛ x 13⅝	1
Q	Movement	La Rose 084015	1
R	Gong		1
S	Dial Plate	LaRose 084210	1
T	Paper Dial	LaRose 133-850	1
U	Hinge	¾ x ¾	1
V	Catch	as req'd	1

(continued on next page)

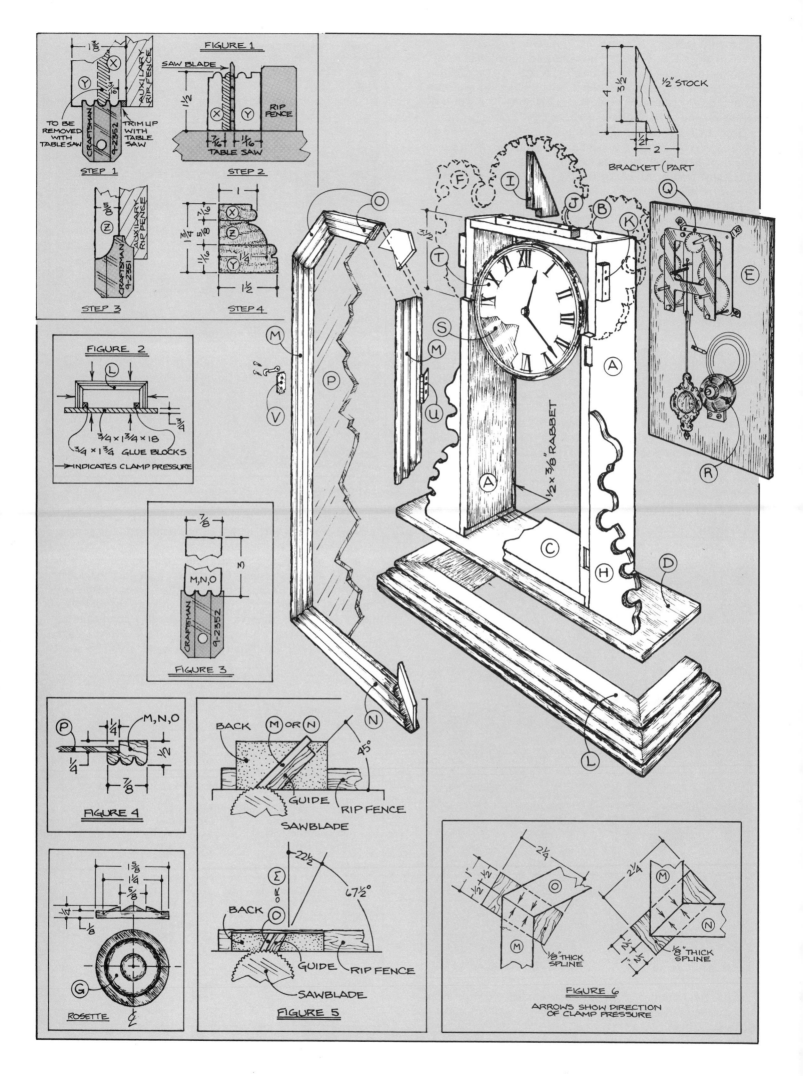

With the case on its back, place the movement inside, then assemble the upper scroll (with part S in place). Align the movement with the holes in part S. Remove part S then join the movement to the back with ½ by #5 pan head screws. Reassemble part S.

To make the beading on the door frame (see figure 3), the molding-head cutter is again used. It's made following the same basic procedure as was used to make the molding. Two 36 in. lengths of beading will provide more than enough stock. For safety's sake use stock at least 3 in. wide. After the beading has been cut it can be ripped to ½ in. thickness. Once cut, use the dado-head cutter to apply the ¼ in. by ¼ in. rabbet as shown in the cross-sectional view (figure 4).

Cut parts M, N, and O to length, mitering the corners as shown. A mitered butt joint, by itself, has minimal strength, especially when there is little surface area for glue as is the case with a small door frame like this. To increase strength, we added ⅛ in. thick splines to each joint. Since the stock is only ½ in. wide, it's important to have a means to support the parts in order to do the job safely. Figure 5 shows two jigs, one to cut the 45 degree angles, and one to cut the 22½ degree angle. The guides are cut from ¾ in. thick stock and glued to a ¾ in. plywood or particleboard back.

To cut the spline grooves, set the table saw to a height of ½ in. and locate the rip fence so that the saw cut will be centered along the ½ in. width of the stock. Clamp the stock

to the jig, then, holding the jig firmly against the rip fence, push the jig through the saw blade. Keep hands away from the blade.

The ⅛ in. splines can now be cut to size keeping in mind that for maximum strength the grain of the spline must run perpendicular to the joint line. Cut each spline to a width of 1 in. and a length of 2¼ (see Fig. 6). Glue the spline to one-half of each joint and allow to dry. Glue and assemble the second half, then apply light clamp pressure perpendicular to the joint line as shown. To apply clamp pressure, clamp a handscrew on each side of the joint line, then use a third clamp to pull the two handscews together. Allow to dry. Follow this procedure for each of the spline joints. Once assembled, the splines can be trimmed and sanded flush. Note that you'll need to cut back the splines where they interfere with the door glass. Stain and finish to match the case.

LaRose sells a stenciled glass (part number 133-8751), although it requires trimming all the way around. They also sell a decal only (part number 112-H243), allowing you to purchase your own glass. Once cut, several glazier (triangle) points are used to secure the glass to the inside of the frame.

The door frame is secured to the case with a pair of small brass hinges (parts U). The addition of a brass catch (part V) completes the project.

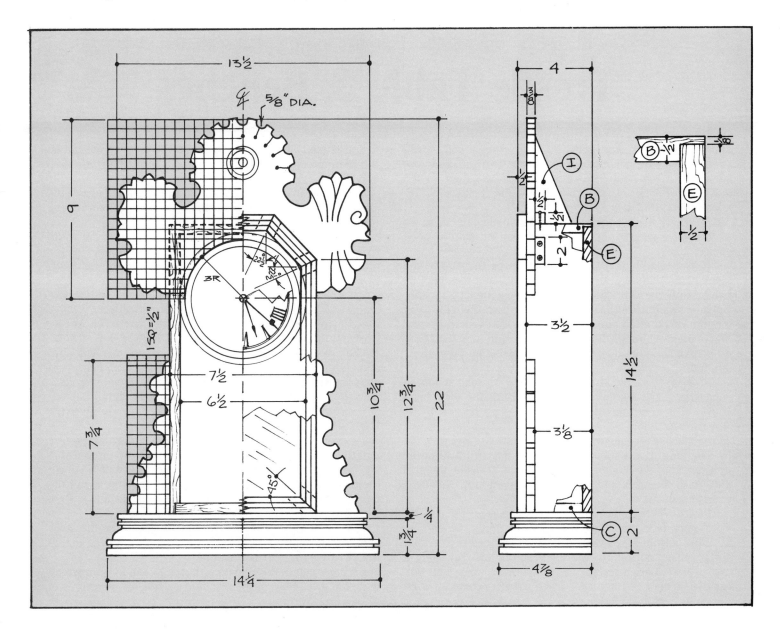

Trestle Table & Benches

In the early days of our country, trestle tables were popular because they could easily be disassembled and moved out of the way when not in use — no small advantage in the one or two room homes commonly found back then. While that feature is not as important today, the trestle table remains a favorite Early American piece.

Those early trestle tables were often made of pine, so we used that wood for our own table. Oak is another good choice.

The two table legs (parts A) can be made first. Since you need 12 in. wide stock, you'll probably have to edge-join two or more narrower boards in order to get enough width. Be sure to allow a little extra stock for both the width and length. When edge-gluing, it's a good idea to add several dowel pins. Although they don't really add strength, they do help to keep the boards aligned when clamp pressure is applied.

The 1 in. thick by 11 in. wide by 1¼ in. long tenon on each end of the leg can best be cut using the dado-head cutter, although repeated passes with a regular saw blade will also do the job.

The mortise for the stretcher (part F) measures 1 in. wide by 5 in. long. Use a sharp chisel to cut out. Work carefully to insure that the edges are square. Next, transfer the grid pattern to the stock and cut out the curved profile using a band or saber saw.

The feet (parts B) are made up of two pieces of 1¾ in. thick stock face glued together. When gluing, be sure to keep the bottom edges flush or else you'll need to joint that surface. The mortise for the leg tenon is best cut using a drill press to bore a series of 1 in. diameter holes. This will remove most of the material. Use a chisel to clean up what

remains.

You'll need a band saw to make the ½ in. deep cut-out on the bottom. If you don't have one, a local millwork shop may do it for you for a nominal charge.

Note that each foot tapers to 2 in. at the ends. Lay out the location of each of the tapers, then use a sharp hand plane to cut to shape.

The cleat (part C) is made next. Cut to length and width from 1¾ in. thick stock, then lay out the location of the mortise. Cut out the mortise in the same way the foot mortise is cut out.

Each cleat has three grooves to accept the table top fasteners (parts I). If your local hardware store doesn't carry these fasteners, they can be purchased from The Woodworkers' Store, 21801 Industrial Blvd., Rogers, MN 55374.

The stretcher (part F) can now be cut to overall length and width from 1¾ in. stock. The tenon on each end is cut with the dado-head cutter or by making repeated passes with the regular saw blade. Referring to the detail, lay out and mark the location of the mortise for the peg (part G). Use a sharp chisel to cut out.

To make the peg (part G), cut 2 in. square stock to a length of about 8 in. Using a push stick, rip the piece to 1½ in., then lay out the taper as shown. Use a hand plane to cut the taper. Assemble the stretcher to the leg and install the peg. Use a mallet to tap it in place. Check the fit-up then trim any excess length on the table saw.

The top is made from 1¾ in. stock. Edge-glue the stock using dowel pins to help keep the boards aligned. Clamp firmly and allow to dry overnight.

All parts can now be given a thorough sanding, finishing with 220 grit. Take particular care to smooth the edges of the curves.

Assemble the leg to the foot and cleat with glue and clamps. Once dry, drill ¼ in. diameter holes as shown, then apply glue to the cleat pins (parts D) and the foot pins (parts E) and drive into the holes. When dry, trim flush and sand smooth.

The project can now be stained and final finished. We used two coats of Minwax's Early American Wood Finish followed by two coats of their Antique Oil Finish.

The top is attached to the base (parts A, B, and C) with the table top fasteners (parts I). One end of the fastener is inserted into the slot in part C, the other end is attached to the table top with round-head wood screws. This method permits the top to change in width as the moisture content changes from season to season.

The benches are made following the basically the same procedure as was used to make the table. The tenon on each end of the leg (parts AA) measures 1 in. thick by 9½ in. wide by 1¼ in. long, and it fits into a corresponding mortise in the foot (parts BB) and the cleats (part CC).

The top (part HH) is attached to the base (parts AA, BB, and CC) with standard 1 in. by 1 in. steel angle stock cut to a length of 10¼ in. Use round-head wood screws to attach.

Final sand all surfaces, then apply a stain and final finish to match the table. To complete the project, apply a coat of paste wax to both the benches and the table.

(continued on next page)

Part	Description	Size	No. Req'd
	Bill of Materials (All dimensions actual)		
	Table		
A	Leg	1¾ x 12 x 23¼ (incl. tenons)	2
B	Foot	3½ x 3½ x 29	2
C	Cleat	1¾ x 2 x 32	2
D	Cleat Pin	¼ Dia. x 1¾	4
E	Foot Pin	¼ Dia. x 2¾	4
F	Stretcher	1¾ x 5 x 42½	1
G	Peg	1½ x 2 x 5¼	2
H	Top	1¾ x 39 x 69	1
I	Fastener	⅝ x 1¼	6
	Bench		
AA	Leg	1¾ x 10½ x 15½ (incl. tenons)	2
BB	Foot	1¾ x 3½ x 15¾	2
CC	Cleat	1¾ x 2 x 11¼	2
DD	Cleat Pin	¼ Dia. x 1¾	4
EE	Foot Pin	¼ Dia. x 2¾	4
FF	Stretcher	1¾ x 4 x 53¼	1
GG	Peg	1½ x 1¾ x 4	2
HH	Seat	1¾ x 11¾ x 67	1
II	Fastener	1 x 1 Angle	2

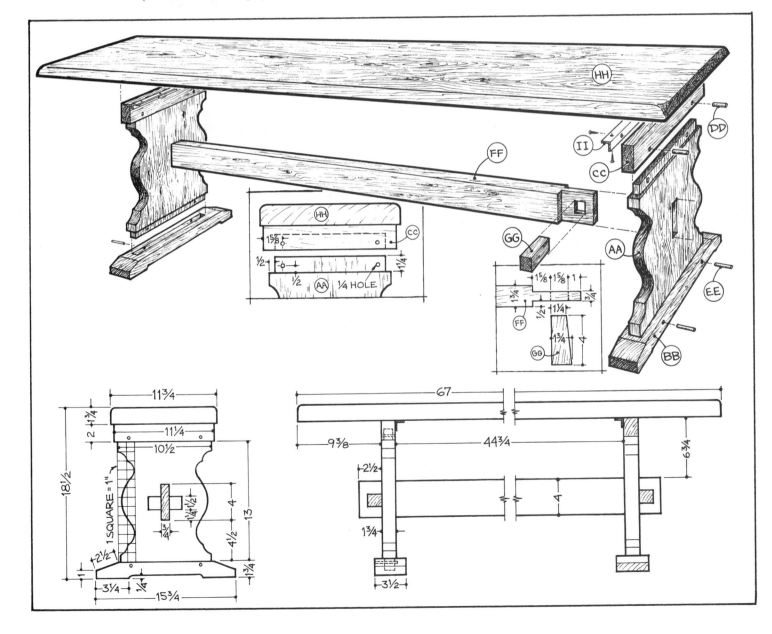

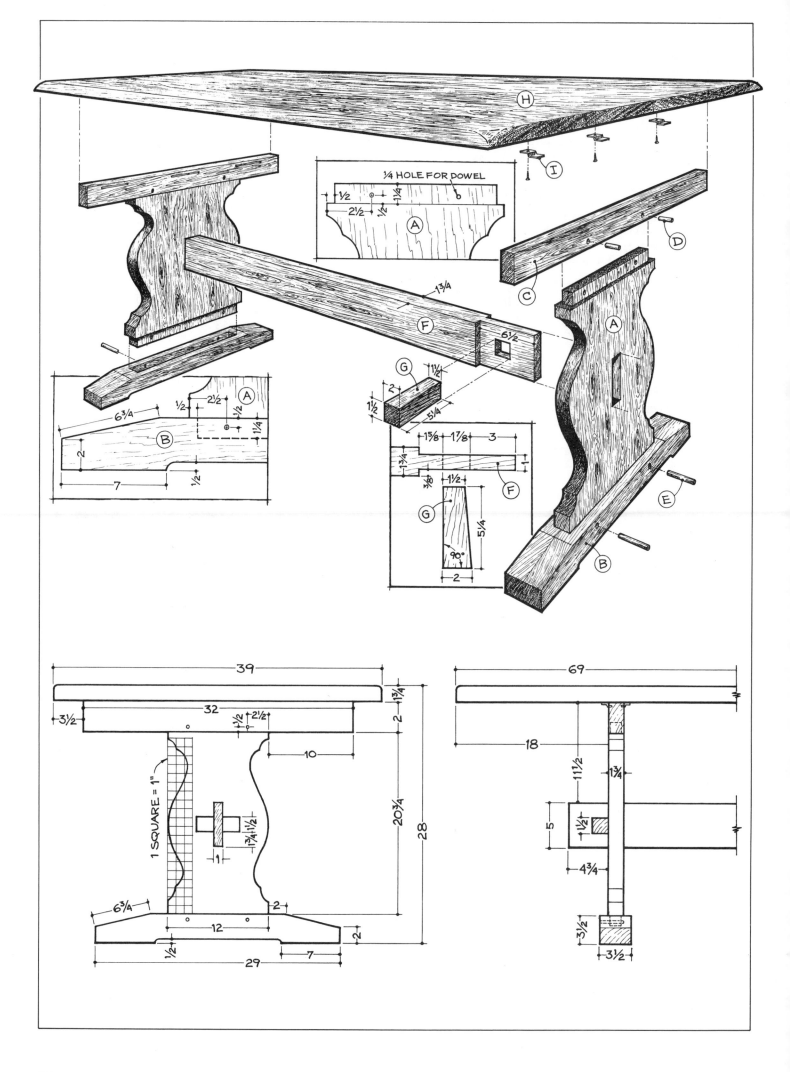

¼ HOLE FOR DOWEL

A

B

1 SQUARE = 1"

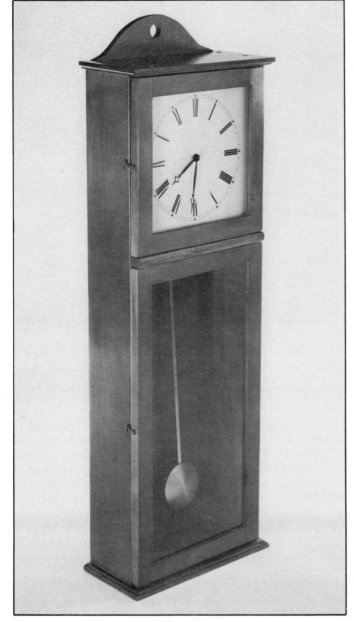

Shaker Wall Clock

This lovely wall clock, made from pine, is very much in the Shaker style. However, with apologies to purists, we modernized it a bit by incorporating a battery-operated quartz movement. These movements keep very accurate time, yet are small and relatively inexpensive, so we feel they are a logical choice for a project like this.

The top and bottom (parts A) can be made first. Cut ¾ in. stock to a width of 5¾ in. and a length of 12 in. Note that the ends and front of each part A consist of a beaded rabbet. The rabbet, which measures ¼ in. deep by 1¼ in. wide, is best cut using the dado-head cutter in conjunction with a table or radial arm saw, although the same results can be obtained by making repeated passes with a regular sawblade.

Once the rabbets are cut, the beading is added. This can be done with a router equipped with a piloted ¼ in. rounding-over bit, although a shaper or router table, if you have one, will make the job even easier. To use the router, clamp the stock firmly to the workbench, then set the bit to form a 1/16 in. lip as shown in the detail. Some readers may find that the length of the pilot is such that the end of the pilot cuts into the workbench. If this is the case with your bit, it will be necessary to include a piece of scrap stock under the workpiece to raise it slightly off the workbench.

To complete work on parts A, a ½ in. deep by 10½ in. long notch is cut along the back edge to accept the back (part T). It can be done using a sharp chisel, or a saber saw or band saw, but the table saw equipped with a dado-head cutter will probably do the job as quickly and accurately as any other way. Set the dado-head to make a ½ in. deep cut, then use the miter gauge to support the stock (on edge) while making a series of cross cuts to form the notch.

The two sides (parts B) are made next. Cut ¾ in. thick stock to a width of 4½ in. and a length of 32½ in. Make the cuts carefully to insure that the ends are square, then use the table saw with a dado-head to cut the ½ in. deep by ½ in. wide rabbet along the inside back edge. The back (part T) will fit in this rabbet when the case is assembled later on.

Parts A and B can now be assembled, but before starting give all four parts a thorough sanding, finishing with 220 grit sandpaper. Add glue to the mating surfaces, then apply light pressure with bar or pipe clamps. Check for squareness and make adjustments as necessary. When dry, remove all clamps and bore ¼ in. diameter holes for the pegs (parts C). Cut the pegs slightly longer than necessary, then add glue and drive into the holes, allowing about 1/16 in. to protrude. When dry, sand flush with the surface.

Next, from ¾ in. thick stock, cut the stretcher (part D) to a width of 1½ in. and a length of 10½ in. Use a ruler and sharp pencil to carefully lay out and mark the dovetail on each end as shown in the detail. Once marked, a dovetail saw or fine-toothed back saw will do a nice job of cutting out the waste stock.

Now that part D is completed, work can continue on parts B. Referring to the front view drawing, note the location of part D on the front edges of parts B. With part D temporarily clamped in its proper position, use a sharp hard pencil to trace the profile of each dovetail. A sharp chisel can then be used to chop out the sockets as shown. Following this, part D can be glued and clamped in place.

To keep weight to a minimum, ½ in. thick stock is used for the back. Most lumber yards don't carry ½ in. thick material, so you'll need to start with thicker stock and reduce it. Many lumber yards have thickness planers, and they are usually willing to plane stock to any thickness for a nominal charge. If your lumber yard doesn't do this, check the telephone book yellow pages for the names of local millwork shops as they also offer this service.

If you have a band saw you can resaw five-quarter stock (which measures about 1⅛ in. thick) to get enough material for the back. Select a piece that measures 5½ in. wide by about 37 in. long, then use a marking gauge to scribe a line along the centerline of the edge. With this as a guideline, the band saw is used to cut the stock in half; each piece now 5½ in. wide, 37 in. long, and slightly more than ½ in. thick.

Of course, there's still another way to reduce the thickness of a board. A sharp smooth or jack plane, and a little hard work, will produce a thinner board in short order. Before you start though, use the marking gauge to scribe the ½ in. thickness all around the stock. This guideline will make it easier to maintain the same thickness throughout.

The ½ in. thick stock can now be edge-glued to get the 10½ in. width that's needed. Apply glue to both mating surfaces and clamp with bar or pipe clamps. When edge-gluing, it's best to allow a little extra length and width of stock. After the clamps are removed, it can then be trimmed to final length and width on the table or radial-arm saw.

Next, mark the centerline of the 1 in. diameter hole as shown. When boring the hole, be sure to clamp a piece of scrap stock on the back side to keep the stock from splintering out. Now, transfer the curved profile of part T to the stock, then cut out with a band or saber saw.

The top and bottom door frames (parts L, M, P, and Q) can now be made. Cut each part to the dimensions shown in the bill of materials, then lay out the location of the mortises on parts M and Q. Most of the waste stock can be removed by making a series of holes using a ⅜ in. diameter drill bit. When drilling though, be sure to keep the bit both square to the edge and parallel to the 1¼ in. wide face surface. And drill the holes slightly deeper (about ¹⁄₁₆ in.) than the 1 in. tenon length. Later, when the joint is assembled, this extra depth will allow room for any excess glue or wood chips that would otherwise prevent the joint from closing tightly.

The tenons on each end of parts L and P are made next. You can hand cut the tenons using a dovetail saw or fine-toothed back saw, but we find it easiest to use the table saw with the dado-head cutter. Set the dado-head to make a ³⁄₁₆ in. deep cut, then use the miter gauge to pass the stock through the cutter. Since the shoulder depth is the same all around, the cutter height need not be changed.

Once the mortises and tenons are cut, both the top and bottom frames can be assembled. Apply glue to each mortise and tenon, then assemble and clamp firmly. Check for squareness and make adjustments as necessary, then set aside to dry.

A ¼ in. wide by ½ in. deep rabbet is now cut into the back of both the top and bottom frames. This rabbet, which serves to accept the glass (parts N and R) and the molding (parts O and S), is cut using a router equipped with a piloted ¼ in. rabbeting bit. Clamp the frame to your workbench (front side down) then rest the router on the back surface of the frame with the bit set for a ½ in. deep cut. Make the cut while moving the router in a counterclockwise direction. You'll need to square the corners with a chisel.

Bill of Materials (All Dimensions Actual)			
Part	Description	Size	No. Req'd
A	Top & Bottom	¾ x 5¾ x 12	2
B	Side	¾ x 4½ x 32½	2
C	Peg	¼ Dia. x 1 Long	8
D	Stretcher	¾ x 1½ x 10½	1
E	Cleat	¾ x ¾ x 10¼	2
F	Divider	¾ x 1 x 11	1
G	Dial Board	¼ x 9½ x 10¼	1
H	Movement (w/ Pendulum)	Klockit	1
I	Paper Dial	Mason & Sullivan	1
J	Side Retainer	¼ x ½ x 10¼	2
K	Top & Bottom Retainer	¼ x ½ x 9½	2
L	Top Door Rail	¾ x 1¼ x 10½ (inc. tenons)	2
M	Top Door Stile	¾ x 1¼ x 11	2
N	Top Door Glass	⅛ x 9 x 9	1
O	Top Glass Molding	¼ quarter-round	As req'd
P	Bottom Door Rail	¾ x 1¼ x 10½ (inc. tenons)	2
Q	Bottom Door Stile	¾ x 1¼ x 20¾	2
R	Bottom Door Glass	⅛ x 9 x 18¾	1
S	Bottom Glass Molding	¼ quarter round	As req'd
T	Back	½ x 10⅜ x 36	1
U	Hinge	Mason & Sullivan	4
V	Hasp	Mason & Sullivan	2

The two cleats (parts E) are now cut to size and screwed in place. Note that they are located ¾ in. from the front edge of parts B as shown in the exploded view. Also, at this time, the divider (part F) can be cut to size and glued and clamped in place.

If you plan to stain the piece, this is a good time to do it. Sand all parts to 220 grit, then stain to suit. When the stain is dry, apply two coats of a good penetrating oil.

To make the dial board (part G), cut ¼ in. thick plywood to a width of 9½ in. and a length of 10¼ in. At a point 5¼ in. from the top edge (and centered along the width), drill a ⅜ in. diameter hole for the movement (part H) shaft.

The paper dial (part I) is available from the Mason & Sullivan Co., 586 Higgins Crowell Road, West Yarmouth, MA 02673. Order part number 2820P (specify an 8 in. dia. time ring).

Next, glue the paper dial to the front face of part G. Make sure that the centerline of the paper dial lines up with the centerline of the movement shaft hole. Part G can then be secured to parts E with four small wood screws.

Parts J and K, which serve as a frame around the dial face, can now be cut and secured to part G with small brass wood screws as shown.

The quartz movement (part H) can be purchased from the mail order company, Klockit, P.O. Box 629, Lake Geneva, WI 53147. Order part no. 11059 which includes a 20 in. long pendulum (measured from the handshaft to the tip of the pendulum bob) and a pair of hands. Be sure to specify the hands — part no. 66977.

The top and bottom door frames are secured to the case with brass hinges (parts U). A brass hook and eye, available from Mason & Sullivan (part no. 2548B), is added to each door as shown. The hinges are also available from Mason & Sullivan. Order part no. 2450B.

The glass (parts N and R) should be cut so that it fits in the rabbets with a little room to spare. If it's a tight fit, and the door frame parts expand, the glass could break. The glass is held in place with ¼ in. quarter-round molding (parts O and S). A pair of small brads in each strip of molding will secure them to the door frame parts.

Now the movement, pendulum, and hands can be installed. With these in place, the back (part T) is added. Note that the screws are located near the center to allow the back to move with a minimum of restriction.

A coat of paste wax and a good rub-down will complete the project.

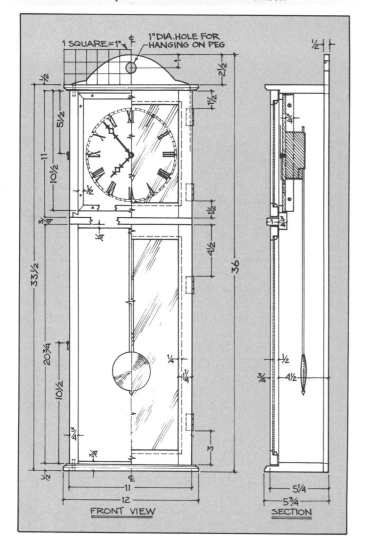

1 SQUARE=1"   1"DIA.HOLE FOR HANGING ON PEG

FRONT VIEW

SECTION

¼ ROUND CUTTER

C

A

B

¼   ¼

TOP VIEW

2½ ¼   ⁴   T   ½

B

A

GLASS

¼ ROUND
MOLDING

DOOR
FRAME
SECTION

¼

¼

1¼

¾

¾

¼

³⁄₁₆

7/8

DOOR
FRAME
JOINERY

D

¾

½

³⁄₁₆

¼

2

Colonial Water Bench

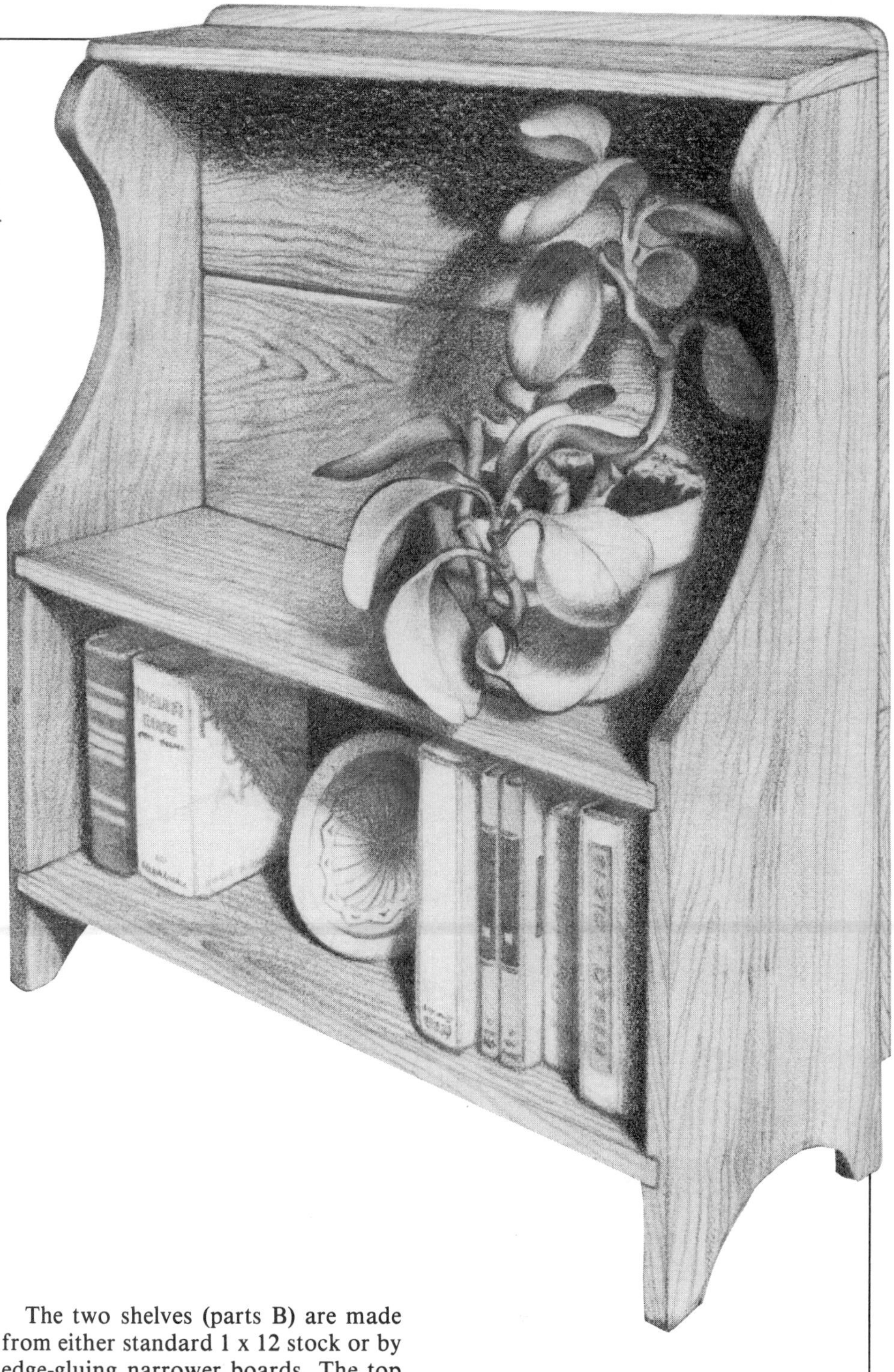

Colonial Americans didn't have the luxury of turning on a tap to get fresh water. Back then, the family's water supply was usually in the form of several large buckets of water, all conveniently stored on a piece of furniture appropriately called a water bench. Filling the buckets was a regular chore, usually assigned to one of the children, and it meant a trek to the well or nearby stream.

We've seen the benches in many sizes and shapes, but this design has to be one of our favorites. We found it in the book *The Pine Furniture of Early New England* by Russell Hawes Kettell, Dover Publications.

We made only minor dimensional changes, the most important one being a change in stock thickness from 1 in. to ¾ in. We felt this change was worthwhile since many of our readers prefer to work with ¾ in. thick stock.

The two sides (parts A) can be made first. Since they measure 11¼ in. wide, you can use standard 1 x 12 lumberyard stock (which measures ¾ in. thick by 11¼ in. wide). Or, if you prefer, you can edge-glue two or more narrower boards in order to get 11¼ in. width. When edge-gluing, be sure to allow a little extra stock for both the width and length. Also, it's a good idea to add several dowel pins to each edge joint. Although these pins don't add strength, they will help keep the boards aligned when clamp pressure is applied. Apply glue to both mating surfaces, then clamp with bar or pipe clamps and allow to dry overnight. Once dry, trim to the length and width shown in the bill of materials.

The ⅜ in. deep by ¾ in. wide dadoes for the shelves (parts B) are best cut using the table saw equipped with a dado-head cutter. Set the dado-head for a ⅜ in. depth of cut, then use the miter gauge to push the stock through the cutter. Once the dadoes are cut, transfer the curved profile from the grid pattern to the stock, then cut out with a band or saber saw.

The back (parts D) can be cut from standard 1 x 8 stock, using the dado-head to machine the tongue and groove joints. Note that all back parts will be 5⅞ in. wide, except the topmost board, which will not require the ⅜ in. tongue. Note also that no groove is machined into the bottom board.

The two shelves (parts B) are made from either standard 1 x 12 stock or by edge-gluing narrower boards. The top (part C) can also be cut to size at this time.

All parts can now be given a thorough sanding prior to assembly. Start with 80 grit paper to remove the planer marks, then progress to 120, 150, and 220 grit.

Assemble parts A to B with glue and clamps. Check for squareness and adjust as necessary. Once dry, remove all clamps and drill holes for dowel pins as shown. Cut each dowel pin slightly over length, then add glue and drive into place. Trim the excess with a dovetail saw before sanding smooth. The top (part C) and back (parts D) are added in the same manner.

The bench can now be final sanded using 220 grit paper. A generous rounding of all corners and edges will simulate years of wear. Some judicious distressing is also in order at this point.

Two coats of Minwax's Early American Wood Finish will produce a good color. An application of their Antique Oil Finish will complete the project.

Bill of Materials

Colonial Water Bench

Part	Description	Size	No. Req'd
A	End	¾ x 11¼ x 34¾	2
B	Shelf	¾ x 11¼ x 30	2
C	Top	¾ x 5 x 30¾	1
D	Back	¾ x 5⅞ x 30¾	6

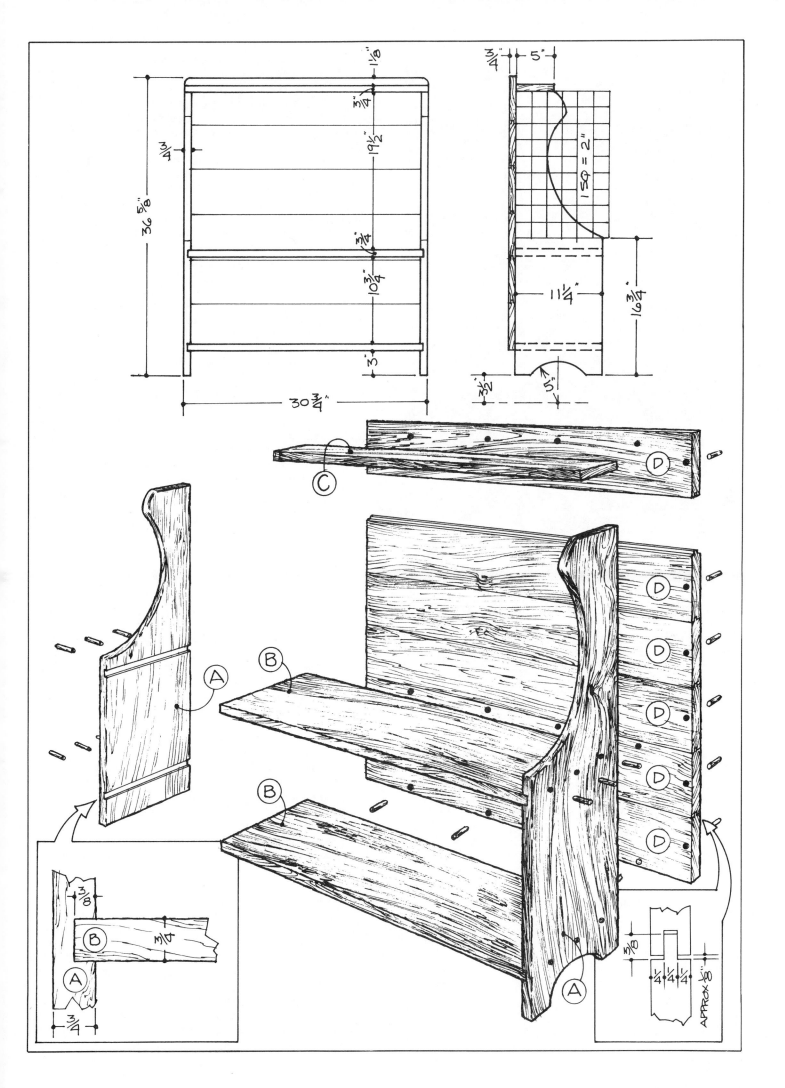

Country Vegetable Bin

Here's a charming reproduction of an old-time country vegetable bin, an item that is as practical in today's kitchen as it was years ago. It also makes a useful general storage cabinet that can be put to use in just about any room in the house. We suspect that many readers will find it serves especially well as a place to keep linens.

Ours is made from pine, a wood commonly used by country cabinetmakers. Oak would be another good choice.

Begin construction by making the two sides (parts A). If you can't locate 1 x 12 stock (which measures 11¼ in. wide), it will be necessary to edge-glue two or three narrower boards to get enough width. Apply a thin coat of glue to the mating surfaces, then clamp firmly with several bar or pipe clamps. When edge-gluing, it's a good idea to allow a little extra length and width of stock. Later, after the clamps have been removed, it can be trimmed to final length and width on the table or radial-arm saw.

Next, lay out the location of the ¾ in. wide by ⅜ in. deep stopped dadoes that are cut to accept the shelves (parts B). A router equipped with a straight bit provides the easiest way to make this cut; simply clamp a straightedge guide to the side stock, offsetting the guide an amount that will properly locate the router bit. If a ⅜ in. diameter router bit is used, you'll need to relocate the straightedge to get the ¾ in. width that's needed.

Note that each dado on part A is stopped at a point ¾ in. from the front edge. The router will leave rounded corners, so a chisel is used to square them off.

In order to accept the back (part E), a ¼ in. deep by ⅜ in. wide rabbet is then cut on the back edge of each part A. This is best done on the table saw in conjunction with a dado-head cutter, although repeated passes with a regular saw blade will also do the job.

Next, transfer the profile of the bottom curve from the drawing to the stock. Use a saber saw or band saw to cut to shape. Cut slightly on the waste side of the stock, then sand to the marked line.

The three shelves (parts B) can be made next. If stock must be edge-glued, follow the same procedure as was used earlier. Once dry, trim to final length and width, then cut the ⅜ in. by ¾ in. notches on each of the front corners as shown.

After the top (part C) has been cut to size, parts A, B, and C can be given a thorough sanding, finishing with 220 grit paper. Apply glue to the mating surfaces of parts A and B, then clamp with bar or pipe clamps. Note that the front of parts B are flush with the front of parts A. Check for squareness; if all looks o.k., set aside to dry. Once dry, bore holes for ¼ in. diameter by 1 in. long dowel pins. Cut each dowel pin slightly over length, then add glue and drive into place. Trim the excess with a dovetail saw before sanding smooth. Part C is added in the same manner.

With part C in place, a router equipped with a piloted ⅜ in. rabbet bit can be used to cut the ¼ in. deep by ⅜ in. wide rabbet along the back of part C. Note that the rabbet is stopped at each end. A sharp chisel can be used to square the rounded router bit cut. The back (part E) is then cut to size and glued in place. A few small finishing nails will hold the back in place as the glue dries.

The door stiles (parts F) and rails (parts G) can be made next. Cut to length and width from ¾ in. stock, then use the dado-head cutter to cut the half-lap joints on each end. Apply glue to each joint and clamp securely. Once dry, a router with a ⅜ in. piloted rabbet bit is used to cut the ⅜ in. deep by ⅜ in. wide rabbet that accepts the screen (part H) and the molding (part I).

We used ½ in. mesh galvanized steel screen (available at just about any hardware store) for part H. Four strips of ¼ in. by ¼ in. molding, each secured with two or three finishing nails, will hold the screen in place.

Final sand all surfaces, then finish to suit. We used two coats of Minwax's Golden Oak Finish followed by two coats of their Antique Oil Finish. The addition of brass hinges and porcelain knobs completes the project.

Bill of Materials
(All Dimensions Actual)

Part	Description	Size	No. Req'd.
A	Side	¾ x 11 x 35¾	2
B	Shelf	¾ x 10¾ x 16¾	3
C	Top	¾ x 11½ x 18½	1
D	Door Stop	¾ x ¾ x 16	3
E	Back	¼ x 16¾ x 33⅞	1
F	Stile	¾ x 1¼ x 10¼	6
G	Rail	¾ x 1¼ x 16	6
H	Screen	As Req'd.	3
I	Molding	As Req'd.	
J	Turnbutton	⅜ x ½ x 1¼	3

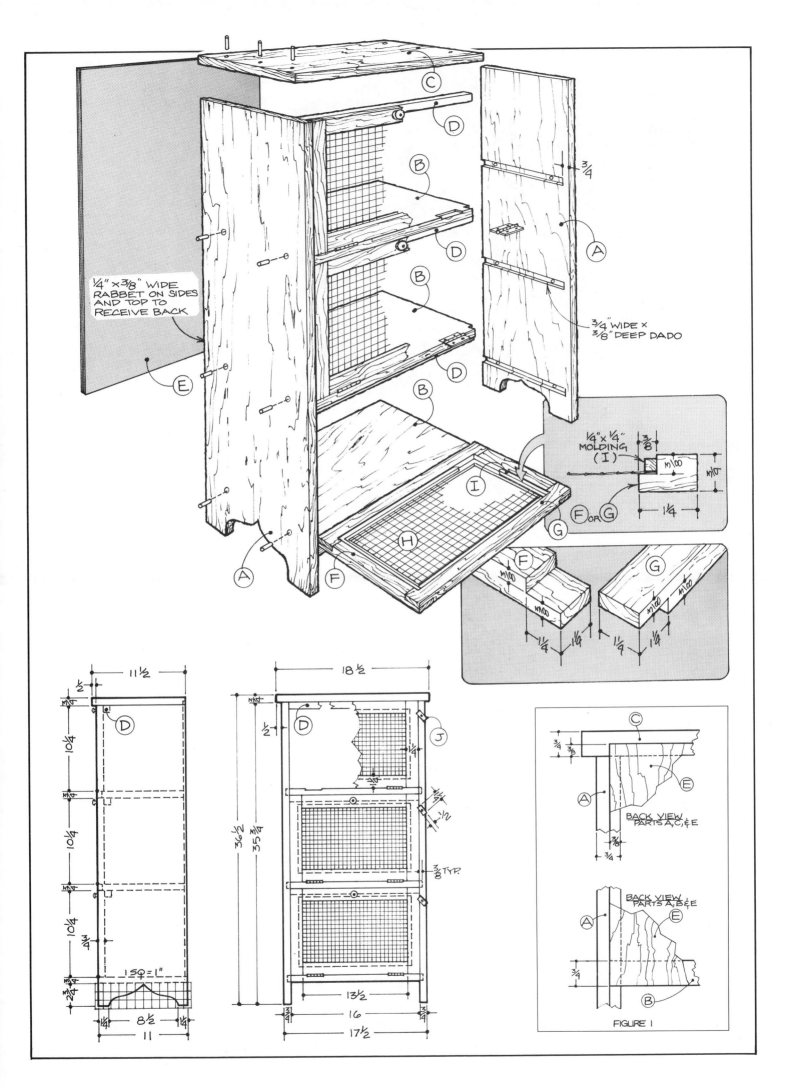

¼" × ⅜" WIDE
RABBET ON SIDES
AND TOP TO
RECEIVE BACK

¾" WIDE ×
⅜" DEEP DADO

¼" × ¼"
MOLDING
(I)

BACK VIEW
PARTS A,C,&E

BACK VIEW
PARTS A,B&E

FIGURE 1

Writing Desk

This writing desk will make a handsome addition to just about any room in the house. The one shown is made of cherry, a logical choice for a piece like this, but mahogany or walnut would also look good.

The four legs (parts A) can be made first. Cut the 1¾ in. square stock to a length of about 30 in., then lathe-turn each leg to the profile shown on the drawing. Once turned, sand to 220 grit while still on the lathe, then remove and trim to a final length of 28¼ in.

Next, lay out and mark the location of the various mortises in each leg, keeping in mind that all mortises are centered along the 1¾ in. leg width. Note that the top mortises measure ½ in. wide by 4⅜ in. long by 1 in. deep while the bottom mortises measure ½ in. wide by 1¼ in. long by 1 in. deep. When making the mortises, you'll find that most of the waste stock can be removed by making a series of holes using a ½ in. diameter drill bit. When

drilling, though, be sure to keep the bit square to the edge so that later, when the desk is assembled, the tenons will fit snugly in the mortises. After the holes are drilled, the remaining waste stock can be cleaned up with a sharp chisel.

The two side aprons (parts B) and the back apron (part C) can be made

next. The tenons can best be cut using the table saw equipped with a dado-head cutter, although repeated passes with a regular saw blade will also do the job. Carefully lay out and mark each tenon, then raise the dado-head cutter or saw blade to a height of ⅛ in. Now, using the miter gauge, pass the stock (5 in. wide side down) over the cutter to establish the 1 in. tenon length. You'll need a second pass to clean up the remaining material; several more passes will be needed if a regular saw blade is used.

Next, flip the stock over and repeat the process on the other side, then check for a good fit-up in the leg mortise. Keep in mind that the tenon thickness is regulated by the height of cutter or saw blade. Following this, the ⅛ in. step is cut on the bottom edge, then the cutter height is raised to ½ in. to cut the ½ in. step on the top edge.

The lower drawer opening, consisting of parts D, E, and F, is made next. Begin by cutting stock to size. From ¾ in. thick stock, cut parts D to 1 in. wide by 35 in. long; cut parts E to 3 in. wide by 3½ in. long; and cut part F to 3 in. wide by 2 in. long. Next, edge-glue part F at the centerpoint (measured along the length) of part D. When dry, measure 13 in. in each direction (see drawing), then edge-glue parts E in place. Allow to dry, then trim each part E to 3 in. long, resulting in an overall length of 34 in. for parts D. Following this, cut the tenon on each end following the same procedure used to cut parts B and C.

Parts J, the two side stretchers, and part K, the back stretcher, are made next. From ¾ in. thick by 1½ in. wide stock, cut part J to 16¾ in. and part K to 34 in. Once again, the dado-head cutter is used to cut the tenons, only this time the cutter height is set to ⅛ in. for all cuts.

Next, use a sharp chisel to cut the mortises for the drawer runners (parts I) in part C and the lower part D. Note

Part	Description	Size	No. Req'd
A	Leg	1¾ x 1¾ x 28¼	4
B	Side Apron	¾ x 5 x 16¾ *	2
C	Back Apron	¾ x 5 x 34 *	1
D	Drawer Frame	¾ x 1 x 34 *	2
E	Outside Spacer	¾ x 3 x 3 *	2
F	Inside Spacer	¾ x 3 x 2	1
G	Cleats	¾ x 2 x 16¾	3
H	Drawer Guide	½ x ¾ x 15¾	4
I	Drawer Runner	¾ x 1 x 16½ *	4
J	Side Stretcher	¾ x 1½ x 16¾ *	2
K	Back Stretcher	¾ x 1½ x 34 *	1
L	Top	¾ x 20 x 36	1
M	Pins	⅜ dia. by 2¾ long	6

Part	Description	Size	No. Req'd
N	End	¾ x 13 x 19	2
O	Back	¾ x 15 x 33¾	1
P	Shelf	¾ x 8 x 33¾ *	2
Q	Divider	¾ x 8 x 3	4
R	Top Drawer Front	¾ x 3¾ x 11¾	2
S	Top Drawer Side	⅜ x 3 x 7¾	4
T	Top Drawer Back	⅜ x 3 x 10⅝	2
U	Top Drawer Bottom	⅛ x 7¼ x 10½	2
V	Bottom Drawer Front	¾ x 3¾ x 13¾	2
W	Bottom Drawer Side	⅜ x 3 x 12	4
X	Bottom Drawer Back	⅜ x 3 x 12⅝	2
Y	Bottom Drawer Bottom	⅛ x 11½ x 12½	2
Z	Bottom Drawer Pull	as shown	2

Bill of Materials
(All Dimensions Actual)

* including tenon(s)

that a total of eight mortises are required. Following this, parts I can be cut to size and tenons cut in each end.

The cleats (parts G) are made from ¾ in. thick stock. Rip to a width of 2 in., then cut to a length of 16¾ in. Use the dado-head cutter to cut the ⅜ in. deep by ½ in. wide notch on each end.

Parts A, B, C, (D, E, and F), G, I, J, and K can now be assembled. Give all parts a thorough sanding, finishing with 220 grit. Begin assembly by joining parts B and J to parts A. Apply glue to each mortise and tenon, then assemble with glue and pipe clamps. As always, use clamp pads to protect the stock, and check for squareness as soon as the clamps are tightened.

Parts C, I, DEF, and K can now be joined to ABJ, Again following the same procedure. Once dry, glue and clamp the drawer guides (parts H) in place as shown.

Next, place parts G in their proper position, then use a sharp pencil to scribe the location of the ⅜ in. by ½ in. notch to be cut in part C and the upper part D. Use a sharp chisel to chop out the notch. Glue and clamp in place, then bore elongated screw holes as shown.

The top (part L), the ends (parts N), and the back (part O) are all made from wide stock, and to get the needed width, you'll need to edge-glue two or more narrower boards. Cut the boards to allow extra on both the width and length, then glue and clamp with bar or pipe clamps. When dry, trim to final width and length dimensions.

Part N has a ⅜ in. deep by ¾ in. wide rabbet cut along its back edge to accept part O. Set the dado-head cutter to a height of ⅜ in., then use the table saw miter gauge to hold part N as it is passed through the cutter.

In addition, part N has two ⅜ in. deep by ⅜ in. wide stopped grooves to take the shelves (parts P). To cut the groove, clamp an edge guide to part N, then equip the router with a ⅜ in. diameter straight bit set to make a ⅛ in. deep cut. With the router held against the edge guide, cut a 7½ in. long stopped groove (see drawing). Two more passes, each one making a ⅛ in. deep cut, will complete the groove.

The profiles of parts N and O are shown on the grid pattern. Transfer the grid pattern from the drawing to the stock, then cut out with a band or saber saw. Cut slightly on the waste side, then sand to the line.

If necessary, edge-glue stock for part P, then cut the tenon on each end as shown. Check for a good fit in the stopped dado. Following this, parts Q can be cut to length and width.

Final sand parts N, O, P, and Q, then assemble as shown with glue and clamps. Check for squareness. Note that part Q is simply a glued butt joint.

Because the top (L) is in cross-grain orientation to the side aprons (B) and ends (N), you'll need to make slotted holes in the top, and use ⅜ in. diameter by 2¾ in. long dowel pins to join parts B and N, with part L sandwiched in between. Wax the area around the slotted holes on part L, and the center section of the outside dowel pins, to prevent glue squeeze out from affecting the freedom of part L to move as it responds to changes in humidity. Round-head wood screws and washers are now added up through parts G, to further anchor the top to the lower leg and frame assembly.

After making the drawers, give the entire project a complete sanding. Two coats of polyurethane provide a durable final finish. If not available locally, the Chippendale-style drawer pulls can be ordered from Paxton Hardware Co., Upper Falls, MD 21156.

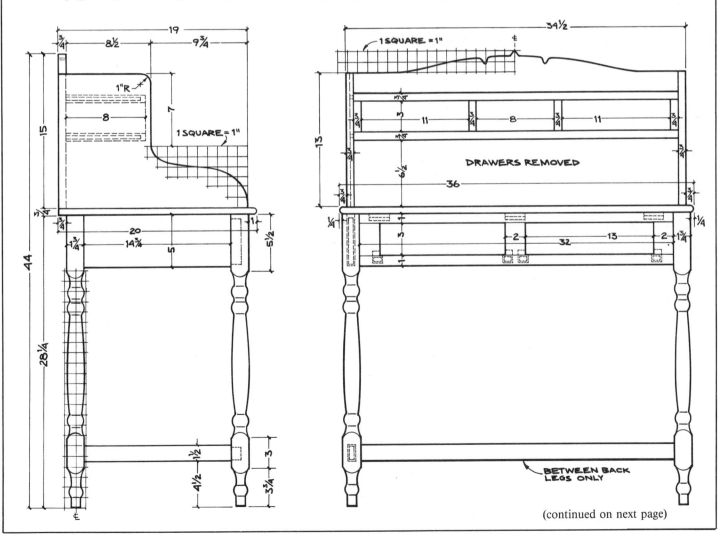

(continued on next page)

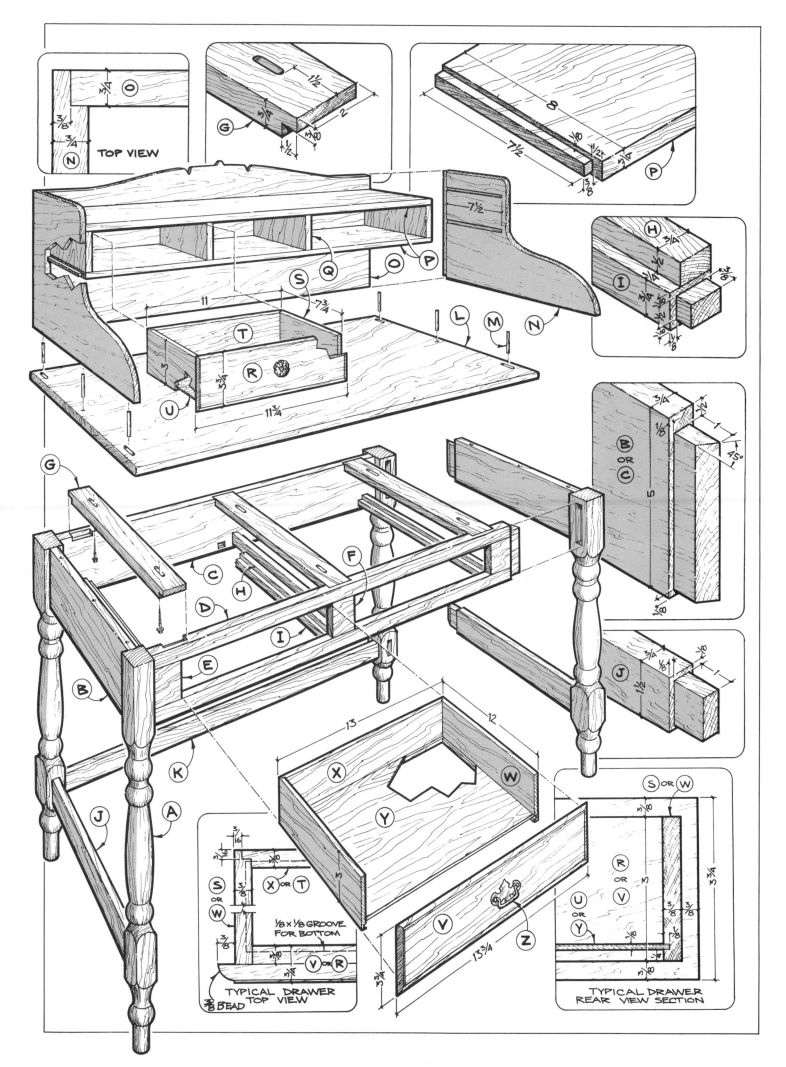

TOP VIEW

7½

45°

11

7¾

11¾

13

12

13¾

¹⁄₈ x ¹⁄₈ GROOVE
FOR BOTTOM

³⁄₈ BEAD

TYPICAL DRAWER
TOP VIEW

TYPICAL DRAWER
REAR VIEW SECTION

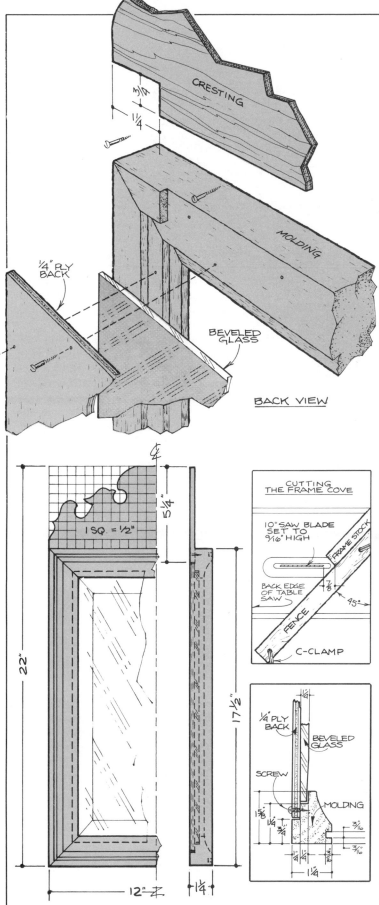

CRESTING

3/4

1¼

¼" PLY
BACK

MOLDING

BEVELED
GLASS

BACK VIEW

1 SQ. = ½"

5¼"

22'

17½"

12"

1¼

CUTTING
THE FRAME COVE

10" SAW BLADE
SET TO
9/16" HIGH

FRAME STOCK

BACK EDGE
OF TABLE
SAW

7/8

FENCE

45°

C-CLAMP

¼" PLY
BACK

BEVELED
GLASS

SCREW

MOLDING

1⅜

¼ ¾

3/16

3/16

¼ ¼

3/16

1¼

Early American Mirror

This Early American style mirror recreates the popular wall mirrors that often graced 18th Century drawing rooms.

Although these mirrors were sometimes made from pine, we believe that hardwoods such as walnut, cherry or mahogany are a better choice. Keep in mind, however, that the plywood for the decorative cresting should compliment the mirror frame.

Start by cutting to size sufficient stock for the four frame sides. Use the dado-head to cut the ¼ in. deep rabbet that will accommodate the plywood back. Next, set the dado-head for a ½ in. depth, relocate the fence, and cut the mirror rabbets. Now cut the 3/16 in. shadow-line groove, and referring to the illustration, set up the table saw jig to make the broad cove cut. Note that the final blade height for this cove is 9/16 in. Be sure to make this cut with multiple passes, raising the blade about 1/16 in. for each pass.

Miter the frame corners, and cut away the back of the top piece as shown, to fit the decorative cresting. This cutaway is made with repeated passes of the dado-head, while the cresting itself is best cut with a jig saw.

The beveled mirror glass is a custom item. Ask your local glass shop to cut the mirror to size, and apply the beveled edge, as indicated. The plywood back is screwed in place, while the cresting should be both glued and screwed. You may wish to add a felt backing under the glass, to cushion the mirror and protect the silvered side.

We recommend a natural finish, using Tung or penetrating oil.

The seasons roll along, and we expect that many of our fellow woodworkers have already laid in a healthy supply of cord wood for the cold winter months ahead. If you burn wood, no doubt you have long ago resigned yourself to accepting the accompanying mess of sawdust, twigs, bits and pieces of bark, leaves, bugs, and plain old dirt. Although there is no way around the fact that there will always be some mess when you burn wood, a wood box will go a long way toward reducing and controlling that mess.

This Shaker woodbox is one of the better woodbox designs that we have seen. In addition to a generous cordwood bin, it features a drawer that is perfect for storing kindling, newspapers, and matches. Our woodbox was crafted from pine, however you may wish to substitute an attractive hardwood instead.

To simplify construction, and make this an ideal project for the beginning woodworker, we decided to use dowel joinery throughout. (The advanced woodworker may wish to substitute dovetail joinery.) The entire piece can be constructed from ¾ in. thick material. Standard 1 x 6 and 1 x 8 pine boards, readily available at any lumberyard, are ideal for this project.

Begin by edge-gluing several 1 x 8 boards to form each of the 2 sides (A). Since 1 x 8 boards have an actual width of only 7¼ in., the two boards should give you exactly the 14½ in. width needed for each side. Also glue up ¾ in. boards to form the base (B), bottom (C), front (D), and drawer bottom (J).

Referring to the illustration, now transfer the top and bottom contours to the two sides, and, using a jig saw, cut the profiles out. The stopped dado for the base, and the through dado for the bottom may be cut with the table saw dado-head.

The back is composed of 5 boards, two 1 x 8's and three 1 x 6's. As shown in the illustration, the boards are ship-lapped for strength. The rabbets in each board, to create this ship-lapped effect, are cut with the dado-head, as are the rabbets along the back inside edge of the sides. After the base, bottom, front, two sides and back boards have all been cut to size, you may begin assembly.

Assemble the sides, base, bottom, back boards and front together first. Do not glue the back boards along the ship-laps or on the ends, however, and leave a ⅛ in. space between these boards (see detail) to allow for expansion and contraction in the wood. Drill out the dowel holes as indicated. Cut the dowels slightly long, so they may be trimmed off and sanded flush. Cut the two small drawer stops (L) next, and glue them in place.

The drawer is also made exclusively from ¾ in. boards. Cut the drawer front (G), sides (H), back (I), and bottom (J) to size. The front and back are rabbeted to fit the two sides, and a ⁵⁄₁₆ in. wide by ⅜ in. deep groove is cut into each piece to accept the drawer bottom. Notch the drawer back as shown so that it will clear the drawer stops, and drill two ½ in. diameter by ½ in. deep holes in the drawer front for the knobs (K). These knobs may either be turned on a lathe or ordered ready-made from: Shaker Workshops, P.O. Box 1028, Concord, Mass. 01742. Order part no. 541.

In traditional Shaker fashion, the drawer bottom is a bevel edged ¾ in. board. The bevels may either be cut on the table saw, or shaped with the hand plane. You will note that the drawer bottom is sized to allow for ⅛ in. of expansion on all sides (see detail). Glue up the drawer carcase, using dowels where shown, however take care that no glue gets on the drawer bottom.

After assembly is complete, sand all exterior surfaces, and gently round sharp edges. The woodbox may be stained if desired, and should be finished with several coats of penetrating oil.

Shaker Wood Box

	Bill Of Materials		
Part	Description	Size	No. Req'd.
A	Side	¾ x 14½ x 35½	2
B	Base	¾ x 13¾ x 25¼	1
C	Bottom	¾ x 13 x 25¼	1
D	Front	¾ x 11¾ x 26	1
E	Back (Narrow Boards)	¾ x 5½ x 25¼	3
F	Back (Wide Boards)	¾ x 7¼ x 25¼	2
G	Drawer Front	¾ x 6 x 24½	1
H	Drawer Side	¾ x 6 x 13	2
I	Drawer Back	¾ x 6 x 24½	1
J	Drawer Bottom	¾ x 12½ x 23½	1
K	Drawer Pull	See Detail	2
L	Drawer Stop	¼ x 2 x 3	2

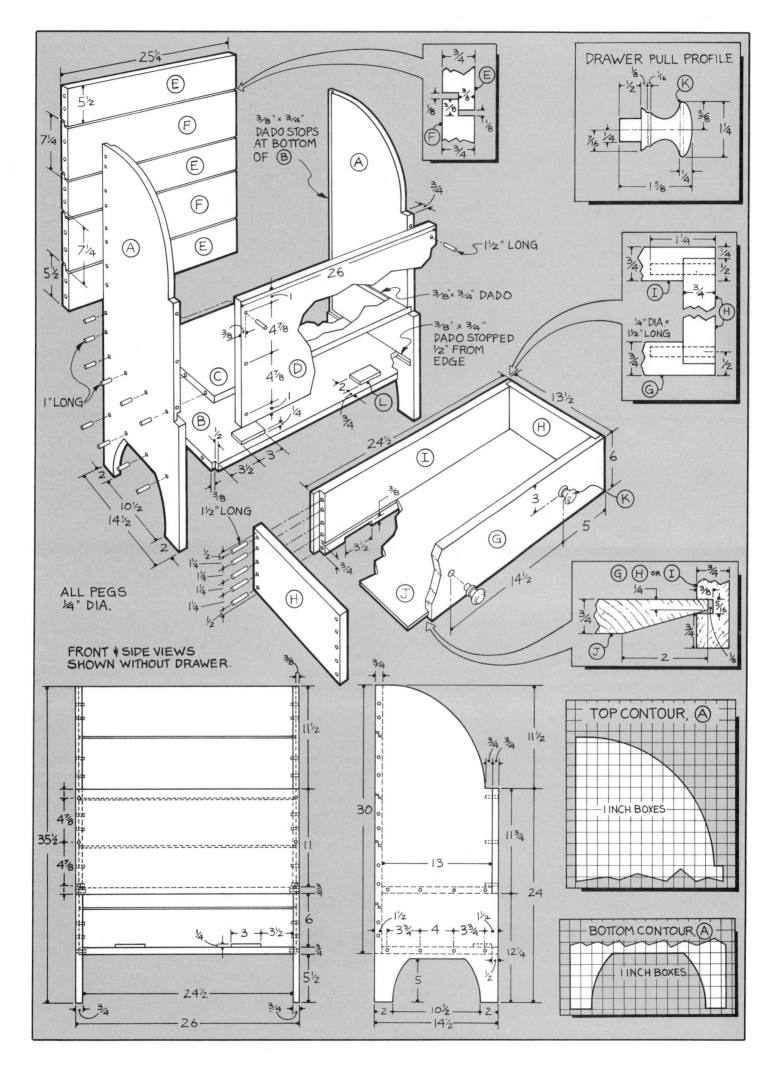

DRAWER PULL PROFILE

3/8" x 3/4"
DADO STOPS
AT BOTTOM
OF B

3/4

1 1/2" LONG

3/8" x 3/4" DADO

3/8" x 3/4"
DADO STOPPED
1/2" FROM
EDGE

1/4" DIA x
1 1/2" LONG

1" LONG

1 1/2" LONG

ALL PEGS
1/4" DIA.

G H or I

FRONT & SIDE VIEWS
SHOWN WITHOUT DRAWER.

TOP CONTOUR, A

1 INCH BOXES

BOTTOM CONTOUR A

1 INCH BOXES

Hall Table

We believe that this handsome hall table will be a popular addition to almost any home, contemporary or traditional. The table's narrow width makes it perfect for placement in an entrance hall, and it can easily double as a sideboard or serving table for buffet-style entertaining. Some folks may choose to use it as a sofa table, to visually soften the effect of the sofa's backside when the sofa is centrally located instead of positioned flush against a wall. Indeed, it is an extraordinarily versatile piece in virtually any room in the house, even the kitchen, den, or sewing room.

This hall table features basic mortise-and-tenon construction. The gently tapered legs and straightforward design contribute to its clean, uncluttered appearance. Although we used cherry for this piece, it would also look good in walnut, mahogany, maple, oak, or pine. The table is not difficult to build, and should be an ideal project for the beginning woodworker. Except for the legs, all table parts are ¾ in. thick.

You may start by cutting the four legs (A) to size. A 28 in. length of 2 x 8 stock is ideal for roughing out the leg blanks. The leg tapers may either be cut with a tapering jig on the tablesaw, or shaped by hand with a plane. Note that the taper begins ½ in. below the apron, and narrows from a 1¾ in. square at that point to a 1 in. square at the leg end.

Next, cut the apron ends (B) and sides (C). With the tenons included, the length of the ends will be 8 in., and the length of the sides will be 42 in. The tenons on the apron ends and sides are identical (See Detail). Although these tenons may be cut by hand, cutting them with the dado-head on the tablesaw will be both faster and more accurate. Note, however, that the tenons are flush with the inside edge of the apron boards.

After the tenons have been cut, mark their corresponding mortises on the table legs. These mortises are located so that the aprons will be set back ⅛ in. (see detail). To cut the mortises first drill out as much material as possible with a ½ in. bit; then square the mortises with a ½ in. chisel.

The table top (D) is locked into the apron frame by means of a series of small blocks (E) that are screwed to the table top and mortised into the apron (see detail). The ¼ in. wide by ¼ in. deep stopped dado for each block may be cut with the dado-head. The 2 screw holes in each block should be countersunk ¼ in. so that 1 in. long flat-head wood screws will extend approximately ½ in. into the table top. The table top itself may be a single board, although most folks will probably have to edge-glue narrower stock to achieve the full 12 in. width.

Assemble the table using glue on all the mortise-and-tenon joints of the leg and apron frame assembly, and clamp securely. Do *not* glue the locking blocks into either the table top or apron, however. The design of the table is intended to permit these blocks to ride free in the apron dados, accommodating changes in humidity that will cause the table top to expand and contract.

Fine sand the table, and rub in several coats of tung oil to achieve a satin gloss finish.

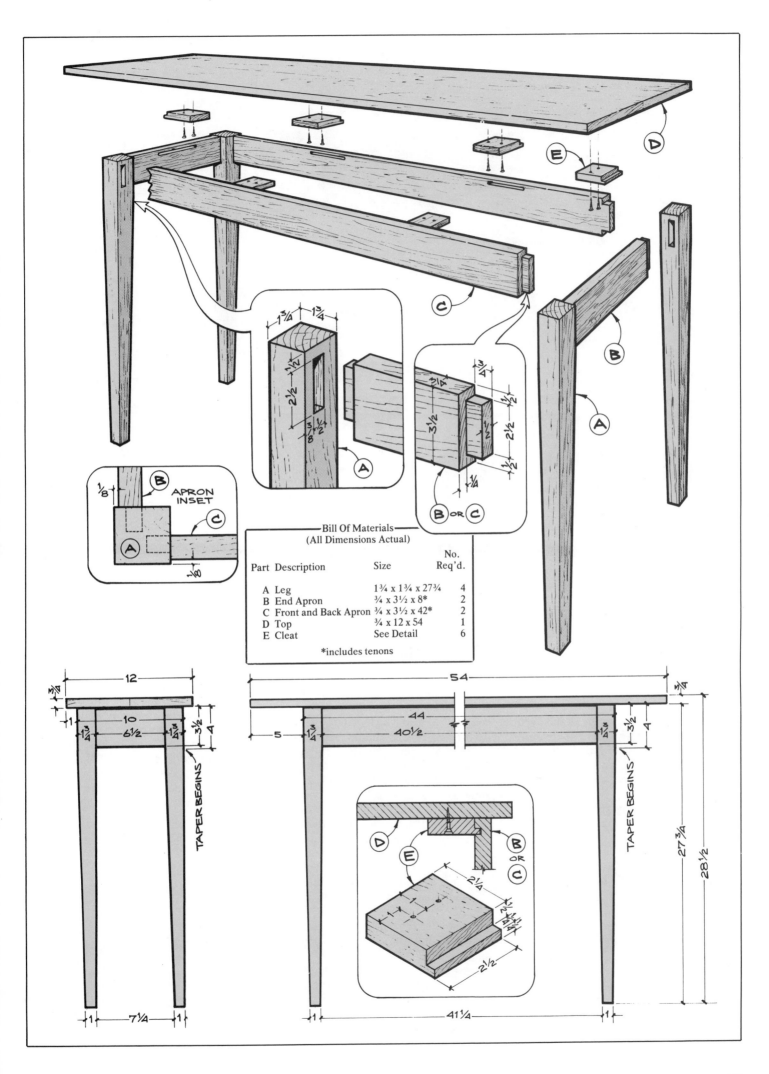

Bill Of Materials
(All Dimensions Actual)

Part	Description	Size	No. Req'd.
A	Leg	1¾ x 1¾ x 27¾	4
B	End Apron	¾ x 3½ x 8*	2
C	Front and Back Apron	¾ x 3½ x 42*	2
D	Top	¾ x 12 x 54	1
E	Cleat	See Detail	6

*includes tenons

APRON INSET

TAPER BEGINS

Shaker Sewing Stand

This twin-drawer Shaker sewing stand is patterned after a mid-nineteenth century sewing stand from Hancock, Massachusetts. It features the traditional Shaker use of dovetailed joinery throughout, and was crafted of cherry, the wood preferred by the Shakers.

Begin by making the pedestal (A). Although you may glue up sections of thinner stock to form the pedestal turning block, we recommend turning the pedestal from a single length of solid stock. If you have no local source for 4 in. thick stock, a 4 in. square by 24 in. long turning block of cherry is available from: Craftsman Wood Service, 1735 West Cortland Court, Addison, IL 60101.

After the pedestal has been turned on the lathe to the dimensions shown in the front elevation, use a sharp chisel to cut the three 9/16 in. deep dovetail slots in the pedestal bottom. Note that these are located 120 degrees apart.

To make the three legs (B), start with three ¾ in. thick by 6 in. wide by 16 in. long boards and lay out the grid pattern as shown in the leg detail. Make the 45 degree end cut at a point 3½ in. from the corner, and set the table saw blade at a 1/16 in. depth to make the cut establishing the dovetail depth (see dovetail detail). This procedure will result in a clean line at the dovetail shoulder, helping to minimize the chance for error in the handwork of chiseling both the dovetail and shoulder undercut. This undercut in the shoulder is important because it accommodates the curve of the pedestal, insuring that the shoulder's outside edge will in fact fit tight. After the dovetails are cut you may cut the legs with a band or saber saw. Shape the ½ in. radius with rasps and files, and sand the legs smooth.

Make the top (C) next. Unless you have access to 18 in. wide cherry boards, it will be necessary to glue up several smaller boards to achieve the total width. The end and center cleats (D and E) may be cut to size, and the cleat rabbets can be cut with the dado-head. Use a hole saw to cut the 2 in. hole in the center cleat that will accommodate the pedestal tenon. Both the top, pedestal and legs should be final sanded before assembly.

Next rip ½ in. square stock and cut to length the stop (F) and the four glides (G).

To make the two drawers, first cut the drawer fronts (H), backs (I) and sides (J) to length and width. The dovetails may either be cut by hand or, if you have the proper bits and jigs, with the router. The ¼ in. square drawer bottom grooves are best cut with the router.

Although the Shakers never used plywood, for convenience we suggest cutting the drawer bottoms (K) from ¼ in. plywood. If you are a stickler for authenticity, however, it will be necessary to resaw a section of ¾ in. solid cherry to make the bottoms. Glue and clamp the drawer carcases, and add the glide strips on either side.

The drawer pulls (L) may either be made as shown, or purchased from: Shaker Workshops, P.O. Box 1028, Concord, MA 01742. Order part no. W531.

When assembling the table, use the drawers as an aid in positioning the cleats so that the drawers will slide easily in and out. You will note that these cleats are screwed, but not glued into the underside of the top. The slotted screw holes are designed to accommodate any seasonal movement of the wood across the top.

The pedestal tenon is glued and fitted into the top assembly and the legs are glued into the pedestal bottom.

The sewing stand is best finished naturally, with several applications of a quality penetrating oil. Because cherry darkens on exposure to light, the wood will acquire a deep, rich patina over the years.

Bill Of Materials (All Dimensions Actual)			
Part	Description	Size	No. Req'd.
A	Pedestal	3½ Dia. x 19⅜ long	1
B	Leg	See Detail	3
C	Top	¾ x 18 x 24	1
D	End Cleat	⅞ x 2 x 16	2
E	Center Cleat	⅞ x 5½ x 16	1
F	Stop	½ x ½ x 21	1
G	Glide	½ x ½ x 16	4
H	Drawer Front	¾ x 3½ x 5¾	2
I	Drawer Back	½ x 3½ x 5¾	2
J	Drawer Side	½ x 3½ x 16	4
K	Drawer Bottom	¼ x 5¼ x 15¼	2
L	Drawer Pull	See Detail	2

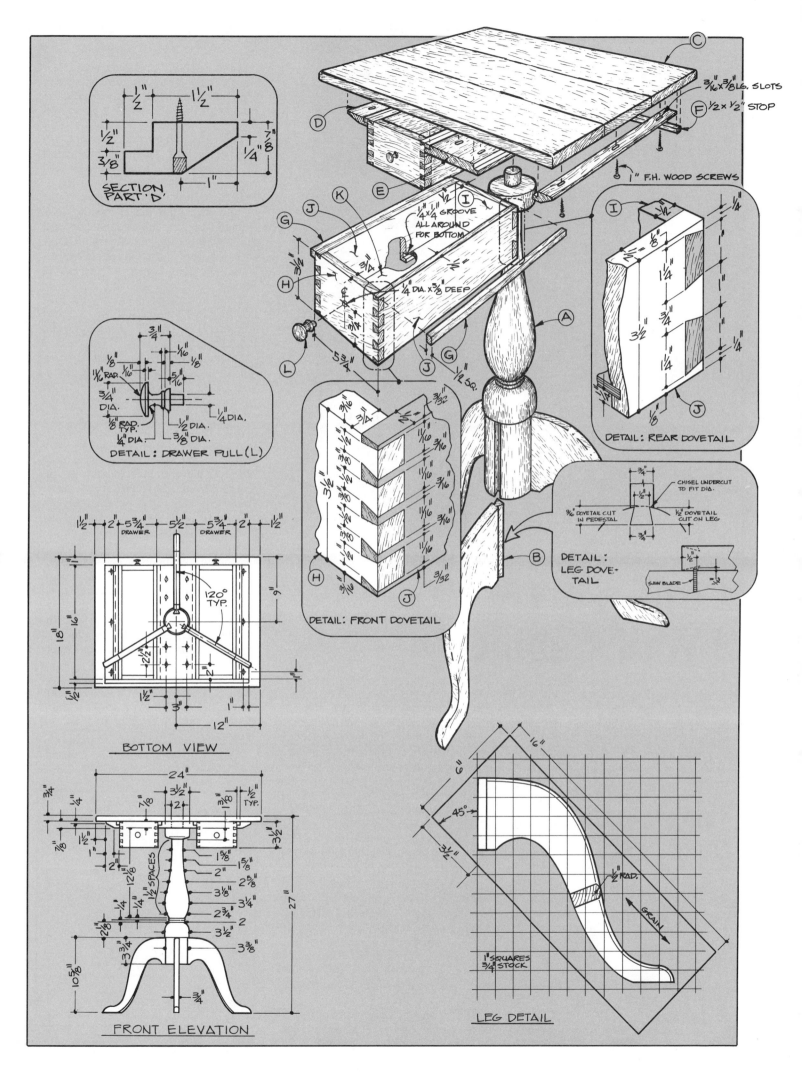

SECTION PART 'D'

DETAIL: DRAWER PULL (L)

BOTTOM VIEW

FRONT ELEVATION

³⁄₁₆" x ³⁄₄" LG. SLOTS

F ½ x ½" STOP

1" F.H. WOOD SCREWS

¼"x¼" GROOVE ALL AROUND FOR BOTTOM

¼" DIA. x ³⁄₈" DEEP

DETAIL: REAR DOVETAIL

DETAIL: FRONT DOVETAIL

CHISEL UNDERCUT TO FIT DIA.

³⁄₁₆" DOVETAIL CUT IN PEDESTAL

½" DOVETAIL CUT ON LEG

DETAIL: LEG DOVETAIL

SAW BLADE

LEG DETAIL

1" SQUARES
¾" STOCK

½" RAD.

GRAIN

120° TYP.

½ SQ.

Pierced Tin Wall Cabinet

This Colonial style pierced tin wall cabinet is an ideal project for the beginning woodworker. Although pierced tin cabinets were traditionally used in the kitchen as pie safes, this cabinet will provide handy storage space wherever there is sufficient wall space to hang it.

This type of cabinet was usually made of pine, as ours is. However, it could also be constructed of an attractive hardwood.

Begin by cutting to length and width the sides (A), top (B), bottom (C), stretcher (D), door rails and stiles (F and G), and the shelves (J), all of which may be cut from a single 8 foot long 1 x 10 board, as shown in the cutting diagram. The ⅜ in. square retainer strips (I) are then resawn from the scrap. The back (E) is a section of ¼ in. thick plywood.

The decorative edge around the cab-inet top and bottom is cut with the router using a ⅜ in. piloted round-over bit, as shown in the edge detail. The ¼ in. radius is then added using a rasp and some hand sanding.

Next, notch the sides to accept the stretcher and drill out the ½ in. diameter dowel holes for the shelf supports. Lay out these dowel holes carefully so the shelves will be in contact with the dowels at all four points, and therefore lie flat.

The cabinet carcase should now be assembled. First glue up and clamp the sides, top, bottom, and stretcher. Next, drill out and counterbore for the 1-¼ in. flathead wood screws, as shown in the screw detail. The stretch-er is both glued in place and secured with several no. 4 finish nails on either side.

The ¼ in. thick plywood back is set in a ¼ in. deep by ⅜ in. wide rabbet that is cut around the inside edge of the cabinet back using the router and a ⅜ in. piloted rabbeting bit. Square the corners of the rabbet with a chisel and then glue the back in place.

The door joinery is known as a mi-tered corner lap. The joints may either be cut by hand, using a fine-tooth backsaw, or with the table saw dado-head. Dry fit the joints to insure a tight fit and then glue and clamp the door frame. The ⅜ in. square rabbet around the inner edge of the door frame is cut with the router and a rabbeting bit. Chisel the four corners of the rabbet square.

The door is sized to accept an 11 x 14 in. tin panel, available from Country Accents, P.O. Box 437, Montoursville, PA 17754.

To punch out the tin panel, first lay out the star pattern as shown in the il-lustration. A prick-punch or even an eight-penny nail will work fine as a punch. With an old piece of plywood under the tin as a backing, punch out the pattern, using one quick firm stroke of the hammer to make each hole. Space the holes about ¼ in. apart. Mount the panel in the door frame and either glue or tack the ⅜ in. square retainer strips in place. Note that these strips are mitered at the corners.

Mortise out the door and side to ac-cept the 1½ in. hinges (L) as shown, then drill through the door stile to ac-cept the mounting screw for the 1 in. diameter porcelain knob (K). Both the hinges and knob should be available at your local hardware or building supply dealer.

Final sand and then finish the cabinet as desired. Minwax Colonial Maple or Natural Pine are two stains that will look especially fine on this piece.

	Bill Of Materials (All Dimensions Actual)		
Part	Description	Size	No. Req'd.
A	Side	¾ x 7¼ x 17½	2
B	Top	¾ x 7⅞ x 15¾	1
C	Bottom	¾ x 7⅞ x 15¾	1
D	Stretcher	¾ x 1½ x 14½	1
E	Back	¼ x 13¾ x 18¼	1
F	Door Rail	¾ x 1⅜ x 13	2
G	Door Stile	¾ x 1⅜ x 16	2
H	Tin	1/16 x 11 x 14	1
I	Retainer	⅜ x ⅜	As Req'd.
J	Shelf	¾ x 6¼ x 12⅞	2
K	Knob	1 in. Dia.	1
L	Hinge	1½ in.	2

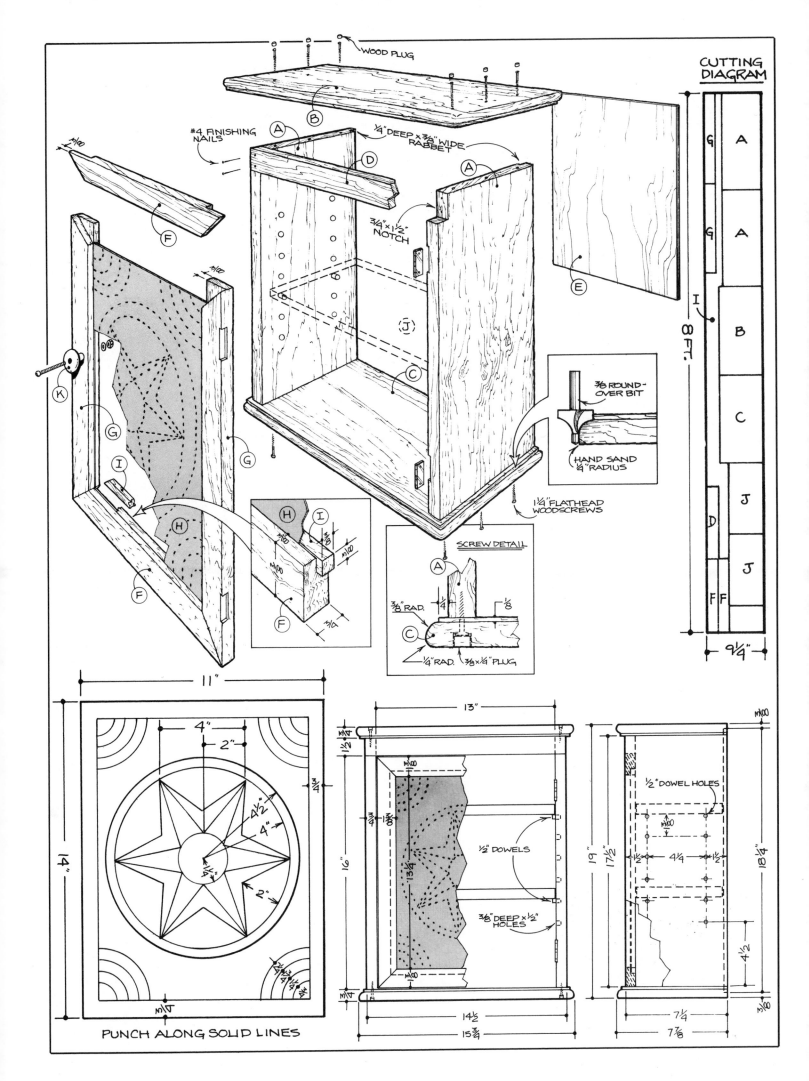

CUTTING DIAGRAM

WOOD PLUG

B

#4 FINISHING NAILS

A

¼" DEEP x ⅜" WIDE RABBET

D

¾" x 1½" NOTCH

A

E

J

C

⅜ ROUND-OVER BIT

HAND SAND ⅛" RADIUS

1¼" FLATHEAD WOODSCREWS

F

K

G

I

G

H

H

I

F

F

SCREW DETAIL

A

⅜" RAD.

¼

⅛

C

¼" RAD.

⅜ x ¼" PLUG

8 FT.

G   A

G   A

I

B

C

J

D

J

F F

9¼"

PUNCH ALONG SOLID LINES

11"

4"

2"

¾"

14"

4½"
4"
4"
¼"
2"

13"

1¼"
1½"

¾"
1¾"

13¾"

19"

½" DOWELS

⅜" DEEP x ½" HOLES

14½"

15¾"

17½"

19"

½" DOWEL HOLES

4¼"

½   ½

18¼"

4½"

7¼"

7⅞"

153

Colonial Pipe Box

The clean lines and simple construction of this colonial-era pipe box mark it as an especially fine example of colonial design. The original is in the Metropolitan Museum of Art in New York City, and was probably used to hold the delicate, long-stemmed clay pipes popularized by the Dutch.

We have found that the box makes an ideal letter holder, and that the small tobacco drawer is perfect for stamps. Pipe boxes were traditionally made of pine, but maple, cherry, or mahogany will serve well for this piece.

Begin by cutting all parts, A through I, to size. Use the dado blade to rabbet the sides (A), base (D), and drawer components (F), (G), and (H). The hourglass shape in the back (C), and curved profile of the front (B), may be cut by hand with a coping saw, or with a saber or bandsaw. The radius on both the base and drawer front is cut on the router table, using a ¼ in. round-over bit.

Refer to the illustration and assemble as shown, using glue on all joints and dowels where indicated. The drawer knob may be obtained from The Woodworkers' Store, 21801 Industrial Blvd., Rogers, Minnesota 55374. Order part No. B1674.

Sand lightly, stain to suit, and finish with a quality penetrating oil.

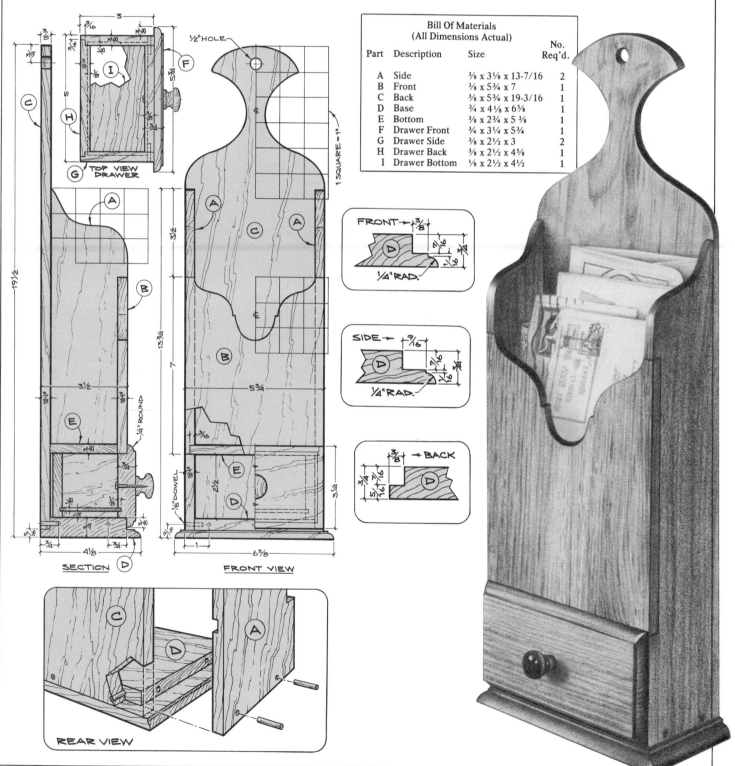

Bill Of Materials (All Dimensions Actual)			
Part	Description	Size	No. Req'd.
A	Side	⅜ x 3⅛ x 13-7/16	2
B	Front	⅜ x 5¾ x 7	1
C	Back	⅜ x 5¾ x 19-3/16	1
D	Base	¾ x 4⅛ x 6⅝	1
E	Bottom	⅜ x 2¾ x 5⅜	1
F	Drawer Front	¾ x 3¼ x 5¾	1
G	Drawer Side	⅜ x 2½ x 3	2
H	Drawer Back	⅜ x 2½ x 4⅝	1
I	Drawer Bottom	⅛ x 2½ x 4½	1

TOP VIEW DRAWER

SECTION D

FRONT VIEW

REAR VIEW

FRONT — ¼" RAD.

SIDE — ¼" RAD.

BACK

Sources of Supply

The following pages list companies that specialize in
mail-order sales of woodworking supplies.

United States

General Woodworking Suppliers

Constantine's
2050 Eastchester Rd.
Bronx, NY 10461

Craftsman Wood Service
1735 West Cortland Ct.
Addison, IL 60101

The Fine Tool Shops
170 West Road
Portsmouth, NH 03810

Frog Tool Co., Ltd.
700 W. Jackson Blvd.
Chicago, IL 60606

Garrett Wade
161 Avenue of the Americas
New York, NY 10013

Highland Hardware
1045 N. Highland Ave., N.E.
Atlanta, GA 30306

Seven Corners Ace Hardware
216 West 7th Street
St. Paul, MN 55102

Shopsmith, Inc.
3931 Image Drive
Dayton, OH 45414-2591

Trend-Lines
375 Beacham St.
Chelsea, MA 02150-0999

Woodcraft Supply Corp.
41 Atlantic Ave.
Woburn, MA 01888

The Woodworkers' Store
21801 Industrial Blvd.
Rogers, MN 55374

Woodworker's Supply of New Mexico
5604 Alameda, N.E.
Albuquerque, NM 87113

W.S. Jenks and Son
1933 Montana Ave., N.E.
Washington, DC 20002

Hardware Suppliers

Allen Specialty Hardware
332 W. Bruceton Rd.
Pittsburgh, PA 15236

Anglo-American Brass Co.
Box 9487
4146 Mitzi Drive
San Jose, CA 95157

Ball and Ball
463 West Lincoln Highway
Exton, PA 19341

Horton Brasses
Nooks Hill Rd.
P.O. Box 120
Cromwell, CT 06416

Imported European Hardware
4320 W. Bell Dr.
Las Vegas, NV 89118

Meisel Hardware Specialties
P.O. Box 70
Mound, MN 55364

Paxton Hardware, Ltd.
7818 Bradshaw Rd.
Upper Falls, MD 21156

Period Furniture Hardware Co.
123 Charles St.
Box 314 Charles Street Station
Boston, MA 02114

Stanley Hardware
195 Lake Street
New Britain, CT 06050

The Wise Co.
6503 St. Claude
Arabi, LA 70032

Hardwood Suppliers

American Woodcrafters
1025 S. Roosevelt Ave.
Piqua, OH 45356

Arroyo Hardwoods
2585 Nina Street
Pasadena, CA 91107

Art Eisenbrand
4100 Spencer Street
Torrance, CA 90503

Austin Hardwoods
2119 Goodrich
Austin, TX 78704

Bergers Hardwoods
Route 4, Box 195
Bedford, VA 24523

Berea Hardwoods Co.
125 Jacqueline Drive
Berea, OH 44017

Maurice L. Condon
250 Ferris Ave.
White Plains, NY 10603

Craftwoods
109 21 York Rd.
Cockeysville, MD 21030

Croy-Marietta Hardwoods, Inc.
121 Pike St., Box 643
Marietta, OH 45750

Dimension Hardwoods, Inc.
113 Canal Street
Shelton, CT 06484

Educational Lumber Co.
P.O. Box 5373
Asheville, NC 28813

General Woodcraft
531 Broad St.
New London, CT 06320

Hardwoods of Memphis
P.O. Box 12449
Memphis, TN 38182-0449

Henegan's Wood Shed
7760 Southern Blvd.
West Palm Beach, FL 33411

Kaymar Wood Products
4603 35th S.W.
Seattle, WA 98126

Kountry Kraft Hardwoods
R.R. No. 1
Lake City, IA 51449

Leonard Lumber Co.
P.O. Box 2396
Branford, CT 06405

McFeely's Hardwoods & Lumber
712 12th St.
Lynchburg, VA 24505

Native American Hardwoods
Route 1
West Valley, NY 14171

Sterling Hardwoods, Inc.
412 Pine St.
Burlington, VT 05401

Talarico Hardwoods
RD 3, Box 3268
Mohnton, PA 19540-9339

Woodcrafter's Supply
7703 Perry Highway (Rt. 19)
Pittsburgh, PA 15237

Wood World
1719 Chestnut
Glenview, IL 60025

Woodworker's Dream
P.O. Box 329
Nazareth, PA 18064

(continued on next page)

Wood Finishing Supplies

Finishing Products and Supply Co.
4611 Macklind Ave.
St. Louis, MO 63109

Industrial Finishing Products
465 Logan St.
Brooklyn, NY 11208

The Wise Co.
P.O. Box 118
6503 St. Claude
Arabie, LA 70032

WoodFinishing Enterprises
Box 10017
Milwaukee, WI 53210

Watco-Dennis Corp.
1433 Santa Monica Blvd.
Santa Monica, CA 90401

Clock Parts

Klockit, Inc.
P.O. Box 542
Lake Geneva, WI 53147

Kuempel Chime
21195 Minnetonka Blvd.
Excelisor, MN 55331

S. LaRose
234 Commerce Place
Greensboro, NC 27420

Mason & Sullivan Co.
586 Higgins Crowell Rd.
West Yarmouth, MA 02655

Newport Enterprises
2313 West Burbank Blvd.
Burbank, CA 91506

Miscellaneous

Byrom International
(Router Bits)
P.O. Box 246
Chardon, OH 44024

Brown Wood Products
(Balls, Knobs, Shaker Pegs)
P.O. Box 8246
Northfield, IL 60093

Country Accents
(Pierced Tin)
P.O. Box 437
Montoursville, PA 17754

DML, Inc.
(Router Bits)
1350 S. 15th Street
Louisville, KY 40210

Floral Glass & Mirror
(Beveled Glass)
895 Motor Parkway
Hauppauge, NY 11788

Formica Corporation
(Plastic Laminate)
1 Stanford Road
Piscataway, NJ 08854

Freud
(Saw Blades)
218 Feld Ave.
High Point, NC 27264

Midwest Dowel Works
(Dowels, Plugs, Pegs)
4631 Hutchinson Road
Cincinnati, OH 45248

Homecraft Veneer
(Veneer)
901 West Way
Latrobe, PA 15650

MLCS
(Router Bits)
P.O. Box 53
Rydal, PA 19041

The Old Fashioned Milk Paint Co.
(Milk Paint)
P.O. Box 222
Groton, MA 01450

Sears, Roebuck and Co.
(Misc. Tools & Supplies)
925 S. Homan Ave.
Chicago, IL 60607

Wilson Art
(Plastic Laminate)
600 General Bruce Drive
Temple, TX 76501

Canada

General Woodworking Suppliers

House of Tools Ltd.
131-12th Ave. S.E.
Calgary, Alberta T2G 0Z9

J. Philip Humfrey International
3241 Kennedy Rd., Unit 7
Scarborough, Ontario M1V 2J9

Lee Valley Tools
Unit 6, 5511 Steeles Ave. West
Weston, Ontario M9L 1S7

Stockade Woodworker's Supply
P.O. Box 1415
Salmon Arm, British Columbia V0E 2T0

Tool Trend Ltd.
3280 Steele's Ave. West
Concord, Ontario L4K 2Y2

Treen Heritage, Ltd.
P.O. Box 280
Merrickville, Ontario K0G 1N0

Hardware Suppliers

Home Workshop Supplies
RR 2
Arthur, Ontario N0G 1A0

Lee Valley Tools
Unit 6, 5511 Steeles Ave. West
Weston, Ontario M9L 1S7

Pacific Brass Hardware
1414 Monterey Ave.
Victoria, British Columbia V8S 4W1

Steve's Shop, Woodworking & Supplies
RR 3
Woodstock, Ontario M9V 5C3

Hardwood Suppliers

A & C Hutt Enterprises, Ltd.
15861 32nd Ave.
Surrey, British Columbia V4B 4Z5

Hurst Associates, Ltd.
74 Dynamic Drive, Unit 11
Scarborough, Ontario M1V 3X6

Longstock Lumber & Veneer
440 Phillip St., Unit 21
Waterloo, Ontario N2L 5R9

MacVeigh Hardwoods
339 Olivewood Rd.
Toronto, Ontario M8Z 2Z6

Unicorn Universal Woods Ltd.
4190 Steeles Ave. West, Unit 4
Woodbridge, Ontario L4L 3S8

Woodcraft Forest Products
1625 Sismet Road, Unit 25
Mississauga, Ontario L4W 1V6

Clock Parts

Hurst Associates
151 Nashdene Rd., Unit 14
Scarborough, Ontario M1V 2T3

Kidder Klock
39 Glen Cameron Rd., Unit 3
Thornhill, Ontario L3T 1P1

Murray Clock Craft Ltd.
510 McNicoll Ave.
Willowdale, Ontario M2H 2E1

Miscellaneous

Freud
(Saw Blades)
100 Westmore Dr., Unit 10
Rexdale, Ontario M9V 5C3

Index

Index

Imperial to Metric Conversion Table

Feet	Inches Centimetres	1	2	3	4	5	6	7	8	9	10	11
		2.54	5.08	7.62	10.16	12.70	15.24	17.78	20.32	22.86	25.40	27.94
1	30.48	33.02	35.56	38.10	40.64	43.18	45.72	48.26	50.80	53.34	55.88	58.42
2	60.96	63.50	66.04	68.58	71.12	73.66	76.20	78.74	81.28	83.82	86.36	88.90
3	91.44	93.98	96.52	99.06	101.60	104.14	106.68	109.22	111.76	114.30	116.84	119.38
4	121.92	124.46	127.00	129.54	132.08	134.62	137.16	139.70	142.24	144.78	147.32	149.86
5	152.40	154.94	157.48	160.02	162.56	165.10	167.64	170.18	172.72	175.26	177.80	180.34
6	182.88	185.42	187.96	190.50	193.04	195.58	198.12	200.66	203.20	205.74	208.28	210.82
7	213.36	215.90	218.44	220.98	223.52	226.06	228.60	231.14	233.68	236.22	238.76	241.30
8	243.84	246.38	248.92	251.46	254.00	256.54	259.08	261.62	264.16	266.70	269.24	271.78
9	274.32	276.86	279.40	281.94	284.48	287.02	289.56	292.10	294.64	297.18	299.72	302.26
10	304.80	307.34	309.88	312.42	314.96	317.50	320.04	322.58	325.12	327.66	330.20	332.74
11	335.28	337.82	340.36	342.90	345.44	347.98	350.52	353.06	355.60	358.14	360.68	363.22
12	365.76	368.30	370.84	373.38	375.92	378.46	381.00	383.54	386.08	388.62	391.16	393.70
13	396.24	398.78	401.32	403.86	406.40	408.94	411.48	414.02	416.56	419.10	421.64	424.18
14	426.72	429.26	431.80	434.34	436.88	439.42	441.96	444.50	447.04	449.58	452.12	454.66
15	457.20	459.74	462.28	464.82	467.36	469.90	472.44	474.98	477.52	480.06	482.60	485.14
16	487.68	490.22	492.76	495.30	498.84	500.38	502.92	505.46	508.00	510.54	513.08	515.62
17	518.16	520.70	523.24	525.78	528.32	530.86	533.40	535.94	538.48	541.02	543.56	546.10
18	548.64	551.18	553.72	556.26	558.80	561.34	563.88	566.42	568.96	571.50	574.04	576.58
19	579.12	581.66	584.20	586.74	589.28	591.82	594.36	596.90	599.44	601.98	605.52	607.06
20	609.60	612.14	614.68	617.22	619.76	622.30	624.84	627.38	629.92	632.46	635.50	637.54

Fractional Equivalents

in.-cms.		in.-cms.	
1/16 = 0.15875		1/8 = 0.31700	
3/16 = 0.47625		1/4 = 0.63500	
5/16 = 0.79375		3/8 = 0.95250	
7/16 = 1.11125		1/2 = 1.27040	
9/16 = 1.42875		5/8 = 1.58730	
11/16 = 1.74625		3/4 = 1.90500	
13/16 = 2.06375		7/8 = 2.22250	
15/16 = 2.38125		1 = 2.54000	

Measures of Length—Basic S.I. Unit—
Metre = 100 Centimetres = 39.37 Inches

Example:

(1) To convert 13 feet 6 inches to centimetres, read along line 13 under feet and under column 6 inches read 411.48 cms. To reduce to metres move decimal point two spaces to left; thus, 4.1148 metres is the answer.

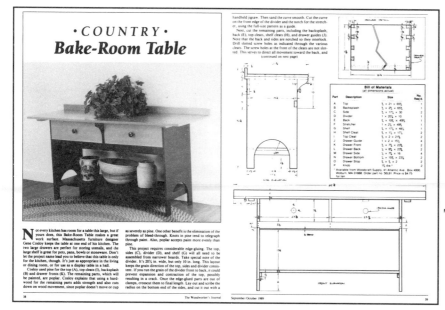